JUDY AND LIZA

One-and-a-half-year-old Liza visits her mother on the set of *The Pirate* in 1947.

JUDY AND LIZA

JAMES SPADA

WITH KAREN SWENSON

A DOLPHIN BOOK
DOUBLEDAY & COMPANY, INC.
GARDEN CITY, NEW YORK
1983

Books of related interest by James Spada

MONROE: HER LIFE IN PICTURES
STREISAND: THE WOMAN AND THE LEGEND
THE FILMS OF ROBERT REDFORD
BARBRA: THE FIRST DECADE

DESIGNED BY LAURENCE ALEXANDER

Spada, James.
  Judy and Liza.

  Bibliography: p.
  1. Garland, Judy.   2. Minnelli, Liza.   3. Singers—
United States—Biography.   4. Entertainers—United
States—Biography.   I. Title.
ML420.G253S65   1983   784.5'0092'2 [B]

ISBN 0-385-18201-5 (pbk.)
Library of Congress Catalog Number 82-45568

PRINTED IN THE UNITED STATES OF AMERICA
FIRST EDITION

Dedicated to Ethel Spada, Anita Felucci, and Mary Scelza,
who have always been very good to me.

—J.S.

For my family, who always give me encouragement
even when they don't realize how; and for my friends,
who put up with the craziness.

—K.S.

ACKNOWLEDGMENTS

A special note of appreciation is due John Fricke. We didn't always agree, but I will be forever impressed with his willingness to help, his concern for accuracy, and his deep affection and regard for Judy.

For their help, enthusiasm, and friendship, thanks to Dan Conlon, Chris Nickens, Vernon Patterson, Guy Vespoint, Rick Summers, Bruce Mandes, George Zeno, Lou Valentino, Terry Miller, Michel Parenteau, Michael Feinstein, Randy Porter, Greg Rice, Jean Booth, Loretta Weingel-Fidel, Marilyn Ducksworth, Craig Zadan, Jeff Schaffer, Doug Bergstreser, Joe Goodwin, J. B. Annegan, Bill Chapman, Bob Chatterton, S.N., Michael Hawks, Lanny Sher, Jeannie Blankenburg.

For their recollections, appreciation to Alma Cousteline, Lionel Doman, Mrs. Ira Gershwin, Tom Cooper, Wendell Burton, Tom Green, Lee Theodore, Robert VanderGriff, Peter Matz, and Tony Manzi.

Very special thanks to Laura Van Wormer, Kathy Robbins, Richard Covey, Jack Dwosh and Larry Alexander for being the kind of people who turn business associations into friendships.

And a grateful nod to the staffs who maintain the theatrical collections at the Academy of Motion Picture Arts and Sciences (special thanks to Carol Cullen and the late Terry Roach), American Film Institute, USC and UCLA libraries and the New York Public Library at Lincoln Center, all without whom very few show business biographies would be possible.

CONTENTS

PROLOGUE:
YOUNG JUDY

"Mother was the worst—the real-life wicked witch of the West."

—*Judy Garland*

Judy and her mother, Ethel Gilmore, appear loving at a "Movie Stars' Mothers" party held in Los Angeles on March 10, 1941.

1

The story of Judy Garland's life, both before and after the birth of her daughter Liza Minnelli, would strain credibility to its breaking point were it the product of a writer's imagination. So rife is it with irony, with the harsh realities behind the American Dream, with hidden sexual secrets, abortion, suicide, drugs, alcohol, triumphs, wealth, power, emotional pain, and ultimate tragedy that only the truth of it separates it from the most sensationalistic "Hollywood novel."

Judy may have been Hollywood's most tragic victim; she in turn could terribly victimize those around her—most painfully her first-born, Liza. It is perhaps only for psychiatrists to fully understand the cycle: Judy considered herself a victim of her own mother, then took on many of Ethel Gumm's worst qualities; Liza was put through Grand Guignol horrors in her life with Judy, only to emulate, as an adult, much of her mother's personality and lifestyle.

The story of Judy Garland's life as a young girl and child movie star is well known; several excellent biographies of her exist, including one concerned exclusively with her childhood years. This prologue is not intended to be a full exploration of Judy's life before Liza Minnelli's birth, but rather an outline, one which will concentrate on the many emotional threads that ran throughout Judy's childhood, into her adulthood and that now continue their inexorable, serpentine advance through Liza Minnelli's life.

Even at the very beginning, there were dark forces at work. When Ethel and Frank Gumm discovered, in 1921, that they were expecting a third child, they were not pleased. Their financial position, they felt, couldn't support another baby. And after eight years of marriage, the relationship between Ethel and Frank had become strained; there were strange inconsistencies in Frank's character that Ethel didn't fully understand, and which deeply disturbed her. This wasn't the time to bring another child into the Gumm household.

Ethel and Frank conferred with a family friend, medical student Marcus Rabwin, and asked if there was something he could do to abort the pregnancy. Rabwin tried to talk the couple out of it, telling them that there was no way to measure the joy and fulfillment the birth of this child might bring them.

Still, Ethel halfheartedly attempted several methods of "naturally" aborting the child, and looked upon it as a burden she would just have to bear. Once the baby girl was born on June 10, 1922, however, the couple's reservations dissolved into love—which, perhaps with not a small amount of guilt, they lavished on the child to the point of excess.

Named Frances (the Gumms had been hoping for a boy they could name after Daddy), the child was born into a family already steeped in show business. Ethel and Frank had been a vaudeville team, "Jack and Virginia Lee," up until the time they began their family. Frank owned the only movie theater in Grand Rapids, a small trading community in northern Minnesota, along the Mississippi River. Ethel encouraged her first two daughters, Mary Jane and Virginia (later nicknamed Suzy and Jimmy), to sing while she played the piano, and one year before baby Frances' birth, the children made their debut on the stage of their father's New Grand Theater, appearing with their parents as "The Four Gumms."

It became quickly apparent that "Baby Frances" was the most outgoing member of the household; wherever she went, she became the center of attention. This was partially because her sisters were beyond the cute baby phase (Mary Jane was seven, Virginia five), but Frances was clearly a special baby.

The Gumm Sisters in Los Angeles, 1929.

Both Ethel and Frank were people who wanted more than their lives were offering them. Frank was a well-educated man, outgoing, gentle, sensitive, a man who loved to sing and loved to laugh. He had been on his own since the age of twelve, when both his parents died. It was a rich suitor of his older sister Mary who saw to it that Frank got through prep school and college, dominions in those days only of the very wealthy. He was no stranger to tragedy; several years after Frank had completed college, Mary contracted a mysterious disease which necessitated her confinement to a wheelchair. Distraught over the burden she had become to the people she loved, she threw herself into a river and drowned.

Ethel Milne was surrounded by a huge family, many of whom were already pursuing careers as entertainers as she grew up. She, too, was forced to earn a living at a very early age, simply because there wasn't enough money to care for everyone. She learned the value of money, and the necessity of resourcefulness in order to survive. She possessed a seemingly boundless energy, and a strong ambition for herself and her loved ones: she was determined that her children would never want for anything. Those who remember her always mention her enormous drive—Ethel Gumm was constantly on the move.

Any dreams Ethel had for her own show business stardom had long before faded; her talents—piano playing, a barely pleasant singing voice—were hardly enough to catapult her into the upper echelons of vaudeville. She had happily traded such dreams for ones of love, home and family, but she had not been fulfilled—not in the way she had imagined.

She loved her daughters, but by the time Baby Frances was born, her marriage existed in little more than name. It wasn't until 1925 that her own fears and misgivings about Frank turned into town gossip. At first, when the stories began about Frank's homosexual inclinations, most of the townspeople who knew him were utterly disbelieving. Frank Gumm was a dedicated family man, happily married as far as anyone could tell, and a religious man as well. In an era when any kind of sexual deviation was thought to be practiced only by the most twisted and degenerate personalities, people would not consider the possibility that the charming, likable Frank Gumm was homosexual.

But, as time went on and the talk increased, and specific instances were named, even Frank's friends began to exhibit some caution around him. They began to doubt the most innocent gesture. The effect of all this was to undermine the comfortable future Ethel had envisioned for her family in this serene community. Her husband's proclivities would have been difficult enough for Ethel Gumm to live with without the added burden of public embarrassment.

She began to withdraw from him, attempting to express herself through her daughters rather than through a loving sexual relationship with her husband. As years went by, she would become increasingly acrimonious toward Frank, often reviling him in bitter arguments between them. And little Frances, who loved her father more than anything in the world, came to hate her mother for the terrible things she would say to him, the awful way she seemed to hurt this gentle, affectionate man who treated his Baby Frances as though the world revolved around her. It was the first of the strikes against her mother in Judy Garland's mind. There would be many others.

Ethel was determined, in spite of everything, to keep her family together. She played the piano during the movies in Frank's theater, and would accompany her daughters as they performed in special stage shows between features. Baby Frances slept in a makeshift box bed backstage. As soon as she could walk, it was inevitable that she would want to see what was going on, what she was missing.

She would head for the stage while her sisters performed, only to be caught by her father and pulled back. But by Christmas of 1924, Ethel knew there was no keeping Baby off the stage. She made her debut at the New Grand by singing eight choruses of "Jingle Bells" while the audience responded with delight at this adorable 2½-year-old child who would not stop singing until her father picked her up and carried her offstage. The show business career had begun.

Judy at the time of her first MGM contract, 1935.

Quickly, Baby Frances became the star of the Gumm sisters; she would perform her songs and "belly dances" apart from the others. She was a precocious child, one who reveled in the attention she was getting. She knew she was cute, she knew people thought her antics funny—although she couldn't bear to be laughed *at*—and she knew she could attract listeners with the sheer volume of her voice.

The Gumms were becoming local celebrities, but it was soon apparent that the family could not stay in Grand Rapids. Ethel and Frank decided to move to Southern California, citing the harsh Minnesota winters and the lure of a warm climate. But the fact was that the gossip and innuendo about Frank were getting out of hand, and Ethel in particular hoped to start a new life in an area as far away from Grand Rapids as possible.

The children, particularly Baby Frances, didn't want to leave. Their friends were here, they'd spent their entire lives here. For the rest of her life, Judy Garland would resent her mother for uprooting them, and for the rest of her life think longingly of what seemed to her tranquillity and "normalcy." From this point on, Baby Frances would not be completely happy ever again.

The family settled first in Los Angeles, where Ethel enrolled all three of her girls in a professional dance school run by Ethel Meglin, whose "Meglin Kiddie Revues" were a frequent and popular attraction in the city. Ethel was determined that the success—such as it was—of her daughters' performing careers would be duplicated in California. Some of Mrs. Gumm's friends thought she was pushing too hard, but others observed that the girls—especially Frances—loved music, loved being in the spotlight, and seemed to be having fun. Who was to say that Ethel was wrong?

While Ethel worked singlemindedly with her girls, Frank Gumm was concerned about making a living. He tried to find a theater in Los Angeles to purchase but could not, principally because he required a stage big enough to produce shows on. (He thought the ability to stage live shows an asset to any movie theater.) Finally, his search brought him to Lancaster, a desert community sixty miles northeast of Los Angeles. He found a theater worth refurbishing, and against the wishes of the rest of his family, purchased it. Once again, the Gumms were uprooted, this time into an arid, hot, and far less friendly community. The townsfolk were suspicious of newcomers, and wary of "show business types."

But Frank and Ethel tried hard to be accepted; Frank particularly felt the family's future depended on it. He became the choirmaster at St. Paul's Episcopal Church, joined Masonic and Kiwanis organizations and got to know every other businessman in town. Ethel made herself available as a pianist at social events and became the church organist.

Once the Gumm family made its debut at Frank's Valley Theater on May 22, 1927, the Gumms were a part of the Lancaster community. The local paper covered the event; the girls would make six more appearances before the end of the year, including one in early December in which Frances came onstage as a black-faced minstrel girl and captured the audience with a rendition of "Mammy" à la Al Jolson.

None of the family really liked Lancaster, but for Frances it was a detriment to her health. She began to experience traumatic hay-fever attacks, brought about by dry desert winds spreading dust and pollen. She would wake up at night, barely able to breathe, and run to her mother. Ethel would put a blanket around her and take her out to the car. Several hours later, they would return—after having driven in and around the San Gabriel mountains until Frances fell asleep in the back seat of the car.

Later in her life, Judy Garland would tell elaborate stories about the terrible ordeals her mother put her though as a child. Some of these stories had elements of truth, others were spun entirely of Judy's need to generate sympathy for herself. While everyone who was around at the time explains these nocturnal rides as well-meaning attempts by Ethel to help her daughter's distress, Judy has said that Ethel would burst into her bedroom in the middle of the night after a fight with Frank, yank her daughter from the warmth of her bed, and announce, "We're leaving

With Toto and the Scarecrow (Ray Bolger) in *The Wizard of Oz*, 1939.

Daddy," ignoring Frances' pleas to let her stay. "Oh, Baby, you don't love me," her mother would accuse as she pushed the terrified little girl into the back seat.

Judy also told of being left in hotel rooms by her mother while they were on the road with a show. She would wait, terrified, thinking her mother might never return, until Ethel felt she had meted out enough punishment to her recalcitrant daughter.

This scenario is one no one but Ethel could confirm or deny; but the truth of Judy's accusations against her mother is largely irrelevant. Even if they are untrue, Judy's need to invent them—and the hatred she must have felt to have invented them—is much more to the point. And it is sadly ironic that, as a mother, Judy would use her children as pawns in battles with her husband, and lock them out of hotel rooms and houses. Whether the stories were true about Ethel, they became true with Judy.

Ethel's reputation—only partially deserved—as a "stage mother" began about this time. Her problems with her husband had not abated—before long, the rumors surfaced again—and Lancaster did not offer her much hope of escaping from her dissatisfaction and lack of fulfillment. She began making frequent trips down to Los Angeles with Baby Frances, leaving early in the morning on the two-and-a-half hour drive. It is perhaps these early morning trips which Judy would later combine in her memory with her hay-fever rides; in any event, she was taken down to Los Angeles for various auditions. Although Judy was to say early in her career that her mother never pushed her, she would later say, "Mother was no good for anything except to create chaos and fear. She didn't like me because of my talent. She resented it because she could only play 'Kitten on the Keys' like she was wearing boxing gloves. And when she sang, she had a crude voice. My sisters had lousy voices, too. My father had a pretty good voice, but he wasn't allowed to talk . . . I enjoyed ‹performing› because, while I didn't get any affection from my family, I got applause from strangers."

Judy did get affection—if not from her mother, then surely from her sisters and her father. She adored Frank, and once again it was what she perceived as her mother's hurtful treatment of him which would foster the hatred she felt for her mother later in her life.

Ethel, enmeshed in a marriage which must have been sexless for years, who had to deal with public whispers about her husband preferring men, sought solace in an affair with William Gilmore, the husband of a friend who had suffered a crippling stroke. Unfortunately, ten-year-old Frances and several of her friends were to accidentally run into her mother and Mr. Gilmore in an abandoned shack near an empty lot in which they were playing. His rendezvous interrupted, the angry Mr. Gilmore ran the children off with a stick, calling them "little brats." Frances never forgave her mother; in her mind Ethel was a hypocrite (sex was a forbidden subject in the Gumm household) and a whore who cheated on her saintly husband. It didn't matter that Frances didn't know the whole story, and never would: her mother was more hateful than she had even imagined.

During the next four years, Ethel's relentless quest for show business success for her daughters was constantly at odds with Frank's desire to have his family at home. And although Baby Gumm enjoyed the attention and the applause, she hated long separations from her father, which were inevitable as the Gumm Sisters went on the road and Frank stayed home to manage the theater.

But the Gumm Sisters were acquiring a reputation, and they were making money. After the stock-market crash of 1929, there was still work to be found in vaudeville, and Baby Frances was becoming a sought-after performer. She had a big voice, danced well, possessed a wonderful stage presence and a knowledge of what an audience liked to see. Ethel concentrated most of her attention on Frances; both because she was clearly the most talented of her daughters, and because Frances seemed to love the performing life much more than either Suzy or Jimmy.

What had been fun for Baby, though, was now threatening to become drudgery. It was work, there was no doubt, but the family needed the money.

A congratulatory kiss from Mickey Rooney as Judy wins a special juvenile Oscar for *The Wizard of Oz*, February 1940.

Judy's insecurity about her looks wasn't helped by the presence on the MGM lot of stunners like Hedy Lamarr and Lana Turner, with whom she co-starred in *Ziegfeld Girl* in 1941.

Mickey Rooney and Judy in one of their first collaborations, *Babes in Arms,* 1939.

The exuberant cast of *Babes on Broadway;* left to right, Ray McDonald, Virginia Weidler, Judy, and Mickey, Anne Rooney, and Richard Quine, 1941.

Ethel needed the fulfillment, and Baby would have to do it. She loved to sing, loved the attention, and so the conflict was within herself as much as it was with her mother. Her reaction was an almost passive resistance. She would invent excuses to forestall a trip into the city, but her mother's will was too strong: Frances could talk her way out of anything but performing.

The Gumm Sisters appeared in dozens of shows throughout the early thirties. In 1933, Ethel took her girls and moved to Los Angeles for good. Frank set them up in a house, then went back to Lancaster, where he gave up the house the family had lived in and rented a run-down apartment on the edge of town.

During that year and the next, Frank and Ethel would come close to divorce several times. "I don't know why my parents decided to stay together," Judy said later. "Perhaps it was for the sake of the children."

In Los Angeles, Frances was enrolled in the Lawlor School for Professional Children. Academically, it was not first rate. Its emphasis was on teaching children the essentials of show business: simple rules of courtesy in the theater, voice projection, how to get work permits— and, perhaps most important to Ethel Gumm—how to act in front of a movie camera. For she had begun to think about the possibility of movie stardom for her little girl. Trying to break her into motion pictures, though, would be a grueling task.

By 1934, Frank Gumm had rejoined his family in Los Angeles. He had wanted to stay in Lancaster, but he found himself increasingly ostracized by "concerned citizens" who decided he no longer "fit in." Feeling alienated and disgraced, he gave up his theater and bought another one in Lomita, twenty miles north of Los Angeles.

Baby Frances was delighted to have her father back, despite his quarrels with her mother, which got more and more bitter. Frank wasn't happy about Frances' being taken around Hollywood to various movie studio auditions which always resulted in disappointment. He was opposed to Ethel's plan to take the girls to the Chicago World's Fair and pay the way with engagements between Los Angeles and Illinois. But Ethel, as always, won out.

The trip East was a fateful one, filled with bizarre events. In Denver, their booking turned out to be a gambling club which had been recently raided. There were few people in the audience, but the club's manager kept them on the payroll. Because Baby Frances was underage to perform in a nightclub, Ethel sent Virginia out to rehearse instead in case a "checker" was around.

Once at the World's Fair, the Gumm sisters had a strong engagement going, for a fee of three hundred dollars per week, when they discovered that the concession they were working in was about to go bankrupt. Over a three-week period, they were paid thirty-five dollars. Ethel moved the girls from a two-bedroom suite in one of the finest hotels in town into a much less expensive accommodation. Reluctantly, she had to spend the traveler's checks Frank had given her to use only as a last resort.

Ethel heard about an open talent night at the Belmont Theater, which was reportedly attended by agents from the William Morris agency. The girls performed, and Baby Frances was a hit with the audience as usual, especially in one number, an inspiration of Ethel's: a baby spotlight focused on the back of Frances' head as she sat atop a piano and sang an uncanny impression of Helen Morgan singing "My Bill," in a rich, mature voice. The rendition prompted cheers from the audience—and gasps when the "woman" got off the piano stool and turned out to be a little girl!

Jack Cathcart, a musician, had met the girls at the World's Fair, and he rushed backstage to congratulate the amazing Baby Frances. He soon became a friend—particularly of Suzy, who later married him.

There was no William Morris agent present that night, but just as Ethel was about to give up and return home, Jack called Suzy to say that one of the acts had just been fired at the Oriental Theater—how fast could they get there? M.C. George Jessel introduced the girls as though they were a comedy act, laughingly stressing their last name. Still, they were a hit.

Judy with Gene Kelly in his first film, *For Me and My Gal,* 1942.

Judy and David Rose as they announced their engagement in June 1941.

Jessel was impressed by the audience's reaction, and he helped the sisters, both in Chicago and back in Los Angeles. But his most lasting contribution was to suggest a name change for the girls: he thought Garland (after his friend, New York theater critic Robert Garland) sounded much nicer than Gumm. And so the Gumm Sisters were rechristened.

Performing again in various cities on the way back to Los Angeles, Frances Garland was beginning to get a reputation. By the time she appeared at the famed Grauman's Chinese Theater in Hollywood in November 1934, no less a publication than *Variety* took note: "As a trio, it means nothing, but with the youngest featured, it hops into class entertainment, for, if such a thing is possible, the girl is a combination of Helen Morgan and Fuzzy Knight. Possessing a voice that, without a P.A. system, is audible throughout a house as big as the Chinese, she handles ballads like a veteran, and gets every note and word over with a personality that hits audiences . . . she has never failed to stop the show, her current engagement being no exception."

It wasn't long before Frances Garland came to the attention of Louis B. Mayer's personal assistant at MGM, Ida Koverman. Ida was impressed, and told Mayer he had to see this girl.

Mayer was so moved by her singing, so impressed by such a beautiful, powerful voice in one so young, that he signed her to a contract without a screen test—something unprecedented at the time. She was thirteen, and had given herself a new name—Judy. She joined the largest studio in the world, one which later boasted of having under contract "more stars than there are in heaven," among them Clark Gable, Joan Crawford, Greta Garbo, Spencer Tracy, and Wallace Beery. Ethel Gumm's dreams had come true.

Judy Garland's rise to fame has been well documented. Her Andy Hardy films with Mickey Rooney, her singing in Ziegfeld-type revues on screen, her wonderful performance in *The Wizard of Oz,* all helped a nation make it out of the Great Depression and through the shadowed days that presaged World War II. Next to Shirley Temple, who dominated the 1930s, and along with Mickey Rooney and Deanna Durbin, Judy Garland was the most popular child star in the country. By 1940, she and Bette Davis would be the only females on the Top Ten Box Office Attractions list.

To the public, Judy Garland was a charmed young lady: talented, successful, wealthy, the envy of girls all across the country. But behind the façade were those dark forces again. Shortly after Judy signed with MGM, her father died. It was a terrible blow to her; she never really got over it. And when her mother married Will Gilmore, himself by then widowed, it was one more thing Judy could not forgive her mother: the wedding was on the anniversary of her father's death. That the day was also her mother's birthday meant little to her: "That was the most awful thing that ever happened to me in my life. My mother marrying that awful man the same day my daddy died."

The death of her father created a vacuum in her life that Louis B. Mayer would soon fill, at least in the sense of being a taskmaster and disciplinarian. Joining MGM might have been a dream come true, but it was also a forfeiture, in many ways, of her individuality. One was part of a stable; the studio knew what was best—one did what one was told to do or there were severe penalties.

Ethel, it seemed to Judy, always sided with Mr. Mayer, as he was invariably called. Perhaps her father would have stood up for her, refused to allow some of the things Ethel permitted—certainly Judy thought so.

There was the work schedule, a grueling one—film after film with little rest between them; hours of rehearsal and filming; schooling whenever there was a free moment. It was tough, especially for kids.

And so there were the pills. Miracle tablets that gave one almost unlimited energy, or helped one sleep at night. No one at the time knew that such pills could be habit-forming and damaging, even deadly; they were looked on as marvelous elixirs.

A series of glamour portraits from the late thirties and early forties show Judy at her loveliest.

Judy took them, supplied by the studio doctor, not only to sleep and to keep functioning during the day, but also to keep her weight down, on orders from Mr. Mayer. The "up" pills, amphetamines, were appetite suppressants. Mayer told Judy she was too fat, and would have to lose weight. She took pills constantly, and they would wrench the rest of her life into a pattern that inflicted tremendous harm on herself and everyone around her.

She grew more and more resentful toward her mother, and the studio. As she grew older, she wanted to play more mature roles; the studio insisted that she continue to play children. At home, Ethel refused to acknowledge that she was able to make her own decisions; she attempted to put up roadblocks whenever Judy was romantically involved. In 1941, when the nineteen-year-old Judy wanted to marry David Rose, Ethel vehemently opposed it, threatening to go to Mr. Mayer and enlist his help in preventing it.

Finally, she relented, but it was one more standoff between mother and daughter, one more example in Judy's mind of her mother's tyranny and lack of concern with her happiness. But the worst was yet to come. When, several months after her marriage, Judy told Ethel she was pregnant, her mother was concerned about what having a baby would do to the fabulous Garland career—after all, she had movie commitments. Ethel went to Mr. Mayer, who agreed that a pregnancy was most inopportune. Judy was told that she would have to have an abortion. She didn't want to do it. Unsure, feeling abandoned, she went along with the decision her "parents" had made for her. She had the abortion. Judy's marriage to David Rose would never be the same. A year and a half after they married, they separated officially after living apart for some time.

Several months later, Judy Garland met Vincente Minnelli. It was an acquaintanceship that would change her life—and it is the point at which the story of Judy and Liza begins.

ONE

"I'm going to have a baby, Mama. Do you mind?"

—Judy Garland to her mother, 1945

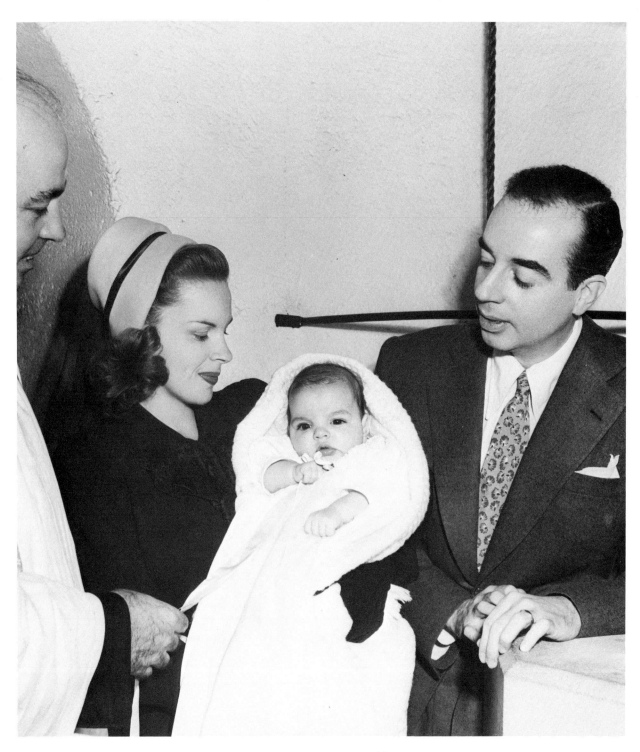

Liza's christening, 1946.

2

The first time she saw him—and for sometime afterward—Judy was not particularly impressed by Vincente Minnelli. There was, in fact, a degree of enmity between them when they were brought together to make *Meet Me in St. Louis*—he as director, she as star.

Minnelli's ascendency at MGM bordered on mercurial. After directing just two films—*Cabin in the Sky,* an all-black musical starring Ethel Waters, and *I Dood It,* a "comic potboiler" with Red Skelton and Eleanor Powell—Minnelli was assigned the major big-star production of *Meet Me in St. Louis.*

Although with his first two films he had batted just .500—*I Dood It* was a box-office flop—Minnelli had enough of a reputation as a Broadway art director to warrant this "big time" assignment. His career had started much like Judy's. His parents, Vincente and Mina (May) Minnelli, produced the Minnelli Brothers Dramatic and Tent Shows, in which, from the age of three on, he often appeared as the family barnstormed across the country. Young Vincente would play all the child parts in pirated productions for which no royalty was ever paid.

By the time Vincente was eight, in 1921, motion pictures had all but destroyed the tent theater—and the elder Vincente reluctantly gave it all up and moved his family to Delaware, Ohio. It was the first real home the Minnellis had ever had. "It wasn't as American Gothic as *Meet Me in St. Louis,*" Vincente says in his autobiography, *I Remember It Well.* "In fact it was rather ordinary. But to Mother it was a marvel. Starting up housekeeping at a late age, she didn't have the Victorian hand-me-downs that other housewives did. She was more modern, with golden oak furniture and chintz fabrics. I learned to appreciate these fripperies by looking at them through her eyes."

Most of Vincente's youthful sensibilities came to him from his mother. He had been her fourth son, and now was her only surviving child—the others having died from what Vincente remembers as "mysterious childhood diseases"—a situation upon which he would later comment, "Little wonder that Mother was overprotective of me."

She taught him to appreciate beauty—something which became of paramount importance in his life. His imagination took him beyond his "ordinary" environment to elegant drawing rooms where English aristocrats would discuss the literature he loved, to glamorous ballrooms which he sketched in minute detail—first from memory, of rooms he had seen in books and on film, then from his imagination. He created rooms more elaborate than any he had ever seen. His fantasy world made his own reality more bearable—and at times completely replaced it.

At sixteen, Vincente left Ohio and moved to Chicago. He studied at the Chicago Art Institute briefly, then, with costume sketches under his arm, was hired by the Balaban and Katz Theater chain in Chicago as a costume designer. When, in 1931, the chain's headquarters moved to New York, Vincente followed. And it was here—as with so many others—that Vincente Minnelli's life and art would take shape and flourish.

His designs, both of costumes and sets, were lavish, extravagant, and beautiful. He possessed a rare talent—the ability to create sumptuousness that did not extend to excess; visual flamboyance tempered by rare good taste. It was a combination sure to make the man a successful art director.

And he became one, at Radio City Music Hall, overseeing splashy productions such as the Ziegfeld Follies, *Cabin in the Sky, Very Warm for May,* and *Hooray for What?*

As Esther Smith in *Meet Me in St. Louis,* 1944.

His talents were well utilized by Broadway, but after eight years, his work for the stage fulfilled him less and less. He began casting covetous eyes at Hollywood—a place with more money to realize his visions, more opportunities for expression. And on film, his work would be immortalized, not torn down to make room for the next show. He took the first opportunity to head west—in 1940, as an apprentice with the Arthur Freed unit at MGM.

It was Freed who first brought to Vincente the idea of making a movie based on a series of turn-of-the-century childhood reminiscences Sally Benson had written for *The New Yorker* and which were later reprinted in book form as *Meet Me in St. Louis.* Warm, sentimental, and evocative, the stories struck Freed as a perfect basis for a movie of the same nature—the kind of film MGM knew the war-weary country wanted to see.

Vincente was excited about the project. He knew the film would be a sizable step forward in his career, and he found the stories humorous and affecting. The first script submitted to him, however, he felt had gone completely off the track, concocting a story of blackmail around the lead character, Esther Smith. "This is hardly the stuff of which lyrical evocations of an era are made," Vincente has said, "so I suggested we get another version."

Both Arthur Freed and Louis B. Mayer wanted Judy to star as Esther Smith. Minnelli was all for it, and Freed commissioned Fred Finklehoffe and Irving S. Brecher to write a script with Judy in mind. They produced a screenplay Minnelli loved, concentrating on one episode in the book: "Though fragile, it had great charm."

The story—about the family's having to move to New York and its effect on each member—was indeed "fragile," so much so that Judy, among others, objected to it as having "no plot." And that was just one of the reasons Judy did not want to make *Meet Me in St. Louis.* She was tired of playing young girls; she felt, at twenty-one, that she should be allowed to play parts more mature than the seventeen-year-old Esther Smith. And the taste that *Presenting Lily Mars* and *Ziegfeld Girl* had given her of on-screen glamour only hardened her resolve not to regress. Her closest friends and associates, among them Joseph Mankiewicz (with whom she was having an intermittent affair) warned her against doing it—"It will set your career back twenty years." Mankiewicz pointed out as well that although Judy was to be the nominal star, the extraordinary seven-year-old Margaret O'Brien, cast as Esther's younger sister, would almost certainly steal the picture away from everyone concerned.

Neither did Judy particularly relish the idea of working on a complete film with Vincente Minnelli. He and Judy had worked together on sequences for *Strike Up the Band* and *Babes in Arms,* and she had been intimidated by his erudition, sophistication, and style; she mistook his natural diffidence and remoteness for condescension. She simply couldn't make this picture with this man at this point in her career. She went to see Mayer.

A few days later, Mayer called Freed. "Judy's been up here raising hell about this, Arthur. She doesn't went to do the picture. For once I have to agree with her. I've read it and there's no plot." Other MGM executives agreed. Judy was exultant. At last, she was not only being listened to but her opinions were being confirmed by top studio brass. But Freed, whom Mayer greatly respected, and Minnelli, in whom he saw tremendous potential, held firm. They wanted to do this picture, and they wanted Judy Garland to star in it.

Judy simply couldn't understand what Minnelli and Freed saw in this script—and she was intrigued by their insistence on its quality. She went to see Minnelli, partly curious to have this film's appeal explained to her, but mostly looking for confrontation and hoping to talk Minnelli out of it.

When she entered his office, she came face-to-face with Minnelli in more than a pass-and-nod fashion for the first time in nearly three years. She still found him intimidating, but his impeccable manners and hostly courtesies even to those discussing business in his office put her off guard and further blunted her hostile convictions. Instead of the harangue she had planned against the script, she merely asked, "It's not very good, is it?"

"I think it's fine," Minnelli answered. "I see a lot of great things in it. In fact, it's magical." Judy was surprised by the strength of his belief in the project, but remained unmoved in her own opinion: "Judy couldn't see the magic," Minnelli says, "neither in my approach nor, I suppose, in me."

The meeting was a stalemate. But Arthur Freed, pressing Mayer for a final go-ahead, convinced him to let Lillie Messenger, a top studio scriptwriter known for her ability to spot a good story, read the *Meet Me in St. Louis* script. She was enthusiastic, thought the story a wonderful slice of Americana, and retold it to Mayer in a crystallized version which made clear to him the charm and substance of the story. He was won over.

Judy was not. If she could be convinced that all her misgivings about the script and the character were unfounded, there was still the fact that she truly didn't want to make this film. It would be a grand musical—the highest-budgeted film of her career—and she did not feel up to the rigors. The diet pills had brought her down to ninety-two pounds—her ideal weight was ninety-eight pounds—and she was weak and tired. Her apprehensions and fears, her feelings of inadequacy, her belief that she was being abused and exploited by the studio—all these came together to harden her resolve. And she held on to a glimmer of hope that should she be able to get out of making this film, another suitable project might not come along quickly. She could take a rest.

But Mayer, now convinced that *Meet Me in St. Louis* had tremendous potential and that Judy would be a perfect Esther Smith, threatened his star with suspension if she refused to make the film. Judy, faced with a cessation of her salary, paid enough attention to her finances to learn, with horror, that she was broke. The Gilmores had invested her money badly, failed to put any of it aside for taxes and—worst of all—her home was about to be repossessed for failure to make mortgage payments on time. As she would so often in the future, Judy found that her indifference to her financial affairs could spell disaster—and that she would be forced to work simply to have her life remain on an even keel.

The first day of shooting on *Meet Me in St. Louis* confirmed all of Judy's worst fears about Vincente Minnelli. Still somewhat intimidated by his mind and his manner, Judy found his direction of her maddening. He was soft-spoken almost to a fault; his low-key approach left her adrift on a sea of uncertainty. The problem began with her very first scene. After the first take, Vincente calmly suggested that they try it again. The cameras rolled, the scene was played, Minnelli yelled "Cut!" Then he indicated that the scene would have to be shot again. He looked at Judy. "I want you to read your lines as if you mean every word," he told her. It was certainly not something a director should have to tell an experienced actress. Judy was mortified and angry. The next two takes were also not to Minnelli's satisfaction. "We'll shoot it again after lunch," he told the crew—and left the sound stage.

Judy went to her dressing room on the verge of tears and called Arthur Freed. "I just don't know what this man wants. The whole morning's gone by and we still haven't got a shot. He makes me feel I can't act."

Freed reassured her, mumbling something about Minnelli's being from New York, and told her that everything would work out if she would trust him.

The problem, as Minnelli saw it, stemmed from the fact that Judy did not want to be playing a seventeen-year-old in another All-American "folksy" picture. Her line readings not only lacked conviction, they faintly mocked the emotions being expressed. "Her intelligence showed through," Minnelli recalls, "and she didn't come off as an impressionable young girl."

After several more takes later in the afternoon, Judy played the scene to Minnelli's satisfaction. Whether it was the actress in her, or simply a desire to get the thing over with that

30

triumphed, didn't matter to anyone. The ice had been broken. "Finally, the message got to her," Minnelli recalled in his autobiography. "I still don't know how. Once she grasped the motivation, she was as brilliant in the dramatic scenes as she'd been in the musical numbers."

But the problem of Judy finding her character's motivation was only part of the clash between director and star. His perfectionism and demands for retakes—many of which related in no way to Judy—exasperated her; she was particularly distressed by Minnelli's desire for lengthy rehearsals of certain scenes. Judy would attempt to leave the studio before Minnelli could announce an after-shooting rehearsal; he would have her limousine intercepted at the studio gate, much to her fury.

During repeated rehearsals of one scene, Judy, in Minnelli's words, "went grousing" to Mary Astor, who was playing her mother. "This is ridiculous," she muttered to the veteran of ninety films after a third run-through of the scene.

Mary Astor looked at Judy. "He knows what he is doing. He's absolutely right. Just go along with it, because it means something."

Slowly, Judy's opinion of the film—and of the director—began to change. Watching an occasional daily, Judy could see clearly that Minnelli was making a beautiful, vibrant film. And it was clear to her that by whatever method, he was drawing out of her a sensitive, warm portrayal of a real, substantive person. Esther Smith might be seventeen and homespun, but she wasn't—like so many characters Garland had had to play in the past—cartoony and cornball. Judy began to respect Minnelli, and to understand him; rather than fearing that he would damage her image on film, she now felt he would enhance it.

She began to work with confidence; Minnelli was amazed when she would flawlessly perform a series of last-minute changes as though she had rehearsed them for hours. And while on too many mornings she had dreaded facing the camera to such a degree that she would retch violently in her dressing room, she now looked forward to days of creativity and accomplishment with Vincente Minnelli.

Minnelli found himself more and more fascinated by this girl. For his entire life, he had thought of women as creatures to be idolized, put on a pedestal. That wasn't possible, of course, with a woman who did not possess sufficient intelligence, talent, or charm. Judy, Vincente was to find after her initial displays of temperament, possessed all three in abundance. She wasn't just a spoiled child star. She was a captivatingly bright, intellectually curious young woman.

For her part, Judy was equally intrigued by Minnelli. He represented quiet strength, a quality she had not found to this degree in any man but her father. She was soon to get the chance to know him socially, not just in a director/actress relationship.

Don Loper, who later made a name for himself as a fashion designer, had been escorting Judy around town—but there was no romantic chemistry between them. Loper took Judy's increasingly frequent conversations about Minnelli as his cue to bring the two of them together outside the work situation. He called Minnelli and asked if he would be kind enough to escort Loper's friend Ruth Brady to a dinner date with Don and Judy. Minnelli agreed.

The foursome had a wonderful time. Judy's wit, as usual in social situations, shone; Minnelli was further impressed by the sharpness of her intellect. And Judy saw another side of this laconic, aloof man: his own sense of humor, an ascerbic wit and heightened sense of the ridiculous which Judy found delightful. He was also a completely on-target—and often devastating—mimic. It was a quality which surprised and delighted Judy.

A newly discovered quality in Judy surprised Minnelli too: her self-deprecating humor. Judy would tell of Louis B. Mayer's introducing her to visitors with, "Do you see this little girl? Look what I've made her into. She used to be a hunchback." And she would tell hilarious stories of trying to hold her own with beauties like Lana Turner and Hedy Lamarr surrounding her.

31

Minnelli was charmed, and touched. "Like everyone else at the studio, I wanted to protect and love her. And Judy was affectionate and loving right back."

The foursome continued to date until the day Loper called Minnelli to say that he couldn't make it that night and would Vincente call Judy to cancel. Minnelli did, and Judy chuckled. "We don't have to go out with Don and Ruth every time, do we?" she asked. "We can go alone."

Their courtship began. Where before Judy had been intimidated by Minnelli's sophistication, she now longed for him to teach her all that he knew about art, literature, style, music. He explained his porcelain collection to her, loaned her art books, taught her what to look for in an antique.

Early in their relationship, Judy shared one piece of information with Minnelli. They were dining at a Sunset Strip restaurant, reminiscing about their childhoods. Judy's mood turned suddenly dark. "I always have to be at my best in front of the camera," she said. "You should know that. You expect it of me too. Well, sometimes I don't feel my best. It's a struggle to get through the day."

Minnelli wasn't sure what she was trying to say.

"I use these pills," she went on. "They carry me through."

Minnelli was aware that many studio people used pills to "carry them through." No one at that time knew, however, that the pills could be harmfully addictive. "Well," he replied, "as long as you don't overdo it, I guess it's all right."

Filming on *Meet Me in St. Louis* was completed in April 1944. By then, Judy and Vincente were living together. She was now a part of his world, a world which included close friendships with Lee and Ira Gershwin, Cole Porter, Harold Arlen, Josephine Baker, William Saroyan, Oscar Levant, Dorothy Parker, and others of this elite, sophisticated, and intellectual world. Although Judy was shy and quiet at first, her natural ebullience and native intelligence won over Minnelli's most erudite friends.

Lee and Ira Gershwin had been Vincente's closest friends since his days in New York. They had known Judy since she'd been introduced to Lee wearing her full Dorothy regalia from *The Wizard of Oz,* but they had not been close.

The Gershwins too were captivated by Judy's humor—but there was more to it than that. "It wasn't funny lines," Lee Gershwin recalls, "it was humorous stories, most of them directed at herself. She was more than bright—she was able to fit in, to hold her own, with anyone. This was one of the most sophisticated households—Albert Camus would come to parties—and Judy would not be out of place. You could talk about any book or author, and Judy would contribute to the conversation. And this after having practically no background at all."

The release of *Meet Me in St. Louis* in November 1944 prompted critical praise and produced tremendous box-office receipts (it soon became MGM's biggest grosser since *Gone With the Wind*). *Time* called it "a musical even the deaf should enjoy. They will miss some attractive tunes . . . but they can watch one of the year's prettiest pictures . . . Technicolor has seldom been more affectionately used than in its registrations of the sober mahoganies and tender muslins and benign gaslights of the period. Now and then, too, the film gets well beyond the charm of mere tableau for short flights in the empyrean of genuine domestic poetry."

Judy's reviews as well were highly flattering, and her fears of being completely outshone by Margaret O'Brien proved unfounded. While audiences found the precocious youngster charming, as usual, there was no forgetting who the star was. Judy was coming into her own as a movie star.

And in her private life, she was on her own. Now that she was no longer living with Ethel, her mother's impact on her life had lessened considerably. (Judy's twenty-first birthday, in June of the previous year, had had a great deal to do with that too.) But Mrs. Gilmore wasn't about to allow the apron strings to be severed completely. When she became aware that Judy and Vincente were cohabitating, she wrote him a lengthy letter, haranguing him for "taking advantage" of her little girl and expressing amazement that an older man would do such a dishonorable thing. She was, she said, sorely disappointed in him.

"I immediately answered the letter as respectfully as I could," Minnelli says, "saying I would never do anything to hurt Judy and we would get married when we could."

That was not to be as soon as Vincente hoped. Judy had begun seeing Joe Mankiewicz again. "She simply gravitated back to him," Minnelli says, "just as she had toward me at the start of our affair. I theorized that Judy must have been flattered by the attentions of such a brilliant man, and intrigued by the fact that he was in analysis. It didn't alleviate my pain."

Minnelli plunged into the "distraction" of directing *Ziegfeld Follies,* a three-million-dollar extravaganza with an all-star cast, sixty-five scenes, and twenty sketches. One of the sketches was "The Great Lady Has an Interview," a musical satire on movie stars with inflated senses of self-importance. The original plan had been for Greer Garson to spoof her stuffy Mrs. Miniver image, but she turned it down, convinced that a real singer would have to perform the role. Kay Thompson, who wrote the sketch with Roger Edens and had performed it for Vincente, suggested Judy. Minnelli agreed, somewhat reluctantly, because he was aware Judy would be perfect. "Any pain I might have been dreading in seeing Judy again simply didn't come to pass. We were no longer lovers, but we could be friends. Shooting the number was great fun."

Judy's reunion with Joseph Mankiewicz was short-lived. Her hopes of a lasting romance with him dashed again, she moved back into her mother's home. Ethel was delighted; she had the entire upper floor of the mansion redone as a suite for Judy, in her favorite colors and with flourishes worthy of a "great lady." There was a tentative truce between mother and daughter despite the dreadful scene engendered by Ethel's letter to Vincente, an act which mortified Judy. The entire family, in fact, was now under one roof—all three daughters, Suzy's husband Jack, Jimmy's daughter, Judalein, and Grandma Eva. Things were the way Ethel wanted them.

After several months of working on *Ziegfeld Follies* post-production, Vincente got a call from Judy. She invited him to lunch. "Curiosity consumed me," Vincente says. Judy told him that *The Clock,* which was to be her first straight dramatic role, had been shelved. The main reason, which she did not elaborate on, was that she did not feel compatible with director Fred Zinnemann, a newcomer. She had wanted Vincente—to direct the picture, and whether her failures to show up for filming were the result of psychosomatic illnesses or a conscious desire to undermine Zinnemann, they had just that effect.

In any clash between Judy Garland and a novice director, Judy had to win. She had walked into Arthur Freed's office one day and told him, "I know Fred Zinnemann is a talented man, but we just can't seem to hit it off together. I can't work with him anymore." Freed knew Judy well enough. "You want Vincente, don't you?" Judy had laughed and nodded.

Now, Vincente told Judy he would look at what had already been shot, to see if he felt he could do some good; but he told her he wouldn't replace Zinnemann without his approval. Minnelli looked at the footage already shot of Judy and Robert Walker as a young couple who meet in New York City as the man is going off to war, have a whirlwind twenty-four-hour courtship and marry just before he leaves. Minnelli liked the story, but felt the footage shot so far did not work. "Each scene . . . looked as if it came from a different picture. It was very confusing. I could see why Metro's executive committee had canceled the project."

Minnelli dropped Zinnemann a note, telling him he would like to take over the picture and asking for his okay. "He was quite put out at Judy, but he gave me his blessings." Filming on *The Clock* began in September 1944. It was a pleasure for Judy, not the terrible grind so many of her previous films had been. With no musical numbers, she did not have to drive herself to the brink of exhaustion simply to keep up. What the film did demand of her, more so than any other, was emotion—the dizzying emotions of a young girl falling crazily in love. And she had a well from which to draw these feelings—she was falling for Vincente all over again. "Some people who see the picture today say it was obvious that I was deeply in love with Judy," Minnelli says. "My feelings for Judy *did* show, as hers about me also did. The script dictated the action, however . . ."

Minnelli as professional—and rapidly ascending MGM star—appealed to Judy as much as Minnelli as lover, sophisticate, raconteur, and friend. For years she had felt it was her against the studio. Certainly it seemed that her mother always sided with Mr. Mayer, and there were precious few people with power and influence at MGM who would side with Judy against him or anyone else of influence. Minnelli, Judy hoped, would be a strong ally in her battles with MGM. It was still another reason to stick with this man.

Although Judy was still living in Ethel's Ogden Drive house, she and Vincente spent a great deal of time together, including occasional nights. Ethel and Judy began frequent quarreling, which culminated in Ethel's phoning Vincente to express once again her vehement disapproval of his relationship with her daughter.

Judy flew into a rage, and, amid a flood of expletives which shocked Ethel into silence, she packed her bags and moved back into Vincente's house. Ethel was devastated—the entire house was practically a shrine to Judy—and she couldn't understand her daughter's anger over something she had done "for her own good."

From Judy's point of view, of course, Ethel was maddeningly meddlesome in matters that were not her concern. Judy was now an adult; she was a big Hollywood star and the family breadwinner. Surely she could carry on a relationship with a man if she so chose. But as she had so many times before, Judy felt Ethel's priorities were her own selfish needs, rather than her daughter's happiness. This latest rift between mother and daughter would last until Judy and Vincente were married.

"We were happy with each other," Minnelli says. "There were the sad times, to be sure, but they were so minor compared to what we usually had. I'd learned to accept those aspects of Judy's makeup that couldn't be changed . . . her frequent swings from moodiness to exuberance . . . a hot temper. She simply couldn't help being what she was, and what she was simply was much more than I ever felt I merited. She gave me so much. I could well learn to live with her occasional moments of despair."

And their professional rapport was something to gladden the hearts of MGM's executives. *The Clock* opened in March 1945 to excellent reviews and good box office. While some critics and audiences missed the musical Judy, most were equally impressed by Garland without a song. *Variety* said, "*The Clock* is a heartwarming and sentimental tale . . . sensitively directed by Vincente Minnelli [which] establishes Judy Garland as a dramatic star, without benefit of singing . . . Miss Garland's first strictly dramatic characterization makes her a double-threat player, capable of undertaking either a singing or straight portrayal . . ."

Judy and Vincente had a lot to feel good about. Three months after *The Clock* opened, and two weeks after her divorce from David Rose became final, they were married. This time, Judy had the blessings of both her mother and Louis B. Mayer. The wedding was held at Ethel's house, a definite—and public—sign of still another patch-up of their differences.

Mayer gave the bride away; Ira Gershwin was best man, and Betty Asher, Judy's publicist and friend, was maid of honor. None of Vincente's immediate family was in attendance. His mother had died several months earlier, and his father was too ill to make the trip from Florida. Before his mother's death, however, Judy had written Vincente's parents of their plans to marry. "We haven't met," she wrote, "but Vincente has told me such wonderful stories about his parents and the tent theater, that I feel I know you and also love you." Minnelli's parents were charmed.

Judy's family made up for the Minnelli absences: Ethel, of course, and Judy's sisters, brother-in-law Jack, niece Judalein, Eva, the Rabwins, and other close Gumm family friends.

34

Mr. and Mrs. Vincente Minnelli pose after their wedding, June 13, 1945.

John Hodiak assists Judy in *The Harvey Girls*, 1946.

For their honeymoon, the Minnellis chose to go to New York, where they had had a wonderful time on a trip (courtesy of Arthur Freed) after the filming of *Meet Me in St. Louis*. Judy had been to New York several times before, but now she was seeing it through Vincente's eyes. He took her to art museums and small antique shops he had frequented while living there; introduced her to his favorite Italian restaurants and the people with whom he had been close.

Judy was happier than she'd ever been. As useful a barometer as any of Judy's state of mind was her use of pills. She and Vincente had discussed this once again since their initial conversation at dinner. Judy had gone into a deep depression, and Vincente asked her if there was anything he could do.

"I think I might be taking too many of those pills," Judy had confessed.

"I know," Vincente replied. "I can't put my foot down and tell you to stop. I know there are times when you're tired and things don't go well at the studio. There are several actresses around who are doing the same thing. And I can always tell when they're on Benzedrine. Just as I can with you. You think you're doing wonderfully, that this is the best performance you've given. But you're not nearly as effective as you think you are." Judy was silent. "Promise you'll stop taking them," Vincente pleaded. "Please try."

"You know I try," Judy replied. And there were times when Vincente was aware that she had forsworn the pills altogether; other days he would return home from the studio to find Judy speaking and moving so rapidly it was clear she had taken amphetamines. He felt helpless to prevent it unless Judy truly wanted to quit.

Honeymooning in New York, happier than she thought she could be, convinced that Minnelli was her knight in shining armor, confident that her battles with the studio would now be won with the powerful help of her husband, Judy felt no need for pills. After just a few days in New York, while she and Vincente were walking in a park along the East River, Judy stopped. "Hold my hand," she said. Vincente noticed a bottle of pills in her other hand. She threw the bottle into the river and turned to him. "I'll never take them again."

Vincente was moved nearly to tears. We love each other so much, he thought. This marriage will last.

Shortly before their planned return to California, Judy learned that she was pregnant. She was overjoyed (Lee Gershwin recalls "Judy wanted a hundred kids") and so was Vincente, but Judy had one gnawing doubt. She had never really gotten over the abortion of her baby with David Rose, nor had she told Vincente about it. Now, when she called her mother from New York to give her the news, she would present it in a tentative way.

"I'm going to have a baby, Mama," Judy said into the telephone. "Do you mind?"

3

Judy and Vincente decided not to let the studio know about her pregnancy for a while. Judy was scheduled to appear briefly as Marilyn Miller in a Jerome Kern biography, *Till the Clouds Roll By,* another all-star extravaganza.

Judy wanted to avoid setting foot in the studio until long after her baby's birth, and she prevailed upon Vincente to convince the studio not to use her. He tried, but rather than replace Judy, producer Arthur Freed simply arranged the filming so that it could be completed before she began to "show." And Vincente, although not directing the picture, would be in charge of Judy's three musical numbers.

She was pregnant enough, however, that some sleight-of-hand was necessary to camouflage her condition. Her first number, "Sunny," took place in a circus, and a double was used when Judy was supposed to jump on a horse. The second piece, "Look for the Silver Lining," Judy sang while standing behind a sink doing dishes.

Only in the third sequence was there no way to hide the fact. The song was called "Who?" and Judy, seeing the footage, roared with laughter. "There I was, sticking out to here. I kept running up to each man in the scene, singing the question, 'Who?'"

Judy's contributions to the film took two weeks to complete, at which time she was four-and-a-half months pregnant. By now, she really was too big to work, and for the first time—after twenty-six films in eleven years—she was to have an extended period away from a sound stage.

Judy was overjoyed at the thought of it—and the idea of her impending motherhood. If she had struggled to be treated as an adult since she was sixteen, here at last was certification that she was indeed that—she was going to be a *mother.* She was sure they could no longer ask her to play naïve teenagers; the whole world would share in her baby's birth. Now, perhaps, she would be treated as a woman, not a little girl.

And she vowed to herself to be the best mother ever. She would never force her will on her child the way she felt her mother had on her; she would never be too busy for her child. Her baby would grow up the happiest, most beautiful, most well-adjusted person in the world.

Part of Judy's new motherly outlook was a brand-new interest in domestic pursuits. She had never had to take care of herself or learn how to run a house; first there had been Ethel, then a plethora of servants. Now that she was going to be a mother herself, she felt she simply had to take part in the daily operations of her household. She did this with little aptitude but much enthusiasm.

Despite the fact that their palatial house with its panoramic view was well staffed with servants, Judy would decide to scrub the kitchen floor, or bake a cake for dinner, or try her hand at needlepoint. Her cake baking was particularly traumatic for the cook. Judy would use every pan in the kitchen, and once the cake was ready for the oven, every surface would be covered with flour. The cook would follow behind her, trying to keep things fairly clean.

Once the cake had been served, Vincente would praise it profusely, assure Judy that it wasn't lopsided, and tell her it was the best cake he'd ever eaten. He quickly learned that Judy was to be praised no matter how inept her endeavors. "Her desire for constant approval was pathological. If she soon became bored with the kitchen floor or the needlepoint canvas had only a half a dozen stitches, then I quickly assured her that was the cleanest half of a kitchen floor in existence and those few stitches were the most uniform ever executed . . . the finishing up would be relegated to the servants."

During the entire term of her pregnancy, Judy stayed away completely from pills, or her "medication" as she had come euphemistically to call them. She was determined that her baby would be perfect and healthy, and she feared that the pills might have some adverse effect on the child.

Shortly before the expected birth date, the decision was made to deliver by Caesarian section, and on March 12, 1946, at 7:28 A.M., a 6-pound 10½-ounce baby girl was born to the Minnellis. They had already decided to name a girl child Liza May, after the Gershwin tune "Liza" and Vincente's mother.

The child was healthy, cried vociferously, and—according to her proud papa, was the prettiest baby in the nursery. Minnelli had once expressed reservations about ever getting married because of "what a child of mine would look like." But this baby seemed to have only the best features of its mother and father—Vincente's large eyes, Judy's alabaster skin. "As for those other wrinkled babies around her," Minnelli says, "all they needed was a cigar in their mouths to look like Eddie Mannix at the studio. There, alone on a table, was a perfect child, with absolutely no wrinkles, letting out a healthy cry—projecting!"

Within a few days, mother and daughter returned home to their house on Evanview Drive. The Minnellis had spent seventy thousand dollars redecorating it, converting Vincente's downstairs study into a sunny, cheerful nursery.

Judy had anticipated Liza's birth with great joy and not a small amount of awe. But she was not immune—in fact she was more susceptible than most—to some of the more negative aspects of first-time motherhood. She suffered a severe post-partum depression, and developed a fear of sexual relations which lasted an inordinately long period of time.

Judy's fear of sex could well be explained by the "Madonna complex": the idea that sex is not something to be associated with a mother. We are, after all, in the mid-forties, long before the *thought* of a sexual revolution had been entertained, much less the fact.

The Victorian notions of sex as something to be ashamed of, endured only for the sake of having children, continued in much of America through the 1940s and the 1950s. Motherhood was blessed, sacred; sex was dirty. The innocence and pureness of a newborn baby could make thoughts of sex create great feelings of guilt.

These new, ambivalent emotions toward her sexuality left Judy anxious and unsure, feelings compounded by the fact that now her baby was no longer an abstraction, but a living, breathing, frighteningly *dependent* reality.

As insecure as Judy was about every other aspect of her life, it is not difficult to imagine how terrifying this enormous new responsibility must have been to her. As much as she wanted to be treated as an adult, she was woefully unprepared to assume the role. She had always been dependent on others—her mother, who made all her decisions for her, the studio, which could solve any problem and which had taught Judy that problems, decisions—even the course of her life and career—were not things to worry her pretty little head about: all you have to think about, Judy, is being your wonderful self on camera.

Now, faced with the responsibility for another human being's life, needing to make decisions, needing to be able to handle a crisis at any time—Judy felt terrified that her practical incompetencies would someday endanger her lovely little girl.

Other complex—and disturbing—emotions were gnawing at Judy. She had been told all her life—by her mother, grandmother, aunts, sisters—that motherhood was the greatest achievement any woman could aspire to; that motherhood would bring total bliss and that mothers love their children totally, always, unconditionally.

She did not always feel that way. Sometimes, she didn't want to care for Liza, wanted to throw off the burden of caring for her. And Judy the actress, Judy the star, Judy the pampered center of attention—this Judy was often jealous of her child, jealous of the attention Liza got from Vincente and their friends, resentful of the time she demanded of her mother.

Liza sits in her mother's chair on the set of *The Pirate*, 1947.

All of these emotions caused Judy great distress: she couldn't be a good mother and feel this way. She did not know that it is a common syndrome with new mothers, especially first-time mothers. Motherhood, idealized to the point where living up to the ideal is often beyond human capability, can leave a woman who believes in the ideal feeling woefully inadequate and guilt-ridden. These feelings confused and frightened Judy. She tried her best to play the motherly role she thought was expected of her. She kept a chart of what Liza ate and when; never failed to tuck her into bed; and bought a baby book in which to record all of Liza's firsts. But it is an indication of Judy's sense of duty rather than a natural aptitude and enthusiasm for mothering that all of the book's entries—from first visitors to first tooth—were made at the same time, after Judy had procrastinated as long as she could about keeping the records.

As her eight-month layoff from work wore on, Judy found herself less and less able to handle the rigors of caring for Liza. More and more, the child's care was entrusted to her nurse. Often, after a period of not being able to deal with Liza—and sometimes not wanting to—Judy would suffer paroxysms of guilt from which she would emerge by showering the little girl with effusive expressions of love. It was a pattern that would be repeated throughout Liza's life.

Her inability to be the perfect mother she had been taught all women should be left Judy less secure than ever, more frightened, more neurotic. She dreaded the upcoming duty of reporting back to work at MGM for *The Pirate*. Daily, the date drew nearer—November 21. She wished the whole thing would go away.

And what would seem to most people an incredible boost, a further certification that one was valuable, wonderful, a success—only reinforced Judy's private demons. MGM rewrote her contract once again, paying her not the $1,000 per week maximum the first contract promised, but over $5,600 a week. And the contract was considerably more humane than the first had been: Judy needn't make more than two films a year.

But to Judy it represented, along with greater wealth and admission of her value to the studio, a further cementing of Metro's grip on her life. There was no softening of the penalties for lack of performance: suspension, cancellation of the contract, withholding of pay. Every day brought her closer to that contractual starting date for *The Pirate,* in which she was to costar with Gene Kelly, with Vincente as director.

MGM allowed Judy a grace period of two weeks if she felt herself unable to report on November 21. Despite the fact that she had had eight months' rest after Liza's birth, she reported on the absolute last day.

To be paid more than $1,000 *per day* to produce put a pressure on Judy unfathomable to anyone who has never been in that position. She didn't want to do the film, and she began preproduction work with little of the enthusiasm Vincente felt for the project. There *were* things to be said for it, as far as Judy was concerned: it would be the most sophisticated vehicle she'd yet starred in, the songs were by Cole Porter, whom she revered, and she was playing an adult role that would, if handled correctly, greatly expand her comedic range. The story line, though slim, was witty; and Judy's part had been played by Lynn Fontanne on the stage.

The role was demanding; Judy needed to sing, be funny—and dance well enough to keep up with Gene Kelly. The familiar patterns reappeared. She was unable to sleep at night, and began taking sedatives again. She would arrive hours late on the set, or not at all. In order to function, she took Benzedrines. Minnelli stood helplessly by, unable to figure out who was giving them to her.

As they would do again and again in her later life, the pills created wild mood swings in Judy, deepening her depression and creating paranoiac episodes frightening in their intensity. Arthur Freed recalls the filming of a number called "Voodoo," which was filmed at night around an open fire. Everyone waited for Judy to appear. No one was prepared for what happened when she did. Her eyes wide with terror, she ran to the center of the sound stage, stared into the fire

41

and screamed "I'm going to burn to death! They want me to burn to death!" She became hysterical; Vincente tried to calm her, but she broke away from him and ran over to a group of extras, begging them for Benzedrines. None of them had any. She laughed, screamed, cried, was completely out of control. Finally she was led away and taken home. The crew was appalled and saddened. They had all heard how bad it had become with Judy. But now they had seen it with their own eyes.

Afterward, Judy would be absent for weeks at a time; often she would come in very late, stay just a few hours, then abruptly leave. Gene Kelly began trying to cover for her; he once feigned sickness for a week so that full blame for delays would not fall on her.

Vincente was in a dreadful state, trying to make a picture, cover for Judy with the front office, and keep his wife on as even a keel as possible. An indication of the strain Minnelli was under surfaced during the running of dailies of a mock fight scene to accompany the musical number "You Can Do No Wrong."

The film's editor had omitted a designated close-up of Judy because she looked spent and haggard. Vincente, normally the most civilized of men, was so enraged he literally jumped up and reached for the editor's throat before stopping himself.

Every day, after filming, Vincente drove Judy to her psychiatrist and waited in the car for her return fifty minutes later. She would come out at the end of the session, her mood unaltered, unwilling to discuss with her husband what had transpired with the doctor. Vincente placed great hope in these sessions as the salvation of his wife's psyche. He didn't see any improvement in Judy's state of mind, but then, everyone had told him that psychoanalysis was no overnight cure. He would be patient.

Judy's emotional problems on the set inevitably affected the Minnellis' home life as well. Judy and Vincente fought frequently, the shouting matches reaching a crescendo as Vincente's temper explosions matched his wife's drug-induced hysteria. Vincente simply didn't know how to handle Judy when she was under the influence; he felt it best to leave her to her own devices, and his alternating attempts to keep his distance and to quietly soothe her were seen by Judy as either indifference or ineffectuality.

What Judy had initially seen as "quiet strength" in Minnelli she now viewed as weakness. She was disillusioned and had lost her respect for him. Somewhere in the recesses of her mind she wanted a man who would discipline her, keep her in line, show his love by whipping her into shape and out of her downward spiral. Such was not Minnelli's style. His love for Judy took the form of caring and solicitation, or of giving her room when he thought she needed it. His quiet manner was now something which often infuriated her.

Their fights frequently resulted in one or the other spending the night at the Gershwins', where Lee more than once stayed up the entire night with a hysterical Judy, trying to soothe her into getting some sleep.

Vincente was tortured by uncertainty. He wondered if he were responsible for her regression, how he had failed. "Submerging the private doubts while presenting an untroubled manner to the world," he said, "was now a permanent way of life."

Part of the world to which Minnelli attempted to present an untroubled manner was little Liza. Her nursery, downstairs and on the other side of the house from her parents' bedroom, shielded her from hearing the sometimes ugly exchanges between them.

By now Liza was sixteen months old, an adorable child with huge brown eyes, a sweet round face and a very feisty, independent personality. Before she was a year old, she had learned to crawl her way up the stairs into her parents' suite, where she would be fussed over and cuddled to excess, especially by Vincente. Her father followed her incessantly with a camera, recording her every movement from very early in her life.

She was still crawling at the age of two, and her first steps were coaxed out of her at a party at the Gershwins'. One of the adults swooped Liza off the floor and told her, "Look at Johnny. He's six months younger than you and he's already walking. Aren't you ashamed that you haven't even started?"

Little Liza looked unhappily at the woman, then climbed down off her lap. The next day, she took her first steps. "That kid has more drive than you and I put together," Judy observed dryly to Vincente.

Judy completed her work on *The Pirate* in July 1947, months after shooting of her sequences should have wrapped. Minnelli continued working, needing to complete filming with Kelly's pirate ballet.

The completion of her work at MGM did little to ease Judy's paranoia, her nervousness, her fear. She was unable to stop taking the pills, although she no longer needed them to perform at her best; by now she was physically addicted to them. Any attempt to stop taking them resulted in severe pain, profuse sweating, nausea, agony. The only way to feel good again was to take more pills. As with all drug addicts, Judy's panacea, her cure, had become her greatest illness.

Now, when she wasn't taking pills, she was nervous, apprehensive, unable to sleep, afraid of the dark, afraid of being alone. When she did take the pills, she might sleep for a time, or be able to function a bit better during the day. But she would also exhibit wild changes of mood, increased fears, paranoia. There were hysterical scenes like the one on the set of *The Pirate* and a suicide attempt after a fight with Vincente, with Ethel in the house.

Always, the day after, Judy couldn't remember that she had acted so outrageously. This frightened her. "What if I hurt our baby?" she cried softly one morning after Vincente had told her of a particularly harrowing night. Clearly, something had to be done. Everyone agreed that Judy needed more help than a fifty-minute visit to a psychiatrist every day could provide. It was decided that Judy would be committed to the Las Campanas Sanatorium in Compton, not far from Los Angeles. "Judy quietly agreed," Vincente says. "She was too tired and too frightened to resist."

Her psychiatrist drove a sedated Judy to the institution, without Vincente. She looked sadly back at him as the car left the driveway, and Vincente wondered when they would be together again. He went to Liza's nursery. "Mama went away for a little while," he told her, "but she'll be back very soon." Liza was too young to understand—but the scene would be repeated, and its effect on the little girl would be far worse later. "I was thankful that a very capable nurse shielded Liza during these formative years," Minnelli says. "Between the two of us, we shielded the unhappy truth from her until Liza was old enough to cope with it."

The largest part of Judy's therapy at Las Campanas was withdrawal from her addiction to pills. The doctors thought this had been accomplished after a week or so, but they suspected that Judy was obtaining pills from other patients. Vincente had told them about Judy's ability to hide her cache of pills (inside the seams of dresses and curtains were two of the more imaginative hiding places) and periodically nurses would enter Judy's private bungalow. Judy protested that there were no pills to be found, and none ever were.

The experience was an awful one for Judy. She was getting off pills, but she was lonely and afraid. Sometimes she would hear terrifying noises coming from the "violent ward," and she would wonder if that was what was in store for her. But she also was aware of a quiet group of patients which would gather by her bungalow every day. Before long, she ventured out to mingle with them. "As far as I could gather," she said in a later interview, "not one of them was demented in the common sense. Most of them were just too highly strung and too sensitive for reality . . . I realized that I had a great deal in common with them, in the sense that they had been concentrating on themselves too strongly, the same as I."

Judy longed to see Vincente and Liza. He visited infrequently. He was hard at work on a major movie, and also felt it better that he leave Judy alone, since his presence had done little to help before. Judy kept asking permission for Liza to visit her, and the doctors finally decided it would be good for her.

Judy anticipated Liza's visit for days. Vincente brought her, and had her walk unannounced into Judy's room. "She toddled into my bungalow and into my arms," Judy said. "I didn't know what to say to her. She wasn't two years old. I just held her, and she just kept kissing me and looking at me with those huge, helpless brown eyes of hers. I jabbered a little but mostly held her. But we laughed, too. After a short while they took her away. I lay down on the bed and started to cry. There have been many blue moments in my life, but I never remember having such a feeling. I almost died of anguish."

The visit did little to help Judy's state of mind. Nor did the fact that her hospital bills— three hundred dollars per day—were given directly to her. Her finances were precarious: the government had placed a lien on her earnings for income taxes the Gilmores hadn't paid, and the studio wasn't paying her any salary while she was unable to work. Vincente's pay, while substantial, wasn't enough to support their lifestyle. Judy's anxieties grew—and so did her disappointment in Minnelli. He was her husband, her protector. She had expected him to take the place of her father, to be a strong pillar on which she could lean, a man who would take control of her life and give her security and comfort.

Minnelli's constitution did not enable him to cope with the problems of Judy Garland. He was a man of quiet introspection, of devotion to beauty, one whose first instincts were to reason a problem out, try to understand it—rather than take quick and decisive action. Minnelli himself has described his inability to deal with Judy as ineffectuality. That may be a more pejorative term than is warranted—but it is clear that Judy's opinion was even worse.

After a brief stay at another sanatorium on the East Coast, Judy returned home. Wanting to rest, she realized that her financial condition demanded that she return to work as soon as possible. She agreed, reluctantly, to co-star in a new film to be directed by Vincente, *Easter Parade*.

4

Once Judy had returned home—"Looking marvelous and in high spirits" according to Minnelli—she tried to restore some stability to her private life. She was as loving and as giving to Minnelli as she had been at the start of their relationship. But she also required constant reassurance, constant attention from Vincente. "I thought I had a bottomless reservoir to offer," he says, "but sometimes Judy found me lacking."

She still couldn't sleep, and was jealous of the fact that Minnelli could doze off in a matter of minutes. Often she would awaken him in the middle of the night and plead, "Be with me." Vincente would put his arm around her and gently rock her until she finally went to sleep.

Minnelli was preparing to film *Easter Parade* with Gene Kelly for several weeks before Judy was set to report to work on it. Sometimes, while Vincente prepared to go to the studio, Judy would entreat him not to leave her, to stay home that day and spend it with her and Liza. Of course, Vincente could not—and Judy would turn cold, kissing him goodbye perfunctorily as she planned a day with Liza and her nurse.

A few days before Judy was scheduled to begin rehearsals, Arthur Freed called Vincente into his office. Minnelli knew something was wrong; he suspected that the picture had been scrapped. He was completely unprepared for what Freed told him. "Judy's psychiatrist thinks it would be better all around if you didn't direct the picture."

Minnelli was practically speechless. "Why not?" he managed to say.

"He feels Judy doesn't really want you as the director . . . that you symbolize all her troubles with the studio."

Vincente had no choice but to acquiesce. He was bewildered by the roundabout way in which this decision had reached him. Why hadn't Judy mentioned this to him herself?

When Vincente returned home, neither made any mention of what had happened. Vincente sat down in his easy chair to read the evening paper. Liza toddled into the den, charming both parents with her attention-seeking antics. Nothing was obviously amiss. Later, as they lay together in bed, the subject hung over them in silence.

Then, as on many another night, little Liza crawled into bed with her parents, snuggling between them. Later she would recall, in *Good Housekeeping,* "I didn't dare move for fear I'd get tossed out. I didn't want that because it was so warm and dark and safe there." It seemed so to a child of two—but in reality her parents' relationship was coming irreparably apart.

Perhaps freed by Minnelli's replacement, Judy presented very little trouble on the set of *Easter Parade,* now being directed by Chuck Walters. She was occasionally late, but she picked up her dance routines in a flash, and her sense of humor and feisty nature had returned. Once, the film's composer, Irving Berlin, suggested how Judy might sing one of the songs. Half kidding, half serious, Judy backed him against a wall with her forefinger and said, "Listen, buster, you write 'em. *I* sing 'em." Berlin, who adored Judy, was bemused and left her to her own devices.

Judy was pleased to be reunited with Gene Kelly, but a few days before filming was to commence, he broke his leg while playing softball. It was one of those unfortunate events with a happy outcome. Fred Astaire was talked out of retirement to star opposite Judy, and they made a wonderful screen pair. Astaire greatly respected Judy's talent, and she was completely in awe of him.

The movie, everyone knew, would be a success. Judy was bolstered by the knowledge that she could still carry a picture and hold her own against Fred Astaire, but her role did little to raise her hopes that MGM would start treating her like a desirable young woman: her character was a plain-Jane chorus girl who must win over Astaire by the sheer force of her personality. It was becoming awfully tiresome for Judy. But it was what the public wanted from her; *Easter Parade* would go on to be one of her biggest hits.

MGM had agreed to give Judy a lengthy vacation after *Easter Parade* wrapped. But seeing how well she had functioned, and anxious to capitalize on this new team and Astaire's renewed popularity, the studio scheduled her to reunite with him for *The Barkleys of Broadway* in just a few weeks' time. It was an assignment she was not up to fulfilling.

Judy wanted to star with Astaire again, but now, as she approached her twenty-sixth birthday, she found herself less and less able to function. She attempted to lose weight for the filming, then could not stop dieting and became emaciated. She couldn't face the cameras. Her marriage had become nothing but façade for the public and for Liza.

Liza had become the one bright spot in Judy's life. When she wanted Liza, she was there for her. Often she would play with her for hours, laughing, becoming as childlike as her baby. She would sing for her, lead her in dances, talk to her about her problems as though Liza were an adult.

Liza was clearly a very precocious little girl. She seemed somehow to know what her mother was going through, those big brown eyes sympathetic and loving. Liza came to long for her mother's attentions. Being with Judy was so much fun, so much love was lavished on her when her mother was around, that the often long stretches when her mother was either absent or unable to deal with her were even more painful than they would have been had her relationship with her mother been more even-handed. Liza seemed to crave attention from everyone, but especially her mother. She would say later, "Millions of people adored my mother, and they never even met her. Can you imagine how *I* felt about her?"

At this point in Judy's life, she was least able to deal with the responsibilities of motherhood. She was too ill to report to work on *The Barkleys of Broadway;* the studio waited several weeks, then suspended her. MGM's action, if it was intended to shock her back to work, had just the opposite effect: it made her depression worse, her paranoia deeper. Ethel had instilled in Judy a great fear of not producing, of not being her best at all times. How good could she be if her studio was willing to suspend her? And clearly this was a failure on her part.

Her remorse frequently gave way to anger: the studio didn't care about her, all they cared about was the money she could bring in to them. They were trying to force her back to work, at the expense of her health, maybe even her life. She convinced herself that the studio was her enemy; even what concern and sympathy the executives did show her was interpreted as insincere attempts to get her back to work.

"By now," Judy once wrote, "I was just a mechanical hoop they were rolling around. I was sure I wasn't going to make it but it didn't matter. The rehearsals began and my migraine headaches got worse. I went for days without sleep but I kept on. Then I started to be late for rehearsals and began missing days. Finally I was fired. They didn't even give me the courtesy of a call or a meeting or a discussion. They sent me a telegram."

Like so many of Judy's recollections of the events in her life, this one has been challenged. Her friend Oscar Levant, who had a part in the film, gave this version of what transpired: "I looked forward to working with Judy, but she never appeared on the set after we were ready to begin. Arthur Freed and Louis B. Mayer both went to her Hollywood hilltop home, but apparently no one could persuade her to show up. Finally, Ginger Rogers was engaged to take Judy's place and the picture proceeded. Then suddenly Judy appeared on the set. When she poised herself behind the camera it was too unnerving—Chuck Walters finally asked her to leave. Judy refused. Chuck took her by the arm and led her out as she hurled imprecations about Ginger."

For days after her suspension Judy was unable to get out of bed. Her weight dropped to eighty pounds. She was fed glucose intravenously. As it did whenever her salary stopped, Judy's financial condition deteriorated to the point of panic. By Vincente's own admission, the entire family's finances were "hopelessly muddled."

Judy came to rely on Carlton Alsop, a close friend along with his wife, Sylvia Sidney. A strong-willed, practical man, he often took charge of situations Vincente was unable to handle, and Judy took to calling him "Pa." Aware of Judy's monetary crisis, and told that MGM had withheld one hundred thousand dollars from money owed her because of her delays and absences, Alsop went to Louis B. Mayer to protest: this was at least unfair, perhaps illegal.

Mayer refused to back down but did make Alsop an offer: if Judy would agree to sing one number in a new Rogers and Hart biography, *Words and Music,* he'd pay her fifty thousand dollars. Alsop wasn't sure Judy would be able to do it, but he brought her the news.

Because Judy's illnesses were almost always psychosomatic, she was able to bounce back from the worst depths when she wanted to. Now, she desperately needed the money; she was being paid a lot to do comparatively little; and the offer indicated to her Mayer's opinion of her value. "I'll do it, Pa," she said to Alsop. "Get me up."

Judy rehearsed and performed the number—"I Wish I Were in Love Again," a duet with Mickey Rooney—in a couple of weeks, and everyone was thrilled by the performance. Judy had delivered, and her optimism returned. In a few weeks she gained over twenty pounds. Mayer, seeing the footage and audiences' reactions to it at previews, offered her another fifty thousand dollars to do an encore. She agreed, performing "Johnny One-Note."

"It's ridiculous when you see the picture," Carlton says. "In the first song, Judy hardly casts a shadow. Then she comes back looking like Kate Smith."

A lifelong pattern was beginning for Judy: incredible highs followed by devastating lows followed by extraordinary rebounds. These dizzying waves in Judy Garland's life could be charted in years, months—sometimes days. Despite her success with *Words and Music,* her problems at home worsened. She remained contemptuous of Vincente for his inability to handle her. They frequently fought, and Judy's psychiatrist suggested that she maintain a separate residence, so that she could be alone when she needed to be.

She rented a house not far from Minnelli's for a thousand dollars per month. Now she had an escape valve, but along with it came the added pressure of paying for an entirely new household. Clearly, though, it was a necessity. Vincente was willing to go along with anything that might help Judy along—even give up his own career. He had not worked at all since *The Pirate;* he assumed the studio wasn't offering him assignments because Mayer knew he had his hands full with Judy. He *was* being paid. Minnelli was prepared to sacrifice his own career if it would help Judy through her troubles. To him, it seemed the least he could do to get her back on an even keel, restore some rationality to her. He tried to keep up enough strength for the two of them, "but I was often found lacking. My own self assurance was at its lowest ebb. A treadmill was transporting us to disaster, and we were running double time in the opposite direction just to keep stationary."

Judy had fallen out of love with Vincente, almost to the point of being unable to summon up remembrance of *ever* having loved him. She would tell Lee Gershwin that she had never loved him, and continually ask her, "Why did you let me marry him?"

Again and again, in moments of despair and repose, she would ask the question. Lee wouldn't answer, or she would remind Judy that it had not been Lee's decision to make for her—she had wanted to marry Vincente. One day, Judy asked the question again. Lee looked out through the glass doors of the living room into the back yard, where Liza was frolicking. "If you'd never married Vincente," she said softly, "you wouldn't have Liza." Judy never brought the subject up again.

It was for Liza's benefit that her parents stayed married for more than two years after their relationship should have ended. Both parents lavished love and attention on the child, in an effort to shield her from the pain they were going through. While Judy's attentions were sporadic, Vincente's were constant, and Lee Gershwin for one thought Liza was being outrageously spoiled. She was uncomfortable with Vincente's constant physical attention to Liza: hugging her, caressing her arms, kissing her, carrying her. To Lee, it bordered on the unhealthy. And there was nothing Vincente wouldn't do for Liza, nothing he would deny her. Finally, Lee spoke out: "You give her everything," she told Minnelli. "You're nothing but a puddle of love. For her own sake, Liza should be disciplined. If she's not, you mark my words. She's going to grow up to be a commuter to an institution."

"I know, I know," Vincente answered. "But you see . . . I just can't help myself."

It had been exactly the same way with Frank Gumm and Baby Frances.

Liza began to crave attention from everyone. In groups, if she felt she wasn't getting enough, she would throw a tantrum. If that didn't work she would faint dead away, panicking the adults around her. Always when Vincente was present, she would be fussed over, soothed, made to feel better. Vincente reacted to Liza's tantrums much the way Frank Gumm reacted to Judy's. And as if to complete the parallel, Judy treated Liza's outbursts with the same disdain that Ethel had Judy's. Liza learned at a very early age that her father's love was something she could count on, something that was hers no matter what. Her mother's love, on the other hand, was harder to earn, rarer. But when it came, it was so special.

Often, when Judy was unable to care for Liza, Ethel would step in, taking her to her house for an afternoon; Liza loved these times with "Nanna," when she would be the only object of attention. Before long, Ethel was driving Liza to dancing lessons at the Nico Charisse dance studio. Judy was wary: now that Ethel no longer had control of her, was she trying to take control of Liza? But she allowed the lessons; they certainly wouldn't do a little girl any harm, and Liza had already exhibited a great affinity for music and dance. And no small factor in Judy's surprising equanimity toward Ethel's taking Liza under her wing was the fact that it helped assuage Judy's guilt over the times when she was unable—or unwilling—to give Liza the attention she so desperately wanted—and often needed.

It wasn't to be long before Liza Minnelli made her motion picture debut. Judy was cast opposite Van Johnson in *In the Good Old Summertime,* a light musical about two shop clerks who cannot abide each other and are each corresponding with their ideal mate. They are, naturally, writing to each other without knowing it. Judy wasn't happy about once again playing a shopgirl, but the movie was another Garland triumph, another of her miraculous achievements, considering her condition. She looked lovely in the film, and *Variety* wrote, "Great troupers come seldom in a theatrical generation, but when one does arrive, there is no mistaking the special magnetism that is their art. If ever there existed doubts that Judy Garland is one of the great screen personalities of the present celluloid era, the opportunity to alter the impression is offered in *In the Good Old Summertime* . . . it is her show from start to finish as she turns in a performance whose acting elements are no less enchanting than the moments of high excitement she provides with her singing."

Liza's appearance in the film came at its end, when Judy and Van Johnson have discovered each other, married, and had a child. Liza was to walk between her on-screen parents, holding their hands, then be scooped up by Van Johnson and carried in his arms. Liza had insisted on dressing herself for the part in a frilly white dress, and she looked adorable. But she appeared nervous and unhappy in the scene—perhaps because, she later said, she had forgotten to put panties on under her dress.

At home, things were worse than ever. Vincente was becoming more and more disillu-

Liza at 2½ makes her film debut with Judy in *In The Good Old Summertime*, 1948.

sioned with Judy, less and less able to handle her drug-induced personality shifts. After a long layoff from work, he was assigned to direct *Madame Bovary,* with Jennifer Jones playing Flaubert's classic character and Louis Jourdan and James Mason rounding out the cast. Minnelli was overjoyed, and anxious to share his pleasure with Judy. She was in the midst of *In the Good Old Summertime,* and her reaction to her husband's stream of enthusiasm shocked him. "Here you are working with these great talents, and what am I doing? Still playing the shopgirl on the corner."

"This time I couldn't deny my feelings," Minnelli says. "We'd been through so much pain together. I'd exulted with Judy as she emerged into renewed periods of triumph. Why couldn't she do the same for me? I was deeply hurt."

All of their problems had resulted in two private separations. Now, a public rift, with an official announcement by Vincente: "We are happier apart." Judy spent all her time in her second house, with Liza in a new nursery on the first floor. Over the next two years, there would be several reconciliations and separations for the Minnellis. They would fight, separate, come together again for Liza's sake, begin to fight again. It has long been said that Judy and Vincente were unusually successful in keeping their marital turbulence from their daughter, but it seems unlikely that a child as precocious, sensitive and vulnerable as Liza was as unaware as her parents may have thought. Their attempts to shield their daughter from the pain they were experiencing were less and less successful the older she got. An indication of Liza's strongly developing personality at this point came with a profile of Judy by Adela Rogers St. Johns. During an interview, Liza entered the room. Ms. St. Johns wrote:

> Miss Minnelli carried a bright red umbrella, although by this time the last of the mist had burned away and there was bright, hot sunshine on the balcony.
>
> Judy said, "But my angel pie, you don't want an umbrella—"
>
> Liza looked her young mother firmly in the eye. She said, "How do you know I don't?" And she walked over to the balcony iron railing, with her umbrella still held high, and stood blandly contemplating the scenery. To herself she was saying, "Don't want an umbrella, Liza, you don't want a bath, Liza, you don't want that dirty old penny. Liza, you don't want that book, that's Mummy's . . ."
>
> Judy held for a moment what I am sure she thought was an expression of stern, maternal discipline. Actually, it was a fatuous, adoring, did-you-ever-see-anything-so-cute-or-hear-anything-so-smart-she's-only-*three*-after-all gaze of pure idiotic idolatry.
>
> After Miss Liza had gone for her nap, Judy said, "How do I know, at that? Imagine her remembering. I said to her yesterday, 'No, no Liza, you don't want a bath at three o'clock in the afternoon.' Obviously she *did* want a bath and obviously she *did* want that red umbrella—it's a wonder they don't think their parents are half-witted, or maybe they do. You do have to walk a tightrope, don't you, between some measure of discipline and some measure of letting them express themselves, and you can't let them put dirty pennies in their mouths . . . well, maybe I'll have more sense by the time I have my next one."

At this point, Judy's life and career were inexorably falling apart. She was addicted to pills, and they were wreaking havoc on her body, her voice, her spirit. Where before she had always been able to summon up enough vocal mastery and sheer gumption to appear her best on screen, she was now embarking on a project that would prove that even the incredible Garland resiliency had its limits.

MGM had purchased the rights, specifically for Judy, to Irving Berlin's smash Broadway musical *Annie Get Your Gun.* It seemed a natural for her. There were great songs and a lovable down-to-earth character in Annie Oakley—a bit of a stretch for Judy, perhaps, but surely she was talented enough to pull it off. The studio's purchase price set a record, and it would be one of their biggest films ever.

Job 99899-09. BERKELEY-
FOR Sc: 30x1 to 30x9
U.S. TRAVEL MONTAGE
CHANGE #2

A costume test for the ill-fated *Annie Get Your Gun* role, 1949.

Things started out badly when Busby Berkeley was hired as director—a mistaken choice for Judy if ever there was one; she had had great difficulty working with him on four prior films. But she wanted the role, and voiced no objections. However, the specter of working with him again added to her ever-present fears of facing the cameras. Her pill intake was so great at this point that for the first time she was performing poorly. Her recordings of the songs were barely adequate, and as she began acting out the role, it was evident that she had not gotten a handle on how to play Annie Oakley. Freed called in Chuck Walters to look at some of Judy's footage. "My God, it was horrible," Walters said. "Judy was at her worst. She couldn't decide whether she was Ethel Merman, Mary Martin, Martha Raye, or herself."

Freed was unhappy too with Berkeley's direction. "Buzz had no conception of what the picture was all about. He was shooting the whole thing like a stage play. Everyone would come out of the wings, say their lines and back away upstage for their exits."

Freed fired Berkeley, and asked Walters to step in. He agreed. But it was too late for Judy. She had seen some of the dailies and was appalled. At one screening, she sank lower and lower in her chair as the footage unfolded and, in the middle of one of her scenes, got up, went over to a water cooler and downed a handful of Benzedrines.

On several occasions, Judy's knees buckled and she fell down during filming. Freed, one of her closest friends and allies, had no reservoir of sympathy left. He began shouting furiously at the prone Judy, as the embarrassed crew moved away off the sound stage.

Judy sought solace in her friendship with Lee Gershwin. Fifteen years older than Judy, Lee was both friend and adviser, a rock of good sense to which Judy could moor the flailing ship that was her life. One day, as her *Annie* troubles engulfed her, Judy asked Lee to take her shopping. They roamed Beverly Hills, returning around nine-thirty in the evening. Judy seemed in a good mood; when Lee stopped for gasoline on Sunset Boulevard, a motorcycle cop sidled up to their car, greeted Judy and asked if they wanted an escort home. "Oh yes, officer, this woman is a very dangerous driver."

Lee laughed, hoping the policeman wouldn't believe Judy: "It was very funny, because I was famous for never driving over thirty miles an hour." The policeman escorted them to Judy's house and bade them goodbye. "It was only nine-thirty," Lee says, "so I asked Judy if she had any plans for the rest of the evening. As she got out of the car, she said, 'Yeah, I think I'll slash my wrists.' Since she had been jesting with me, I thought it was a macabre joke, and I dismissed it."

The next morning, Lee got a call from MGM asking if she knew where Judy was. Alarmed, Lee told them of Judy's "joke" of the night before. A studio representative went to the house to discover that Judy had indeed tried to cut her wrists the night before, but wasn't seriously hurt. It was an incident, unlike subsequent ones that did not get into the papers.

"I was shocked," Lee says. "And I felt very guilty that I had ignored Judy's cry for help."

After less than three weeks of shooting, there was very little good footage, and Judy's condition was worse than it had ever been. The prognosis for completing the film with Judy was very poor. The studio had no recourse but to fire her. An executive walked into her dressing room one afternoon and handed her a suspension notice.

She was furious. "Those bastards," she kept repeating. "Those bastards." Then she fell to the floor, crying hysterically, sobbing, "No. No. No." A half hour later, Judy's hairdresser emerged from her dressing room. "Where is everybody?" she asked the assistant director. There were just a few people left on the sound stage. "Get them all back. Judy is on her way."

A few minutes later, Judy came out, ready to act before the cameras. By that time everyone had left.

5

My first horrendous recollection was when Mama had to go away. Daddy and I drove with her to the train. When it came time for her to leave, she cried and carried on so much that Daddy hopped on the train and went with her. I sobbed and screamed to be taken, too, but all I could do was stand there and watch the train pull away.

—Liza, in a *Good Housekeeping* interview by Muriel Davidson, July 1968.

Judy's condition had deteriorated so badly that it was again recommended that she be hospitalized—this time three thousand miles from home, in the Peter Bent Brigham Hospital in Boston.

There really was no alternative. She was chronically depressed, unable to sleep, afraid to do her job; she would fly into hysterics at the slightest provocation; she thought often of suicide.

Her physical condition was now as bad as her emotional state. Her weight was down below ninety pounds, she suffered from excruciating migraine headaches and rashes on her skin. Worst of all, her hair was falling out.

MGM, aware that there was a serious problem with one of their biggest stars—that this was not just a spoiled child being insolent—agreed to pay her medical bills at Brigham. They wanted her back.

Judy arrived at Brigham on May 29, 1949. There, she was weaned from the pills, given proper food and made to eat it. She began to sleep without medication. Her weight increased, her rash cleared up, her hair stopped falling out. Her medical treatment was successful (she was in perfectly good health in every other respect) but her psychiatric treatment was less so. Her doctors felt that her best chance for emotional health was to realize that too much of her life was absorbed in fantasy; that the adoring crowds and mass approval she lived for were worthless; that it was herself—Frances Gumm, not Judy Garland—who was important, and that coming to grips with that reality was her best hope for emotional stability.

It was impossible for Judy to separate the real from the unreal. The unreality of public adulation had been the only reality she had ever known. Whether it was her family cheering her on around a piano, or millions of moviegoers paying to see her on screen, she had been taught that Judy Garland—the voice, the personal—was who people loved. She knew at an early age that her best chance for love and success and approval was to perform—to be lovable, charming, and in good voice.

She had come to believe that Frances Gumm was nothing, Judy Garland everything. From her mother to Louis B. Mayer, her signals were that she was worthless unless she was performing—and she'd better do it well.

Her larger complexes were barely penetrable; the doctors attempted to help her with some of her smaller ones. Their most realistic goal was to get her functioning again. That they seemed to be doing.

Her doctor, trying to restore her self-confidence, allowed her to be an outpatient, and she moved to a nearby hotel in Boston. There, she suffered relapses. One night her nurse called her doctor. Judy must have obtained pills somewhere—she was under the bed, screaming. The doctor went over to the hotel at 3 A.M., crawled under the bed to coax Judy out, and spoke with her until dawn to calm her down.

Less than two weeks after she had arrived at Brigham, she observed her twenty-seventh birthday. Liza and her governess had traveled by train, and Judy and Carleton Alsop, who was staying in Boston to be near her, met them at South Station.

Judy and Liza, who was three years and three months old, met the press, posed for pictures, hugged each other joyfully. They spent days together exploring Boston, riding in the swan boats in the public gardens, taking long rides around the outskirts of the city; they went sightseeing to the historic buildings and famous locales of Boston.

A few weeks later, they went on a "vacation" to Cape Cod, where they swam in the ocean, rode the merry-go-round at an amusement park, took long walks together.

Wherever they went, admiring crowds would gather, oohing and aahing at Judy, waving hello; some people came up to her expressing their admiration in gushy, stuttery ways. Liza was both frightened and fascinated by the crowds. Her mother was obviously someone very special— everyone loved her just as much as Liza did. She would never have to be away from her mother ever again; this wonderful play time would go on forever.

Of course it could not, and Liza was brought back to California. Her life pattern was established quite early: joyful happiness, loving attention from her mother, then—it seemed— desertion. How could her mother love her and not be with her all the time? Then her father's almost smothering attentions, which never could match the rarer solicitations of Mama; then complete happiness again as Judy re-entered her life and in her singular way made her daughter seem like the most important person in the world.

Judy spent thirteen weeks in Boston, the last month without visits from Vincente or Liza. She missed her daughter, but there was an outlet for her maternal cravings which was to prove extremely significant for her.

She had gone to the nearby Children's Hospital for a battery of tests, and her presence quickly became known to the young patients. Many of them had seen *The Wizard of Oz;* the others, caught up in the excitement, longed to see this very special celebrity, although they might not really know who she was.

Judy agreed to pay the children a visit. She at first shrank away from them in pity as she entered the ward; there were children who couldn't walk, some whose minds were completely infantile even as they bordered on their teens. Judy was apprehensive. "What'll I do, Pa?" she asked Carleton Alsop. He told her just to be with the children, talk to them, sing them a few notes. He pointed to the signs at the foot of each bed which read "TLC": "Give them what the signs say—tender, loving care."

She tentatively went up to the first bed, and the pure, unrestrained joy of the child at seeing her touched Judy deeply. She had feared that being surrounded by so many unfortunate children would depress her, but rather she was elated by their simple generosity of spirit. And the happiness that she could bring them with a held hand or a few notes of "Over the Rainbow" seemed more fulfilling to Judy than reams of reviewer raves.

She went back to visit the children often. Only one child—who reminded Judy of Liza—failed to respond to her. The girl, five years old, was mildly retarded, and her family had rejected, even beaten her, because of her difference. She had not uttered a word in the two years she had been at the hospital.

Every day Judy sat next to the child, talking of her life in Hollywood, and Liza. The child would huddle in a corner of her bed, eyes wide, listening to Judy but never responding.

Now, as Judy prepared to leave Boston, she made one last visit to Children's Hospital. She was again taken aback as she entered the ward: the children had been spruced up for her farewell visit—each was specially dressed and had a small bouquet of flowers for her.

Judy once again sat by every child, bidding them goodbye. Finally, she came to the little girl who reminded her of Liza. She started to say goodbye to her, when the child jumped up, screamed out "Judy!" and fell sobbing into her arms. She spoke in a stream of words which made little sense, but the entire room was caught up in the incredible emotion of the moment. As Judy said later, "Everybody was crying, the nurses were crying, I was crying, and this child was talking at the top of her lungs and I was holding on to her and rocking her."

Judy would have had to leave just then in order to catch her train, but she stayed with the child another hour until she calmed down. "I guess it was one of the great moments in my life when that child spoke like that," Judy said. "I felt I had . . . I just didn't give a damn how many pictures I'd been fired from, or how much humiliation . . . I'd done a human being some good! I felt right on top of the world."

As Judy was leaving, the child murmured, "I love you, I love you." Judy kissed her and said, "If you love me, you must promise me you'll talk to the nurses, because they love you very much, too." The little girl nodded her head in agreement.

Sitting in a train speeding toward California, Judy thought of that child and how much she had changed the little girl's life. The entire episode made her miss Liza enormously, and she felt more guilty than ever about the times she hadn't been with her daughter. She vowed to herself that she would be a better mother to Liza—and that she would make a go once more of her marriage to Vincente.

The staff at Brigham had had serious reservations about Judy's release; they felt she needed at least three more months of treatment. But she was anxious to return home. The studio had already paid over forty thousand dollars in hospital bills, and Brigham's physician in chief accompanied her back to California to help her adjust once again to life in Hollywood.

She returned to Vincente's house in early August with tears of joy and effusive hugging of Liza. Judy and Vincente were now officially reconciled. Vincente wrote, "Judy's condition was as normal as it would ever be. Her only medication was a series of glucose injections prescribed by her physician to keep up her energy."

It was, though, an awkward time. As Vincente put it, "We were getting to know each other, and Liza was getting to know Judy, all over again." Judy continued to keep her second residence, and would occasionally spend a night or two there, but for the most part the Minnelli family was back together as a unit.

Judy was scheduled to begin work on a new film, *Summer Stock,* in November, a scant three months after her return to Hollywood. She didn't think much about it, preferring to rest and enjoy Liza's company. She and Vincente worked hard at restoring a semblance of romance to their marriage; every night they would dine by candlelight, and Liza would climb the stairs to their part of the house and eat with them often.

She was a completely adorable child. Usually attired in a long white dressing gown which skirted the floor and made her look like an angel atop a Christmas tree, Liza was so sweet to look at, so bright, so intensely interested in everything, that her parents and visitors to their home would involuntarily laugh with delight the minute she approached them. Not understanding the reasons behind this laughter, Liza became very upset by it, thinking she was being mocked.

Vincente took great delight in making Judy laugh, as did almost everyone who crossed her path: her laughter was loud, infectious, and a sign that she was in a good mood. But Vincente and Judy had discovered that Liza often thought Judy was laughing at her, and Judy would have to be careful, sometimes stifling her laughter completely.

Judy thought it was "cruel," but Vincente took to trying to make her laugh in Liza's presence. He delighted in Judy's often futile attempts to keep a straight face, while Liza watched them both with a fixed stare. It's safe to assume that all this made little Liza even less secure.

As Liza got older, it was clear that she was a singular child. One day when she was about four and a half, Vincente came home from the studio, lay on the couch, and began reading the newspaper. Liza was playing at his feet, and he absently murmured something to her about his discomfort with the De Gaulle regime in France. Liza ran looking for her mother and when she found her delightedly cried, "Mama! Mama! Daddy is *talking* to me!" It was the first time Vincente had addressed her as anything but a baby.

Such examples of Liza's delight at being treated as something more than a baby were frequent. Once, Vincente took her to the Ice Capades, a drive of over an hour. After they had arrived and parked the car, Liza decided she didn't like the dress she was wearing. Vincente drove all the way back home, let her change her dress, then drove back. While on their way the second time, Vincente says, "She said something that I've never forgotten: 'Daddy, you really do understand me, don't you?'"

"And," Minnelli marvels, "she was only *four*."

It needn't be stressed too heavily that as unusual a child as Liza was, her upbringing was pretty rarefied, too. For all the times Mama was away, and for all the insecurities being Judy Garland's daughter inevitably created, there were extraordinary privileges for any child brought up in the center of world glamour. Liza remembers being taken by her father to the sound stage of his latest production, riding with him on the camera boom—"It seemed a long way off the ground"—and watching with rapt attention as some gay, colorful musical number unfolded in front of her.

Dramatic scenes didn't interest her—if Vincente were filming a love scene she would run to another set until she found someone who was singing or dancing. Dancing especially appealed to her. She was still taking lessons with Nico Charisse, Cyd's ex-husband. She adored watching Fred Astaire, and mimicked his dance steps. Cyd Charisse was another of her favorites. "I always thought if I could grow up and dance like her, I'd be in heaven. I wasn't all that fascinated watching Mama. After all, I could always see and hear *her* at home."

In the July 1950 issue of *Photoplay,* a photo spread entitled "Ballerina" featured the four-year-old Liza performing in a ballet recital at Nico Charisse's dance studio. "In her powder puff skirts, she's absorbed in a whirl of her own," the blurb read. "She's Liza Minnelli—Judy Garland's talented daughter. Ask Liza what she wants to be and she'll tell you—a ballerina!"

Candice Bergen, another celebrity daughter (of ventriloquist Edgar Bergen) has described growing up in Hollywood as ". . . on the highest level of the absurd . . . all highly surrealistic, like living in a big playroom."

Many of Liza's recollections are indeed surreal: "I can remember playing in the Beverly Hills park with Mia Farrow and Candy Bergen and Tish Sterling, and while we sat in the sandbox we could hear our English nannies talking about picture deals and costume direction and whose employer was going to win the Academy Award."

While for many children fantasy is a diversion, for Liza it was often a major part of her life. She would visit sound stages and see glamorous, colorful sets and costumes, created worlds that to a small child represented the ultimate in excitement. Most children, when exposed to such fantasy, return home to reality. Liza was able to bring the fantasy home with her: Vincente would have exact replicas of famous costumes made in miniature for his daughter. At a party, or while trick-or-treating, Liza would appear as Scarlett O'Hara or Madame Bovary in an outfit by top studio designers and sewn by some of the world's finest seamstresses.

And she was given access to innumerable props—wigs, hats, fake swords, canes, parasols. It wasn't too big a jump for Liza to use these accouterments exactly in the way in which they were intended to be used: in theater. She was fascinated by her parents' work, had an aptitude for dancing and a penchant for singing, and all the wherewithal in the world at her command. She and her friends Tish Sterling, Amanda Levant, and Candy Bergen would plan, rehearse and perform mini-musicals, costumes and sets supplied by Vincente, with songs straight from the movies and dance routines—more often than not—of Liza's own devising.

Judy would sit with the other parents and watch the show, all the time shouting directives to Liza. "Kick higher," she'd yell. "Sing louder!" Judy undoubtedly felt she was lending a

Vincente and Liza on the set of *Lovely to Look At*, 1952.

helping hand, but her exhortations made Liza feel all the more insecure about her performing abilities. It was a situation that would be repeated several times after Liza became a professional.

Liza's early commitment to dancing—for most of her life she aspired to a dancing career—may have been the result of her mother's belief that there was no way her daughter could follow in her footsteps as a singer. Liza was not naturally gifted with a beautiful voice as Baby Gumm had been at the same age. Judy's friend John Carlyle recalls a party at which Liza followed Judy with a song. "My God," Judy whispered to Carlyle, "she's got a voice like chalk on a blackboard!"

But even at four or five, Liza was clearly star material. The voice could be worked on. The natural presence one had to be born with. Carlyle remembers that Liza danced after her singing stint. "She was lovely, all in white, and she was startling—incredible-looking, with those huge eyes and her hair held back with a white ribbon. She danced all over the room like a beautiful white butterfly."

Her parents were frequent partygivers, and goers. Parties at the Minnelli house would turn into private cabarets, with Judy, Sammy Davis, Jr., and Frank Sinatra singing their latest hits, David Niven and Lauren Bacall telling anecdotes, and Humphrey Bogart taking it all in. As Sammy Davis put it, "Bogey never needed to do a star turn. He was cabaret just sitting there."

Sometimes Liza would hide under the piano until she was discovered, to much acclaim. Other times she would peek through the banister, hoping to be allowed to join in. Sammy Davis recalls pleading with Judy to allow him to bring her in, and Judy relented. Liza sat on "Uncle Sammy's" lap watching all these famous, talented people entertain each other. "Then she couldn't contain herself," Sammy says. "She had to sing. She got up in the most natural way, when everyone else had done his turn, and gave us a version of the latest hit of the day. It was totally natural and spontaneous, and despite this star-studded audience, she stole the show."

Despite her "chalk on a blackboard" voice, Liza clearly had potential. Davis remembers saying to Judy, "With friends like this and talent like that, this girl has just got to be a star."

Judy replied, "She'll either be a star, or turn her back on the whole damned mess and get a nice husband and a safe job. You know what we've done, Sammy? We've thrown her right into the middle of the Atlantic Ocean, and she's either going to swim or drown."

It was an apt metaphor, especially as it concerned Judy. Back now from her hospitalization, preparing to star in another MGM musical, she herself would have to swim or drown. Offers for her film services were not pouring in as they once had. Few producers were willing to risk millions of dollars on a woman with as spotty a record of reliability as Judy. But Joseph Pasternak, preparing to produce *Summer Stock*, did want her. He had told her, "If you're half-dead, you're still better than anyone else. Any time Arthur will let you go, I'll use you in anything, if you'll just work for me."

As so often in the past, Judy needed to work if for no other reason than to pay her rather considerable bills. She felt good too, and wanted to prove to herself and to others that she still had it in her.

But somehow, at this point in her life, the fates always seemed to conspire against Judy. Whenever she was reasonably happy, she would gain weight. Now, as she began preparing for *Summer Stock,* she was told she would have to lose fifteen pounds, and quickly. The only way she knew how was to take diet pills. She lost some weight, but not enough. Finally, it was decided that Judy needn't be all that slim—she was playing a farm girl, after all.

But by then, it was too late. Unable to sleep well under the best circumstances, Judy unfailingly needed barbiturate help to sleep while she was on diet pills. Dr. Rose, the physician from Brigham, refused to give her pills of any kind, but he was fighting a losing battle: Judy had sources. Lee Gershwin recalls late-night telephone calls from her: "Lee, I can't sleep. Won't you please give me just one Seconal?"

"Well, I suppose one won't do you any harm. How can I get it to you?"

"Leave it in your mailbox. I'll have someone pick it up."

Lee would leave the pill in her mailbox, and fifteen minutes later she would hear a scurry of feet as the pill was retrieved. Lee was never sure who it was who came after the pills; it may have been Judy herself. "It never occurred to me," Lee says now, "that Judy may have made the same request the very same night of any number of her friends. Who knows how many pills she was taking?"

Many of Judy's friends would discover, after a party, that their medicine chests had been raided of whatever pills were on hand. Nothing was ever said to Judy, but a number of them began locking their cabinets.

The terrible maelstrom of pill dependency was once again engulfing Judy, and it affected her work on *Summer Stock*. She would be in the middle of a scene, performing well, then break out into a cold sweat and be unable to continue. Dr. Rose was on the set every day, there to counsel her and calm her fears. Rose tried to explain to Mayer, Pasternak, and director Chuck Walters that Judy feared failure, found it hard to interact with people, could not handle the pressure.

Gene Kelly found it particularly hard to deal with Judy this time around. Not that he was surprised by her behavior; he had in fact been talked into taking on a role he didn't really want when it was explained to him that his presence might make the difference in Judy's being able to fulfill the role.

The film's premise was not something that appealed to him; it was a silly yarn about a farm girl and a troupe of traveling performers. The girl (Judy) falls in love with the head actor (Gene) and proves herself a fabulous performer in a show they put on in her barn.

As filming progressed, Kelly couldn't see how his presence was making Judy any less of a problem. He simply hoped that she would hold up long enough to complete the picture. She did, but at great expense—this time not only to herself, but to her mother and daughter as well.

Judy's relationship with Ethel had been deteriorating for years. By now, their every encounter was at best icy and at worst resulted in a terrible screaming bout. Lee Gershwin recalls a battle so bad between Judy and Ethel while they were in Lee's home that she and Ira left.

Judy's hatred for her mother was no more rational than many of her other fears and psychoses. But it was not altogether unfounded. She deeply resented Ethel's interferences into her life. Beginning when she was Baby Gumm, a part of Judy felt like nothing more than a commodity, something to bring some luster to her mother's reputation, or some money into the family coffers.

Always it seemed to Judy that her feelings, wants, and needs were the last things on her mother's mind. Whether Ethel was siding with the studio "for Judy's own good" or butting into her personal life with phone calls to her suitors, she had a knack for infuriating Judy.

And Judy could never forgive her mother for her treatment of Frank. Their bitter battles over Frank's sexuality and Ethel's affair with Will Gilmore, left Judy hurt for her beloved father and angry toward Ethel. Now, it seemed, every little thing was enough to send Judy into uncontrollable rage at Ethel.

Finally, the breaking point came. Judy and Ethel had an unutterably violent argument, a vindictive, hurtful exchange that ended with Judy ordering Ethel out of her house. "I never want to see you again!" she screamed. "And I don't want you seeing Liza either. You stay away from us!"

Ethel had run from the house. She had taken all she could as well. Judy was everything she had in Los Angeles; Grandma Eva was in a rest home; her other daughters lived in other states. Ethel decided to move to Dallas, where Jimmy, Judalein, and Jimmy's new husband lived. There, she began managing a movie theater, carving out a brand-new life for herself.

Liza, too, was to experience Judy's wrath around this time—and it would have a deep emotional effect on her. As much as Judy's laughter was loud and infectious, her voice when angry was a terrible thing. In her *Good Housekeeping* interview, Liza said: "There is only one real trauma I have and that's a complete horror of angry, screaming voices. When my mother is angry, her voice is absolutely terrifying."

Liza first heard it one day when she and her father were watching Milton Berle on television and eating pumpkin pie. Judy was pacing back and forth, telling Vincente about all the problems she had faced on the set that day. She was very agitated. Liza was wearing her Hopalong Cassidy suit and boots; her energy level being what it was, she couldn't stay in one place on the couch very long. She decided to do a back flip. She kicked out her legs and hit Judy square in the head. "She started to cry and scream at me," Liza said. "She screamed and screamed and it seemed as if the yelling went on for hours." Liza burst into terrified, hysterical tears.

Vincente told Liza to go to her room, calmed Judy down for a few minutes, then went down to see Liza. Judy's rage was irrational, but he couldn't explain that to Liza. Instead, he asked her to understand: Mama had had an awful time at the studio that day, and her temper had just gotten the best of her; it wasn't really Liza Judy was screaming at, but all the problems she was facing these days. Liza started to cry again. "Oh, Daddy, I'm sorry—"

After a while, Judy herself went down. Liza could see that her mood had changed the minute she walked into the room, and the child ran to Judy in tears, begging forgiveness. Judy sat her little girl down and tried to explain to her the pressures she was under, that when she went to a set it wasn't to play and have fun—as Liza was used to—but to work. She didn't always want to do what she had to, Judy explained, and sometimes she just wasn't able to. But she *had* to, and that made her very nervous and upset sometimes.

It was a scene that would be repeated throughout the relationship of Judy and Liza—Judy acting badly, terribly—then asking Liza's forgiveness. Throughout the ensuing years, there would be tearful hugs and apologies and great professions of love following the most dreadful incidents. That would change as Liza's independence grew, but it was a pattern in their lives for more than ten years.

After Judy completed *Summer Stock,* she took a trip to Carmel, California, and put herself in the hands of a diet guru who promised to slim her down in a matter of weeks, without medication. Within three weeks, she had lost nearly twenty pounds, healthfully, and looked wonderful. She planned to stay in Carmel several months more, but after about a month she got a call from Chuck Walters asking her if she would agree to film a dance number for the end of the film: the front office thought the picture needed a sensational Garland finale.

Judy agreed, if Walters could get her a song of Harold Arlen's she had heard him sing at a party—"Get Happy." Walters did, the number was filmed, and it came off sensationally—but many critics and audiences would wonder whether the number had been pulled from stock footage filmed years before: Judy looked so much thinner than she had a few minutes earlier in the film. The number would remain one of the highlights of her career.

As so often with Judy, a performing triumph was but a momentary upswing in a degenerative pattern that was taking her inexorably toward the dissolution of the life she had known for nearly fifteen years. The chain of events that was to ensue would end her career at MGM, her marriage, and very nearly her life.

After she completed *Summer Stock,* Judy expected considerable time off. But MGM, as always, wanted to use her as much as possible. When June Allyson became pregnant and had to bow out of *Royal Wedding,* Mayer asked Judy to please step in, help the studio out. Judy liked the idea that the studio *needed* her, and it was a chance to work with Fred Astaire again. She accepted.

But once again, she found the thought of sparkling before a camera unbearable, and she repeatedly canceled rehearsals. Once again, she was suspended; this time the notification came

Judy's appearance in *Summer Stock* (1950) began to show the mature Garland to audiences.

from New York, from the corporate bigwigs who were wrestling power little by little from Louis B. Mayer. It was clear to everyone that where Judy was concerned, Metro was at the end of its rope. In the studio's view, it had been patient, coddling; Judy had cost them millions; they had paid for her hospitalization in Boston. Alsop, in a confrontation with one studio executive, asked to see the books to ascertain exactly how much Judy had made for the studio: the executive had complained of how much she cost them. But the studio was in the business of making money, not losing it, and Judy's unprofessional behavior could not be tolerated any longer.

The telegram had arrived on June 17, 1950, a Saturday, and over the weekend an agitated, bone-weary Judy and many of her associates talked about her options: she needn't stay with the studio; she could do Broadway shows, or concerts, or work for other studios whenever she wanted to. Judy was noncommittal; she didn't know what she wanted to do; at that moment all she cared about was sleeping—she would stay in bed for days. On the Monday after the suspension, while in conversation with Vincente and her secretary, Myrtle Tully, in Vincente's house on Evanview, Judy got up and went to the bathroom. A few minutes later, there was a scream. Vincente jumped up and ran to the bathroom. The door was locked. Inside, Judy screamed. "Leave me alone. I want to die!" Vincente heard a glass shatter and panicked. He tried to break down the door with his body, but wasn't strong enough. He picked up a chair and battered it against the door, finally breaking it open and shattering a mirror on the other side.

Judy stood with a piece of broken glass in her hand, her throat glistening with blood. As she tried to cut herself again, Vincente took the glass from her and Myrtle held her. Judy was sobbing hysterically; Myrtle attempted to calm her. One of the servants called a doctor, then phoned Carleton Alsop, who was on the scene within a matter of minutes.

He came upon an incredible scene: Judy lying on the floor, with Myrtle pressing a towel against her throat to stop the flow of blood; Vincente pacing frantically back and forth, alternately crying "Where did I fail her?" and "They've finally killed my beautiful wife!" Alsop brushed past Minnelli and looked at Judy's wound. It was long but not deep; the blood had already practically stopped. He realized Judy was in no real danger. She whispered in his ear, "Take care of Vincente, Pa."

Alsop rose, called out "Vincente!" ran into the hall, and punched Minnelli in the mouth. Whether the action was simply to calm him or a result of a natural fury at such an inept response to a crisis must be left to the imagination. "That brought me out of it," Minnelli says. "There was no time to indulge my own sorry feelings. We had to help Judy."

For some reason even Minnelli is now hard-pressed to explain, he and Alsop felt that Judy had to be moved to the 10000 Sunset Boulevard house, which was "officially" her residence. She was bundled up in the back seat of the car and taken there, where a doctor was waiting. He looked at Judy's cut. "It's only a scratch," he told Vincente and Carlton. "But suicide attempts are desperate cries for help. You must realize that."

They did. And soon, so would the entire country. Where before, descriptions of Judy's actual condition had always been couched in euphemisms, it was now impossible to keep the full story from the press. By the time Alsop got to the nearby Mocambo Club on Sunset to call an ambulance—he didn't want to tie up the house phones—a gossip columinist accosted him. "It's on every news desk in town that Judy tried to kill herself. Is it true?"

Alsop denied it, but when he got back to the house, reporters were surging around. Before, MGM could make sure that the "proper" story got into the papers. Now, they no longer cared. A studio press agent was one of the first to come to the house, and after conferring with Vincente (who had been denying a suicide attempt) went outside with Alsop. A reporter asked what happened; the publicist ran his hand across his neck in a cutting gesture.

Alsop was furious and pushed the man back into the house. "You stupid son-of-a-bitch!" Alsop screamed. "All you've done is put them on twenty-four-hour duty." The publicist left in a snit, leaving Alsop as Judy's press liaison, as well as agent/manager, father figure/protector, and ofttimes psychoanalyst.

The "sob sisters"—as Minnelli calls them—had a field day with the story. It was front-page news in the nation's largest circulation paper, the New York *Daily News*. Under the curiously worded headline "Judy Garland Fails in Suicide Attempt" (one can imagine Judy's reaction to that particular perspective on the event), Florabel Muir painted with wide purple strokes a portrait of the broken Judy: "Judy Garland, despondent over being suspended by her studio, attempted suicide last night by slashing her throat with the shattered edge of a waterglass in the bathroom of her pink alabaster mansion . . . the 29-year-old actress, hollow-eyed, highly nervous and suffering from physical and mental exhaustion, was resting under a doctor's care today."

Ethel, reading the news in the Dallas paper, flew immediately to Los Angeles to be near her daughter. Judy refused to see her. Ethel returned to Dallas, telling friends "They don't want to let me see her. But I'll get in if I have to kick the doors down. I'm going to see my little girl." Ethel's pride would never allow her to tell her friends it was Judy herself who didn't want to see her; she packed up her things and moved back to Los Angeles.

Judy still would not see her, and Ethel got herself an apartment. She had trouble finding work at first, attempted a career in real estate, and later took a job on an assembly line at Douglas Aircraft in Santa Monica. When this—and the fact that Ethel was being paid little over a dollar an hour for her labors—was reported in the press, the story was that the rich, successful Judy Garland had abandoned her mother, forcing her into menial labor.

But now, confined to bed, Judy was showered with good wishes. Katharine Hepburn came to visit, using her inimitable gumption to try and snap Judy out of it. Some of her friends tried turning her sometimes macabre humor on her: "So glad you cut your throat. All the other girl singers needed that kind of break." Judy looked up from the card and said to Alsop "Isn't that sweet, Pa?"

The studio was completely unsympathetic. They issued a legalistic statement, detailing all of Judy's transgressions. A reporter read the statement to Alsop, asking his reaction. He reserved comments on the accusations, but asked the reporter if he noticed that there wasn't one word of concern about Judy's condition, not a wish for her quick recovery, in the entire thing. The reporter was startled, and wrote a piece lambasting the studio for its heartless treatment of such a vulnerable girl.

It was all moot, however. Judy's relationship with MGM was at an end. She asked to be released from her contract, and the studio readily agreed. To them, Judy Garland was now more trouble than she was worth.

Finally free from MGM, Judy was relieved—and terrified. The options open to her—concerts, Broadway shows, films for other studios—were no less frightening than appearing on an MGM sound stage had been.

She tried not to think about it. She stayed in bed a lot; when she was up she usually played with Liza. Knowledge of Judy's suicide attempt had been kept from Liza; she was aware only that Judy was ill and needed to stay in bed. Alsop told *Newsweek* at the time: "We tell (Liza) Mommie's sick. And we try to keep her entertained with television and by letting her sing. That little doll can carry long tunes now. Thank God she can't read the papers."

Judy's first three death tries hadn't impinged on her daughter's world, but in time Liza would become a bizarre supporting character in Judy's future attempts—serious and staged—to kill herself.

As Judy's life was about to change, so was Liza's. The relatively predictable life she had known would come apart, and Liza would grow up very quickly indeed: her parents were heading for divorce.

In reality, the marriage had been unsalvageable for years, but both Judy and Vincente

63

harbored hope that something could be worked out—if only for Liza's sake. Perhaps now that Liza was approaching five years old, or simply because the entire relationship was untenable, Vincente came to realize that the marriage was over.

Just as Judy had fallen out of love with Vincente years before, he now felt concern and sympathy rather than affection. A conversation with Judy had proved Minnelli's last straw. Someone at the studio told Judy that she had been to a total of sixteen psychiatrists. "So what?" she retorted. "I never told any of them the truth. There's more than one way to get even with you people."

"Her admission deepened my depression," says Minnelli. "The months of near nervous collapse we'd both suffered had been for naught. She hadn't even tried . . . It was damn near impossible for me to forgive Judy for this. I opted for sanity. Liza's well-being would be better served if she had one stable parent living apart from his mate than having two emotionally wounded parents living together."

Three days before Christmas, 1950, Judy left Vincente's house for good. Liza would remain with her father. Liza had pleaded with Judy to stay until after Christmas; she couldn't understand why Mama had to leave right at that moment. As Vincente put it, Christmas is "the day when families renew their loving bonds. But we needn't pretend any longer."

Judy and Liza spent Christmas together after Liza watched her mother re-create the role of Dorothy for a live Lux Radio Theater broadcast of *The Wizard of Oz* for CBS.

But a few days later, Judy left California for a trip to New York. Whatever her feelings about leaving Liza, she was expectant about her sojourn in New York. She felt it was going to be the start of a good new life for her. She couldn't have expected that it would also be the beginning of a love affair, and result in a new "papa" for Liza.

TWO

"*Before Mama did something she knew would drive me nuts, she'd warn me. 'Watch this,' she'd say. 'I'm going to have to do something crazy.'*"

—*Liza Minnelli*

Liza gravely blows a horn at her fifth birthday party, March 12, 1951.

J udy had met Michael Sidney Luft during an earlier trip to New York, and they were by now seriously—albeit secretly—involved. In March 1951, Judy began divorce proceedings against Vincente Minnelli, but until then her liaison with Luft had been handled discreetly. Luft himself was embroiled in divorce proceedings.

They had met briefly in the mid-forties, again in a restaurant in the 1950s, then again later at a party. Judy was fascinated by Sid Luft—he was unlike most of the men she knew in Hollywood, and completely different from the two men she had married. He was brusque, swaggeringly masculine, the kind of man who would as quickly knock an adversary's teeth out as discuss the problem. He carried a gun, and a chip on his shoulder from years of fighting "Jew-boy" slurs.

Judy, adrift professionally and emotionally, felt safe around this man; secure that he would protect her in the ways Minnelli had failed to do. And her physical attraction to Luft was the strongest she had felt since a teenage fascination with Artie Shaw: he was big, muscular, sexy. She would later describe her arousal as "love at first sight."

Luft was a man with no discernible profession; he had been described as an "entrepreneur" and a "businessman"; others, less sympathetic, called him a hustler and a con artist. Several of Judy's friends who knew Luft warned her vigorously against getting involved with him, but she would hear none of it.

Judy was fascinated as well by Luft's background. He was raised in Bronxville, New York, an affluent community with restrictions against Jews. His childhood was spent defending himself against slurs, to the point where he enrolled through the mail in the Charles Atlas body-building program in order to fight back. Before this, he had been picked up by police at the age of twelve for carrying a .22 revolver. He had learned quite early that the best way to avoid being hassled in life was to fight—and he never hesitated to do so whenever provoked.

He attended several universities, never graduated, was briefly married, and by twenty was involved in the production of an aquacade in Ottawa, Canada. He liked the taste of show business this venture gave him. He enlisted in the Royal Canadian Air Force and, after his discharge, went to Hollywood, looked up old Bronxville friend Eleanor Powell, and for a time worked as her secretary.

In the mid-forties, Luft used his air-force experience to get a job as a test pilot for Douglas Aircraft, where he also worked as a technical adviser for the flying sequences on a grade-B movie starring Lynn Bari, "Queen of the B's." He and Lynn fell in love, got married, and planned for Luft to guide Bari's career into the upper echelons of stardom. It wasn't to happen, and after eight years and one child, the couple were involved in a bitter divorce case and custody battle.

Now, although neither Sid nor Judy was free to wed, Luft became her constant companion and, later, her "manager." Whatever her friends' feelings about Luft, the relationship was very good for Judy; Minnelli himself acknowledged it: "She was now leaning on Sid, who'd seemingly discovered the secret to keeping Judy sane and healthy."

The secret was that Judy was in love; and as terrified as she was of making her stage debut, Luft convinced her it was the logical next step in her career. Judy began making plans to make her concert debut at the famed Palladium theater in London. But first, she would have to begin divorce proceedings against Vincente.

On March 23, 1951, she appeared before Superior Court Judge William McKay and recited a litany of complaints against Minnelli: ". . . without any explanation, my husband withdrew himself and shut himself out of my life . . . I was terribly lonely, I frequently became hysterical. I had to go under a doctor's care. I just couldn't understand [my husband's] attitude. He lacked interest in me, my career, my friends, everything."

The truth of her testimony was irrelevant; Vincente had told her that anything she did to gain the divorce was all right with him. They were now legally separated, and a divorce would become final in one year if there was no reconciliation.

Custody of Liza was granted to Judy, with the stipulation that the child was to spend six months a year with Vincente and he was to pay five hundred dollars a month child support when Liza was with Judy. The agreement went on to state, ". . . The child will be given utmost 'freedom of locomotion' and changes from one home to the other will be irregular to avoid the child developing a feeling of regimentation."

Considering the course of Liza's life over the next ten years, this fear of "regimentation" was quite unnecessary.

Liza's was to be a life of wild extremes and unpredictable crises, a nomadic existence following Judy from hotel rooms to mansions and back again when Judy toured, sometimes being evicted for nonpayment of her bill. Her life with Vincente would be secure, predictable. And filled with love.

Vincente pointed out the dichotomy in Liza's life after her parents' divorce. "If I spoiled Liza outrageously, the fairy tale quality of our relationship achieved a balance with the starkness of her life with Judy. Much as Liza loved her mother, Judy represented duty and worry. I required nothing but love. As a result, I shared Liza's most carefree times. Judy was sadly short-changed."

Immediately after her custody was decided, however, Liza had no need to worry about leaving her father anytime soon: she was left with Vincente as Judy prepared to go to London and her debut at the Palladium.

Judy arrived in London aboard the *Ile de France* in early April. The British press was astonished at how she looked: she was plump, matronly; she looked closer to forty than twenty-eight. The press commented on her weight, but otherwise her greeting was warm and affectionate: Britons would not forget that in the blackest hours of World War II, Judy Garland movies brought them some respite from their horrendous plight.

Judy had begged Sid to accompany her, but he had decided against it. She persisted, though, and after several transatlantic telephone calls, he relented. He surprised her as she went backstage after a rehearsal, and she was joyous at having him there: he could supply her with most of the emotional strength she needed to go through with this.

Still, she was terrified. She couldn't sleep the entire night before the concert; her body ached with fear. "I kept rushing to the bathroom to vomit," she said. "I couldn't eat, I couldn't sleep, I couldn't even sit down."

Despite her fears, and a somewhat rocky start, Judy's Palladium concert was a triumph. Her reviews were ecstatic, her audiences rapturous in their adulation. She was as astonished as delighted by the overwhelming reception the British gave her. It was clear that an entirely new career outside pictures was possible for Judy Garland.

Not that doing concerts—especially on tour, night after night, as she now planned for the British provinces—was any easier than film making. In many ways, it was much harder. But concertizing did not create the psychological stress for Judy that making films did. She didn't feel used, or forced to work; she wasn't doing this to please Mr. Mayer or her mother, she was doing it to please Sid—and herself. This was *her* career—and as difficult, as terrifying, as exhausting as it could be, it was, in Judy's mind, much more worthy of the trouble.

After Judy had done a four-week stand at the Palladium, Sid put together a tour which

Judy on her way to London and her first Palladium date, March 1951.

Vincente comforts an apprehensive Liza as she is about to leave aboard the *Queen Elizabeth* to join Judy in England.

took her to Glasgow, Edinburgh, Manchester, Liverpool, Dublin, and Birmingham. Everywhere she went, even the smallest towns with the most spottily attended theaters, sold-out houses cheered her lustily.

Judy was happier than she had been for a long time. She and Sid had discussed marriage, which Judy very badly wanted. She was at heart quite old-fashioned; when she loved a man it seemed logical to her to get married. Sid was somewhat reticent; he had been burned twice by marriage and was still not divorced from Lynn Bari. But he made a commitment to Judy that ultimately they would wed, and it made Judy's happiness complete. Sid had proven his loyalty to her on this tour; he was a fighter in her corner. She was not going to let this man out of her life.

A few weeks before the end of the tour, Judy's longing to see Liza got the better of her, and she telephoned Vincente, asking to send her over. It seemed extravagant and unnecessary: Judy would be back in the States in less than two weeks. But word of Judy's English triumph had been prominently played up in the American press, and her friends—Vincente among them (he had suggested she sing "Swanee" when she asked for his advice)—were delighted that Judy had pulled herself together. Vincente wanted Liza to see her mother now, at her best.

"Though I'd selfishly wanted Liza for myself," he wrote, "now was the time she should be with Judy, during the period of one of her mother's greatest triumphs. Only then could Liza, who'd lived through so many of Judy's down periods, begin to understand her mother's staggering talent."

For Minnelli, there were two Judy Garlands—a woman he couldn't live with and a performer whose ability he greatly admired. It was a dichotomy that would run throughout Liza's life—although for her, there were often not just two mamas, but three or four. And some were as hateful as the others were lovable.

Now, though, Liza was excited about going to see her mother, sailing on a ship for the first time, and visiting England, a place her father had told her about in his inimitable, colorfully detailed way. She and her governess, Cozy, arrived in Birmingham in July.

Everything around Liza was new—including the man constantly at her mother's side. He was introduced to her as her mother's very dear friend Sid, and Luft noticed that the child was reticent with her feelings, watching him carefully with her wide brown eyes. Luft kept his distance, rarely impinging on the time mother and daughter spent together.

Judy showed Liza her favorite spots in Birmingham, and the little girl—just five a few months before—sat with Sid to watch her mother's performances and listen to the great waves of love and applause that swept from the audience every night. Liza was caught up in the mass love for her mother, and when they were together at home, she clung to her, wanting for herself the love the audiences felt from Judy when she was performing. Judy returned all Liza's affection and more—hugging and kissing her, subjugating all her own needs and desires to her daughter's. Sid was amazed and touched. He had never before seen Judy so selfless, so outgoing.

Liza and Cozy spent a week in England, then joined Judy aboard the *Queen Elizabeth* for the trip back to New York (Sid had flown ahead). Once more, Liza was the center of Judy's attention. But as before—and so often again in the future—Judy's devotion to Liza proved short-lived. Judy was incapable of going for long periods without being the center of attention, and once her longings to be with her child were satisfied, she could conveniently pack up Liza and send her back to Vincente. Once Judy arrived in New York, she did just that—Liza and Cozy boarded a train for California the very night the *Queen Elizabeth* docked. Judy and Sid would remain in New York indefinitely, eventually—Judy hoped—tying the knot. And there were a lot of plans to be made—Sid was determined that Judy's success in England be duplicated in the United States.

7

In the smothering heat of a New York August, Sid Luft went to work to find engagements for Judy Garland. To his surprise, there was little interest. Hadn't everyone heard about her triumph in England? Yes, they would tell him, they'd heard, but that was England, not the United States, and there had been so many reports about Judy's lack of professionalism, all the extra money she had cost film producers. Luft would counter all their objections but get nowhere. He began to feel as though it were a lost cause, and he and Judy, cooped up in a stifling hotel room with broken-down air-conditioning and getting more and more impatient, began to bicker for the first time in their relationship. Something would have to break soon.

The idea came to Luft as he walked, dejected, along the street in front of the Palace Theater. "The Palace" had been the pinnacle of show business, the place where only the greatest entertainers appeared. In ten of her films, Judy had played characters whose dream was to someday play either the fabled Palace specifically or Broadway in general.

Luft entered the theater, his mind racing. What he saw depressed him. The building was run down, filthy; there were five acts of vaudeville and a movie for $1.25. Only a few patrons sat in the seats, most of them winos sleeping it off. But Luft had more show business vision than his detractors gave him credit for: he could see Judy in concert, restoring a refurbished Palace to its former grandeur and at the same time re-establishing herself as a first-rank star in the United States—where it mattered.

Luckily for all concerned, Sid knew Sol Schwartz, a vice-president of RKO, which now owned the Palace. Sol shared Sid's enthusiasm, and a deal was put together for Judy to open at the Palace in October, performing for nearly an hour following an hour of vaudeville acts. Judy was thrilled by the prospect, and left immediately for Los Angeles, where Roger Edens and Chuck Walters helped her whip an act into shape.

They worked to make it the biggest thing ever to hit New York. Judy wouldn't just sing, she would dance, take part in elaborate production numbers, re-create her most famous movie scenes on stage. Judy worked harder than she ever had before at the Nico Charisse dance studio, where Ethel had brought Liza for her first dance lesson several years before.

Although Judy was in California, Liza remained with Vincente; Judy saw her several times, but her rehearsal schedule was backbreaking: the act would debut in less than two months.

Judy Garland's opening at the Palace was, without exaggeration, the biggest event to hit Times Square since the celebration at the end of World War II. Everyone wished Judy well; they had heard about her English successes but were skeptical about her staying power; if she could pull this off it would indeed be the start of a gigantic new career for her. And all New York show business was caught up in the excitement of the Palace's revival.

Judy did indeed pull it off. Not only was she in wonderful voice, summoning up the most treasured memories of her film appearances, but there was the added pathos of her dramatic triumph over the problems which had made headlines less than sixteen months earlier. Her fans came ready to cheer her on, help her through what many feared would be a pathetic display of the remnants of Judy's battered talents.

That she was brilliant, charming, in big and glorious voice despite an almost startling smallness on stage; that she had risen from illness and breakdowns and suicide attempts and divorces to give perhaps the best performance of her life; put her fans—and thousands of others—into a rapturous euphoria.

Judy listens in rapture as her Palace audience sings a farewell song, "Auld Lang Syne."

It was the first of many times that Judy's personal travails would combine with her talent and amazing recuperative powers to make her performances almost mythical in their effect on her audiences. And it was, clearly, the start of the Judy Garland cult, a following of fans, many of them gay men, who were devoted to her—more completely, more intensely, and for a longer period of time than for any other performer before her.

Judy's gay following was rather ironic, considering the aversion to homosexuality she appears to have had since the disturbing rumors about her father. Her feelings on the subject, though, were not publicly known until after her death; and she in fact may have ultimately found personal as well as professional solace among gay men: there were published implications in newspapers that her husband after Sid Luft, Mark Herron, was homosexual.

Later, published reports would appear that Liza shared her mother's disdain for gay men while at the same time surrounding herself with them and marrying a man, Peter Allen, about whom such implications would also be published.

These fascinating contradictions—just a few of the many surrounding Judy and Liza—were, however, far in the future in 1951. Gay men responded to Judy initially for a variety of reasons. She sang about unrequited love ("The Boy Next Door"); a better life just ahead ("Somewhere Over the Rainbow") and, later, lost love ("The Man That Got Away.") Thousands of lonely, misunderstood men, who needed to conceal their most important emotions in order to function in the repressive society of the 1950s, empathized with Judy's despairs, her feelings of alienation, her thoughts of ending it all. And when she sang a heartrending ballad, many in her audience, men and women alike, felt not only that she was singing it about herself, but that she was singing it about *them*. And she could put across happiness and jubilation in an unequaled manner, despite her personal travails. She was living proof that even someone as emotionally fragile as she could triumph against adversity.

Judy Garland was now at the height of her career. The Palace engagement was a sellout, and lasted over four months, the all-time long run record for the Palace. But Judy Garland's life could never stay at a peak very long. Sometimes the descents into valleys were precipitous, sometimes almost indiscernible, but they always came. Three weeks into the Palace run, weak from dieting after some unkind references to her weight had appeared in the press, Judy collapsed in the middle of a show. She was taken to a sanitarium with "nervous exhaustion." It was clear that two hour-long shows a day, six days a week, was too much. Her schedule was cut from thirteen shows a week to ten, and she returned five nights later, planning to take another week-long break at Christmas to spend the holidays in California with Liza.

Judy had not taken any pills during most of the time she knew Sid Luft. Now, under the strain of a difficult work schedule, and trying to lose weight again, she began seeing a doctor who supplied her with a variety of pills. Luft found out, and forbade the doctor ever to return. He told Judy, who to his surprise agreed that it was the best thing. But she began seeing another doctor, and Luft—then as later, and throughout their relationship—could never be entirely sure whether she was taking pills, or how many she was taking. Luft, in this instance, let the issue pass.

Once again, Judy took a break by visiting Liza, using her daughter almost as therapy, as part of her R&R. Once again, Liza was the center of Judy's world, and they spent a wonderful holiday together. Then, Judy was gone again for another indefinite period, and Liza was back to being a one-parent child, her life with Vincente as predictable as the morning sunrise.

Judy's closing night at the Palace was February 24, and she and Sid left in early March for a two-week vacation in Palm Beach, accompanied by the Duke and Duchess of Windsor. Their golf playing and restaurant going were amply covered by the press, and Judy played the chanteuse/socialite role with verve.

Her sojourn in Palm Beach caused Judy to miss Liza's sixth birthday party, a fact which was reported in the press, since the party was quite an elaborate affair and amply covered by

Liza welcomes Judy back from New York after her Palace engagement, 1952.

reporters and photographers. It was held at the Gershwins', and Lee and Vincente spared little to make it one of the more memorable birthdays of the season.

The guest list was a Who's Who of Hollywood: Humphrey Bogart and Lauren Bacall, Joan Bennett, Paul Henreid; and the children of Jimmy Stewart, Ray Milland, King Vidor, and Betty Hutton, among others, were present. Also there was Timmy Getty, the son of J. Paul Getty, who was little Liza's first crush. Vincente remembers fleetingly fantasizing about becoming a part of such a wealthy family, but the relationship was not to last.

Dozens of children crowded the Gershwin home; there were clowns and other performers milling about, then a scary cartoon was shown. Later, a magician held the children, especially Liza, in thrall with his act. The opening of presents was accomplished with great fanfare, Liza politely thanking everyone individually. Her father gave her a satin-topped tutu for her dance classes, then she blew out the six candles on her birthday cake with a great flourish.

With her mother not there to give her the parental attention she needed, Liza was ever more covetous of Vincente's time and ministrations. At one point in the party, while Liza was preoccupied with some of her friends, Vincente was talking with Lauren Bacall and some of the other parents present. A little girl came over to him and pulled herself up onto his lap. He made a fuss over her, and kissed her. Vincente didn't notice that Liza was watching.

She marched over to her father and without a word punched him in the nose. Vincente says he saw stars, but Liza wasn't punished—everyone thought her jealousy very cute, and it was, after all, her birthday party. Vincente was more careful in the future about paying undue attention to little girls other than his Liza. "The attitude was 'That was for nothing. Now watch it!' " Vincente says.

Judy and Sid returned to California late in March to put together her appearance at the Los Angeles Philharmonic Auditorium. It was now time for Judy to show this company town that she had indeed come back, had succeeded without the support of the omnipotent MGM. And she did just that. Everyone she had ever worked with, it seemed, turned out for her opening night, and she was a smash. There was nothing but joy for Judy, and the wheels were put in motion for her return to motion pictures. At the end of her show, Judy told the audience, "This is the happiest night of my life. I've missed you all . . . "

Sid worked on booking Judy for an appearance in San Francisco. The couple's life together was wonderful. She credited him with restoring her career; his entrepreneurial spirit and faith in her ability had, after all, made all this happen. Their sexual relationship was better than ever, and she had gotten along with him, on a day-to-day basis, better than she had with either of her previous husbands. She began thinking seriously, and often, of marriage. She didn't mention her thoughts to Sid, but she did talk to Liza about them.

Liza was staying with Judy, and one night, as the six-year-old watched her mother put on her make-up to go out, Judy asked her nonchalantly, not taking her eyes off the mirror, "What would you think if I married Sid?"

Liza was puzzled by the question, and thought for a few seconds. "I don't think I'd like that. Why would you want to do that? What about Daddy?"

Judy stopped applying her make-up and turned to her daughter. "Well," she said. "We're not married anymore." Liza said nothing. Then Judy asked her, "Wouldn't you like to have a little brother or sister?"

Liza's face brightened. "Oh, yes, I'd like that very much." She ran over to her mother and sat on her lap.

"Well," Judy told her, "If I marry Sid, then we could have a little baby in the house."

Later, Liza would say, "That made good sense, so I gave her my permission." But after Judy left for the evening, Liza experienced mixed emotions. She wondered what life would be like with a new daddy, and she worried that somehow her own father would go out of her life.

A portrait of Liza, 1952.

But she grew excited about the prospect of a baby in the house, and began thinking about the wedding, sure that she would be a flower girl and take part in an elaborate ceremony.

That isn't how it turned out. Judy had gone up to San Francisco to bring her show to the Curran Theater, where she opened on May 26. On June 3, Judy had confirmed by a doctor what she had suspected when she spoke to Liza about marrying Sid: she was pregnant. She told Sid, who agreed that marriage was necessary; but he was apprehensive. His divorce from Lynn Bari, like Judy's from Vincente Minnelli, had just become final in March. Lynn was in court demanding additional child-support payments from Sid, and he knew that his marriage to Judy Garland would give Lynn's lawyer new ammunition. More than that, though, was his fear of another marriage so soon after one so bitterly failed. Still, there was nothing else to be done.

On June 11, Liza was sitting with her father watching the six o'clock news. A picture of her mother and Sid Luft appeared on the screen. Three days ago, the announcer said, they had been secretly wed. "I was shocked," said Liza later. "And I think Daddy was, too." Louella Parsons had broken the story before Judy had a chance to tell Liza, and Liza was hurt. Her mother had gotten married without telling her, and she hadn't been a part of the ceremony. Liza was more afraid than ever that she and her father would forever be peripheral to Judy's life. She tried to reason it out, realizing even at six that perhaps the reason she wasn't there was precisely because her mother was getting married and wanted to be alone with her new husband. But it was difficult for her to accept this rebuke: she had learned on *television* that her mother had a new husband. Liza reports that she comforted herself that night with Eskimo pies.

A new chapter in Liza's life was beginning. Her custody was with her mother; and when Judy and Sid returned from San Francisco, they moved into a big new home on Maple Drive. Judy's finances were now in excellent shape; she had made quite a bit of money from her ten concert engagements over the past year, and a new album, *Judy at the Palace,* was selling extremely well. Mr. and Mrs. Sid Luft could afford a lovely home, and they moved into it with Liza, her governess Cozy, a psychiatric nurse hired to help Judy through her pregnancy, and a full staff of servants.

Liza was again part of a family unit, but its head was a virtual stranger to her. She didn't know exactly how she felt about Sid Luft. He seemed a nice enough man, but her precocious and always aware mind had picked up some of the negative intimations about Sid being expressed by Judy's associates. Still, she was willing to give this man the benefit of the doubt, for her mother's sake: she was thrilled to be back as a part of her mother's life on what seemed to her a permanent basis.

They had talked about Daddy. Judy explained to Liza that Vincente would always be her father, and would always love her, but that Sid wanted to be like a father to her, too. It was like having two daddies, Judy explained, and that seemed like not such a bad thing to Liza. Judy was anxious that Liza accept Sid, and the first day they moved into the Maple Drive house, Judy asked her daughter if she would call the new man of the house "Papa Sid." That seemed like a good compromise to Liza, and she agreed.

When Sid drove up and came into the house, the first thing Liza said to him was, "Hello, Papa Sid." Sid was taken aback, blushed, and took Liza in his arms as Judy laughed with delight. They would be a real family, together awaiting the new arrival.

8

Judy's pregnancy was even more difficult than her first one had been. She put on a great deal of weight, ballooning with what her doctor explained was water retention. She found it difficult to get around, and hated the way she looked. At one point, she lost all feeling in her right arm, and had to keep it in a sling for a week.

She was not at all happy with her condition. "Oh, God," she sighed four months into her pregnancy. "Five more months of this!" Unlike the time she was carrying Liza, Judy did not give up her "medication," and—despite Sid's attempts to keep her pill-free—she was able to obtain Seconal and Dexedrine. Several times, he searched the house, but couldn't turn up any of the pills. Still, he could tell immediately upon speaking to her whether or not she was medicated. Like Vincente Minnelli before him, Luft often felt impotent in trying to deal with Judy's pill use. But unlike Minnelli, Luft in the future would frequently take definite steps to do something about it.

Although Judy was now a part of a family—Luft's son Johnny, a year and a half younger than Liza, lived with them—she was totally estranged from her mother, and rarely saw her sisters. Things with Ethel weren't improved when she went to court, claiming nonsupport from her "high salaried" daughter. Just before Judy's wedding to Sid, the story broke that Judy Garland's mother was working at Douglas Aircraft for sixty-one dollars a week. The intimations were cruel; Judy was making twenty-five-thousand dollars a week in concert, and she couldn't help out her poor mother?

Judy had ignored that publicity, but a lawsuit was a serious matter. Ethel's action infuriated her: it was one thing for Judy to refuse to see her mother, as she had done several times while on tour, but quite another for Ethel to publicly air their differences. Judy fought the suit, claiming that Ethel was capable of earning quite a bit more if she wanted to. She also showed proof of all the money she had paid to Ethel since the start of her career, and accused her of mismanagement. Ethel lost the suit, and the estrangement between mother and daughter was worse than ever. On July 19, Ethel gave an interview to gossip columnist Sheilah Graham. The picture Ethel painted of Judy was not flattering. "Judy has been selfish all her life," Ethel said. "That's my fault. I made it too easy for her. She worked, but that's all she ever wanted—to be an actress. She never said, 'I want to be kind or loved,' only 'I want to be famous.'"

The rift between mother and daughter was not healed by the birth of Judy's second daughter on November 21, 1952. Ethel attempted to see her newborn grandchild, but Judy refused to allow it, instructing the hospital staff not to grant Mrs. Gilmore access to the maternity ward.

Judy and Sid named their baby Lorna, and she was a pretty, fair, six-pound four-ounce child. Liza was thrilled at having a little baby sister—she and Sid's son, Johnny, were often at each other's throats. Now, she would have someone she could care for and, later, play with.

Sid was delighted the child was a little girl—now, he was the father of a son and a daughter. For Judy, however, there was a repeat of the severe post-partum depression she had suffered with Liza—only this one was considerably more severe.

Several days after Lorna's return home, Judy's condition had deteriorated to the point where she cried almost constantly, rarely venturing out of bed. Sid was sure she was on pills—her moods shifted crazily, sometimes in midconversation. He tried to talk her out of using them, but his efforts resulted only in an argument. He instructed the butler to keep a close watch on Judy, and to phone him at his office if anything seemed amiss.

Later that day, the butler phoned: there was no answer to his knock on Mrs. Luft's bedroom door. Sid was home in a matter of minutes, and broke down the door. No Judy. The bathroom door was locked, and after three tries to break that door down, it gave. Sid came upon Judy, lying in a pool of blood, her throat cut. He was stunned, incredulous—but he retained the presence of mind to wrap her wound in a towel. Her doctor arrived a few minutes later and stitched the cut up on the spot. Coming to, Judy asked what had happened. She had no recollection of having done this to herself.

The incident didn't make the newspapers, but word spread around Hollywood that something untoward had happened at the Luft house. To help scotch the rumors, Sid gave a dinner party for dozens of Hollywood notables, less than a week after the incident. Judy, with a high collar to hide her bandages, not only appeared, but sang. Sid watched her, marveling at her resiliency, hoping against hope that the stitches wouldn't pop. They didn't, and Judy seemed to be snapping back from this depression which again had almost cost her her life.

On Christmas day, Sid, Judy, baby Lorna, and Lorna's nurse left for New York, where Judy had agreed to perform for charity. Johnny spent the holiday with his mother; Liza was visiting her father. As happy as she had been at Lorna's arrival, it didn't do much to alleviate an unpleasant feeling Liza was having: that she was an outsider in the Luft family. The man of the house was Johnny and Lorna's dad; Liza had to go away to see *her* father. And as happy as she was to spend Christmas with Vincente, Liza, soon to be seven, couldn't have failed to observe which family unit took the trip to New York. But Liza's resiliency was beginning to rival Judy's, and she had a wonderful time with her father.

While Judy and Sid were still in New York, on January 5, Ethel Gilmore was found dead between two parked cars in the Douglas Aircraft parking lot. She had suffered a heart attack as she arrived for work. Sid got the news by telephone and broke it, as gently as possible, to Judy. She became hysterical; then, calming down, arranged to meet her sisters in the Maple Drive house. Heavily sedated, Judy flew back to Los Angeles despite her great fear of flying.

At the funeral, Judy became hysterical again, collapsing into the arms of her brother-in-law, Johnny, and sobbing, "I didn't want her to die."

The family could muster little sympathy for Judy, after the way she had treated Ethel. All Johnny would say was, "Judy, you better straighten up. You have a lot to live with. I wouldn't want that on my conscience."

Judy's treatment of Ethel stayed on her conscience for years to come; often she would wake up after nightmares in which her mother cried for help. Although Judy surely had good reasons to resent certain things about her mother, the intensity of her hatred can be explained no more readily than some of her other behavior; surely neither of Ethel's other daughters harbored similar feelings.

Perhaps to assuage her guilt, Judy began, more than a decade later, to tell horror stories about her mother's treatment of her. She was, she said, awakened in the middle of the night to drive long distances to attend auditions she wanted no part of; Ethel, she claimed, would lock her in a hotel room while they were on tour, and leave her there, fearful of permanent desertion, for hours. Ethel was painted as a shrill harridan who must always have her way, a stage mother in the extreme who forced her daughter into a life she never wanted to fulfill her own unrealized show business aspirations.

Whatever Ethel's shortcomings—she certainly misused much of Judy's money and took sides with MGM in disputes with her daughter—most of Judy's Dickensian tales of her treatment at the hands of Ethel have been denied both by her sisters and friends of the family. Just as with her tales of being force-fed pills and worked into exhaustion by MGM—stories which have been denied by Mickey Rooney, who should know—Judy manufactured these facts to create sympathy, and to somehow justify to herself and others her treatment of Ethel.

Her mother's death was a body blow to Judy, and she was consumed with guilt, espe-

Judy, Sid, and her sister Suzy attend the funeral of Ethel Gilmore, January 1953.

cially because Ethel had never seen Lorna. Her depression returned; her pill use increased; she kept herself isolated from the children.

Sid knew he would have to do something to make Judy snap out of it, and he thought a new film would help. For over a year, he had been negotiating with Warner Brothers for Judy to star in a remake of the 1937 Janet Gaynor/Fredric March film *A Star Is Born*. It was something Judy had wanted to do ever since she had played the role—that of a rising star married to an alcoholic actor on the skids—on a radio program while at MGM. Louis B. Mayer had nixed the idea of Judy's doing the film because he was convinced audiences wouldn't want to see adorable Judy Garland as the wife of an alcoholic. But now the goody-goody image was gone forever, it was a juicy role—and if Sid could get the project off the ground, he would be the film's producer and have his own source of income for the first time in their relationship.

Preparations for the film diverted Judy's attention from her emotional travails, as did the purchase of a palatial new home on Mapleton Drive in exclusive Holmby Hills. Its nineteen rooms included complete suites for Liza and Lorna, a forty-foot living room, separate suites for Judy and Sid for private moments, and servants' quarters to house the butler, cook, and maid. Other employees included governesses, chauffeurs, nurses, and a gardener.

Pre-production work on *A Star Is Born* was slow and fraught with problems. Often Judy would be alone in that huge house, with Sid at some meeting or another; she would be bored and lonely. She didn't work at all during 1953 until the start of *Star* filming; she spent most of her time with Liza and Lorna.

Liza turned seven in March 1953, and was attending an exclusive private school, finishing first grade, and doing very well, especially in subjects relating to the humanities. Although high-spirited and energetic, she was capable of a seriousness far beyond her years, a condition helped along by frequent household exigencies. The first of these was on a night when, with Sid out of town, Judy had a violent argument with Lorna's nurse. When Judy was angry she could be a horrifying spectacle, and many a servant would experience her wrath. She would call them the most vile names, accuse them of incompetency, dishonesty, and worse, and order them out of her house. Sometimes, things would be patched up; more often, the servant left whether asked to return or not.

This night, Judy reviled the poor woman in whose care Lorna was entrusted, and stormed out of the house. The nurse, shaken and unable to summon up the slightest caring for any member of the Luft household, packed up her belongings and left for good. Liza was panicked. She was barely seven years old and hadn't the vaguest idea what to do with a screaming baby.

Finally, Liza roused the soundly sleeping cook, who helped her cope with baby Lorna until Judy returned. Liza would be forced to care for her siblings—and later her mother—many times, and it was these sometimes traumatic experiences that went far toward making Liza a little girl who could sometimes be described only as "grave."

It was not easy for Judy to begin work on *A Star Is Born*. It was the first time she had set foot on a sound stage in over three years, and her fears weren't lessened much by the fact that it was with a new studio, Warner Brothers, and was her husband's production of a project she had developed herself.

As before, she was often late, sometimes refusing to come out of her dressing room for hours. Director George Cukor agreed to film some of her scenes at night, when she was often at her best. But despite these difficulties, it was clear that Judy was giving a magnificent performance as Vicky Lester opposite James Mason's Norman Maine. Her musical numbers were thrilling, her dramatic scenes heart-wrenching. Here at last was a full-bodied adult role in which the wide range of Judy Garland's enormous talent would be revealed.

But it would be revealed at tremendous emotional cost to Judy. For in fact Judy was deeply feeling not only the Vicky Lester role but the Norman Maine character as well. As Vicky

On the set of *A Star Is Born*, Judy and Sid celebrate his birthday, 1953.

A Star Is Born costume test.

Judy, James Mason, and George Cukor on the set.

Lester, she was called upon to act a stable, optimistic young performer on the road to success who falls in love with an actor consumed by self-doubt, facing a failing career, and suffering from an emotional and physical dependence on alcohol. Judy certainly could relate to Maine's emotional dependency.

Her role became increasingly difficult to play, increasingly painful for her. But she came through brilliantly. When Jack Warner saw the first rushes, he was convinced he had one of the greatest movies of all time, and upped the budget from $1.8 million to $4.5 million, an enormous sum at the time. Ultimately, the film cost $6 million, with much of the overage blamed on Judy. But no one really cared; *Star* would be a great film, put Judy Garland back at the height of Hollywood stardom and make millions for Warner Brothers.

The terrible pressures of making this film—and there were problems completely unrelated to Judy—put a great strain on the Luft marriage. According to Judy, the honeymoon hadn't lasted long. She said after the marriage ended in the early sixties, "From the beginning Sid and I weren't happy. I don't know why. I really don't. For me it was work, work, work; and then I didn't see much of Sid. He was always dashing off to places lining up my appearances."

If they truly weren't happy in their marriage, they certainly stuck it out; despite several separations, reconciliations and ugly court fights, they remained man and wife for eleven years. Their wills frequently clashed, but Luft was one of the few people who could handle Judy, who did not wilt under her furious tirades.

In fact, Judy later claimed in court Luft's temper sometimes erupted into physical violence against her. At a custody hearing in 1964, Judy testified that their children were so frightened of Luft that she was forced to seek psychiatric treatment for them.

Whatever the circumstances, Judy needed Sid Luft's firm, sure hand, even if that hand might occasionally rise up and strike her. *A Star Is Born,* she felt, would be their great triumph, bringing renewed film stardom to her and lofty status as a producer to him. *Star* was indeed a triumph, but it failed to have either result.

The film opened at a huge Hollywood premiere attended by practically every celebrity in town. Praise for Judy was effusive, and the critics agreed with her friends: it was a staggering performance. Bosley Crowther in the New York *Times* called the film "One of the grandest heartbreak dramas that has drenched the screen in years" and added that director Cukor "gets performances from Miss Garland and Mr. Mason that make the heart flutter and bleed. Miss Garland is excellent in all things but most winningly perhaps in the song 'Here's What I'm Here For,' [sic; it was actually 'Someone at Last'] wherein she dances, sings, and pantomimes the universal endeavors of the lady to capture the man . . . It is something to see, this *A Star Is Born."*

Time reviewed the film in the guise of a background article. "*Star* is a massive effort . . . The producers assumed enormous risks . . . The star, Judy Garland, was a 32-year-old has-been as infamous for temperament as she is famous for talent. What's more, all the producers' worst dreams came true. Day after day, while the high-priced help—including Judy's husband, Producer Sid Luft—stood around waiting for the shooting to start, Judy sulked in her dressing room . . . but after Judy had done her worst in the dressing room, she did her best in front of the camera, with the result that she gives what is just about the greatest one-woman show in modern movie history . . . An expert vaudeville performance was to be expected from Judy; to find her a dramatic actress as well is the real surprise, although perhaps it should not be . . . Judy Garland makes a stunning comeback . . . "

She was the toast of Hollywood; the talk was that she was a shoo-in to win the Best Actress Academy Award, and best of all, she was expecting another baby. Her doctor told her that delivery would come sometime in mid-April of 1955, and the Oscar show was scheduled for March 30. Judy and all those around her looked forward to a very joyous spring.

Judy and James Mason in *A Star Is Born*.

She was also off pills once again. After principal photography had ceased in March of 1954 and the pressures of filming had eased up, she and Sid took a trip to Ojai, a beautiful Southern California vacation town. Once they had settled into their cabin, Judy told Sid that she wanted to get off the medication, that she feared she was overdoing it. She asked him to help her. He agreed, not really knowing what to expect. Gerold Frank, in his brilliant biography *Judy*, reconstructs the event based on interviews with Sid Luft:

> They unpacked the bags. He ordered breakfast. She ate nothing. He had lunch. She did not eat. By nightfall she was beginning to perspire. Sid thought, *My God, she's going to do it cold turkey.*
>
> She began to tremble. "Just hold me," she said. He put his arms around her. She was trembling and perspiring. "Don't worry about it. Just hold me." She shook, and it took all his strength to hold her. It was now nearly 11 P.M. No, midnight . . . The sweat started pouring from her. Her trembling increased. "Judy, I better call a doctor," Sid said, as gently as he could . . . "No! Don't! Don't call a doctor! No needles, no needles, no doctor, nothing, for God's sake, don't!"
>
> For the next twelve hours, from midnight until nearly noon, they went through mutual agony, he holding her, she screaming into a pillow, into his chest, gritting her teeth, holding onto the wall as he supported her, he taking her back to the bed, holding her down, she suddenly unconscious, then coming back again, fighting, fighting, fighting, until, around noon, whatever it was broke, and she lay limp, her eyes open, no longer struggling, in a kind of peace.

It was an experience to bring husband and wife as close together as humanly possible, and the bonds between Judy and Sid were immeasurably strengthened. Several months later, she was pregnant again, and the Luft marriage was as solid as ever.

Since few things in Judy Garland's life went according to plan, it isn't surprising that she began to experience labor pains two weeks early, and was admitted to the hospital two days before the Academy Awards ceremony, on March 28.

By two in the morning of March 29, Judy had given birth to her first boy. She was overjoyed—she had wanted a boy, especially since this would be her last child: she had asked her doctor to tie off her Fallopian tubes after the child was born.

Sid was delighted to have another boy, but Judy's doctor warned him that there was trouble—the baby's left lung hadn't opened, he was in an incubator, and there was only a 50 percent chance the child would live.

The next morning, with his baby's life still in jeopardy, Sid entered Judy's room. They expressed their joy to each other, chose the baby's name—Joseph Wiley—and failed to let each other know they knew of their son's precarious position. When Judy was told, she refused to accept that her baby would do anything but recover fully. She called Liza—who had just turned nine—to tell her it was a boy. "Oh, Mama! That's what you wanted!" Liza exclaimed. Judy told her, strength in her voice, "They tell me he's going to die, but he's not going to—I promise you that. I won't let him."

Liza would never be able to forget her mother's voice at that moment, or the way that she herself felt on hearing the news, and her mother's determination that it not happen. She couldn't think of anything to say to Mama. Judy simply reiterated before hanging up. "I just wanted to call you and tell you that. It won't happen."

If Judy prayed for her son to live, it worked. By the next morning, little Joey's lung had opened normally and he was completely out of danger. The first time Joey was brought to her, Judy cried.

A serene, happy, maturing Judy in 1954.

The next scene in Judy Garland's life might have come from a bad movie—and might have been funny if it weren't so sad. She was up for an Academy Award; if she won it, it would be the final and most glittering symbol of her complete comeback to film stardom. And the Oscars had, year by year, become more and more important; this year's ceremony would be broadcast coast-to-coast over national television.

The contest, observers agreed, was between Judy and Grace Kelly, whose excellent performance as a haggard wife in *The Country Girl* had come as a pleasant surprise.

James Bacon, in an Associated Press report less than two weeks before the ceremonies, set the stage for Hollywood's biggest night: "It wasn't planned that way, but the fight for the films' top feminine Oscar might be called a class struggle. It's Judy Garland, born in a vaudeville trunk, versus Grace Kelly, born into a Philadelphia mansion.

"At this writing, the contest between Little Miss Showbusiness and the debutante actress looks like a draw. Hollywood, perhaps unconsciously, is taking sides strictly on the class basis. Performance-wise, both were superb.

"Sentiment, perhaps, is on the side of Judy. One of the greatest of child actresses, she had led a heartbreak life—a has-been and near suicide at 28, an Oscar favorite at 33. It's the kind of story Hollywood loves and one that needs an Academy Award for the happy ending."

Judy told Bacon, "I admit I want to win very badly." Because she would be unable to attend the ceremonies, she agreed to allow a film crew into her hospital room so that she could make an acceptance speech to the public should she win. All day on March 30, technicians wired the room, Judy's bed and Judy herself, running cables up her housecoat. "My God, they're wiring me up like a radar," Judy said at one point, unable to turn her head for fear she would disconnect something.

Finally, everything was ready, and the interminable show which preceded the announcement of Best Actress dragged on. Finally, with Sid holding her hand, Judy waited to hear if she had won. The envelope was opened, the winner announced: Grace Kelly. Judy shrank back into her pillow, Sid patted her hand and vented his anger. "Fuck the Academy Awards," he seethed, "you've got yours in the incubator. Why, those sons of bitches . . . they wouldn't give it to my baby!"

Worse for Judy was the reaction of the film crew and technicians. All day, she had been solicitous of them, asking if they wanted anything, ordering up coffee for them. When Grace Kelly's name was announced, not one of them said a word to Judy. The chief technician yelled, "Okay, wrap it up!" and his crew began unceremoniously—and gruffly—dismantling all their equipment. "Boys, don't short me," Judy said, only half jokingly—there were tears in her eyes. Their treatment of her was so cold; the intimation that winner was all and loser nothing made Judy feel worse than she already did. To Judy, being denied such a richly deserved Oscar merely confirmed to her that Hollywood was against her, would never acknowledge her real talents. Lauren Bacall, a close friend and neighbor, recalled Judy's deep disappointment. "She knew it was then or never. Instinctively, all her friends knew the same. Judy wasn't like any other performer. There was so much emotion involved in her career—in her life—it was always all or nothing. And though she put on a hell of a front, this was one more slap in the face. She was bitter about it, and, for that matter, all closest to her were."

It *was* then or never. Because, despite the triumph of her performance in *A Star Is Born*, it was not a big box-office hit; Judy would not make another film for seven years, and Sid would never produce another film. Judy's life would become a series of concert tours, wonderful highs and dreadful lows, weight gains and losses, riches and poverty, happy moments and brutal fights with Sid. All the horrors of Judy Garland's life to this point would seem rehearsals for what was to come.

And nine-year-old Liza's life, fairly stable for nearly three years, would become a harrowing series of crises to test the mettle of the strongest adult.

9

Over the next five years, Liza would attend fourteen different schools, bear responsibilities far beyond those a girl of her age should have had to face; suffer feelings of loneliness and alienation; make attempts to save Judy from suicide; have fights with schoolmates who ridiculed her mother; and develop an emotionally protective device, "wafting." As she would later explain it, wafting "is when you pretend that you're not really you. You're like a cork bobbing on the ocean. No matter how rough the water is, the cork stays afloat. Nothing can stop it." At times, "wafting" was the only way the young Liza Minnelli would be able to deal with the terrible absurdities of her life.

The arrival of Joey Luft was followed just a few weeks later by the birth of Vincente Minnelli's second daughter, Tina Nina. Minnelli had wed his second wife, Georgette Magnani, in February 1954.

Now, Liza felt like an outsider in her father's home as well as her mother's. Although Vincente continued to treat her like a princess, she was no longer the object of his undivided attention.

She began to withdraw more and more into herself; she became moody and aloof. She continued to build up defenses. As she recalled it, "I didn't belong totally to anybody."

Liza was forced to carve out an independent stance; dependence on Judy would have left her sorely in need, and, far more often than not, Judy's dependence on Liza was almost suffocating for the child. As Judy's oldest, Liza received the brunt of the Garland storms, while Lorna and Joey, as toddlers, were there for Judy to dote over—when she did any doting at all.

Joey particularly was the apple of Judy's eye. He was a beautiful baby, and became an unusually handsome boy. His being Judy's only boy gave him a special place in her heart. As for Lorna, Judy would frequently tell anyone who would listen that although Liza seemed at the time to be the one headed for a show business career, Lorna was the more likely to become an enduring star. Later, Judy would in various ways indicate jealousy on her part toward Liza, and perhaps the seeds were being sowed even as Liza grew up. But her mother's lack of confidence in Liza's potential couldn't have helped her daughter's self-esteem; although it may have made her even more determined to succeed.

Judy's own self-esteem was being battered, too, this early summer of 1955. *A Star Is Born* was not enough of a box-office hit to justify its cost; its rave reviews were based on a 182-minute version, but Harry Warner decided to shorten it to 153 minutes so that it could play the maximum number of times per days at theaters. Director George Cukor was appalled: "It was edited brutally, stupidly, and arbitrarily, and many of Garland's finest moments were taken out."

Audiences, disappointed that this much-praised film wasn't all it was cracked up to be, generated poor word-of-mouth, and the box office flagged. There were recriminations between Judy and Warner Brothers, and their multipicture deal was off. Hollywood, in its inimitable way, blamed Judy, deciding that she was no longer a box-office draw; Sid could not put together another picture deal for her. Instead, he worked up a twenty-city tour which replicated her Palace show, and negotiated for her to make her television debut on a "Ford Star Jubilee" special to be broadcast live September 24.

Two days before, things seemed fine, and Liza and Lorna visited the CBS studios, which resulted in a *Life* magazine photo layout. But the morning of the special, despite the fact that Sid had hired a nurse to watch her, Judy took an overdose of sleeping pills and was nearly unconscious. Sid spent the entire day giving her coffee, walking her, talking to her, trying to rouse her. The dress rehearsal was nothing more than a walk-through, and once the show began, broadcast live, Judy's words were slurred, her movements practically in slow motion. But Judy slowly began to come around. As the show progressed, her adrenalin flowed, and by the fifth or sixth number, she was performing at her best.

It was a pattern which had been with Judy for some time and would stay with her: an incredible fear of performing would lead her to take sleeping pills or amphetamines, or both; and her physical dependence on the drugs created a need for them at all times, in varying degrees. Every so often, Sid would go through her bedroom quarters and search for pills; he'd find them sewn into the lining of drapes, hidden in bottles of talcum powder, in the bedsprings, under the carpets. Each time he found them, he'd clean her out; but always she would replenish her supply.

And she had begun to drink heavily. A maid, at a later custody hearing, would testify that Judy was often drunk and "spoke in a loud and intoxicated voice to the children." Judy and Sid fought, often so loudly and violently that neighbors complained. They fought about Judy's pill and liquor use, about Luft's gambling, about money, of which there was always a shortage; about how each treated the children; about the myriad details of Judy's career.

Liza's life during this period is a mosaic of impressionistic memories for her, some of them ugly, some funny, some tender, some bordering on the surreal.

One day, Liza and a schoolmate were watching television in the Mapleton Drive house; Sid had been away for a while, and Judy was holed up in her bedroom suite, where she would often stay for days, having her meals brought to her. Suddenly, Judy stormed out of the bedroom, announced that she was going to kill herself, ran into the bathroom—and locked the door.

Beside themselves with fear, the two children pounded on the door, pleading with Judy to let them in. "Mama, don't kill yourself," Liza begged hysterically. She ran for the butler, who managed to open the door. The three of them came upon Judy standing in front of the toilet bowl. She had emptied a bottle of aspirin into it. "All she wanted was attention," Liza later said.

Periodically, Judy would pull the same stunt, but never did Liza assume it was a hoax: this time, her mother might mean it. She took to using garden shears to cut through window screens to get to Judy when there was no other way in. Sometime later, Liza took the added precaution of getting a stomach pump in case it should ever be needed. As Liza wryly commented later, "That life with her was theater of the absurd."

It was also terribly frightening for a young girl barely into adolescence. It was about this time, as she was entering her teens, that Liza began to develop her now familiar nervousness, that taut psychic energy that can often make those around her extremely uncomfortable. Liza never knew what to expect next: a fight between her mother and Papa Sid; Judy flying into an irrational rage against one of the servants or, sometimes, her children; and, of course, there was always the possibility that Judy might not be bluffing this time about committing suicide.

One morning, a drugged Judy let a cigarette fall under the cushion of a chair in her bedroom. Sid smelled smoke, and was able to get her out of her burning bedroom in time. The children were not endangered, because their bedrooms were on the other side of the enormous house, but it was a frightening episode for them, and left Liza with something more to worry about: might Judy do the same thing again, sometime when Papa Sid wasn't around to save her and roust everyone else?

With the awful tension of her home life, Liza's personality became skittish and jumpy, particularly around Judy. Observers noticed a reservation on Liza's part during happy times, an uncertainty about whether she could let herself go, be entirely happy around her mother. She had learned at an early age that her own happiness was quite tentative, and now, a little older, she realized that her mother's was, too. "I remember those moments," Liza said in an interview. "I think what I was doing was trying to find out from my mother whether that was the sort of time

A publicity shot for Judy's first TV special, Fall 1955.

when it was all right to laugh all you wanted to. You see, I was remembering the times my mother laughed and was happy and then later, I'd see her crying. And that was something I did not want to do—cry. So I was always in the middle, torn between the laugh and the invisible caution that if I dared to be happy about some things, I would pay for it in tears, later, a hundred times over.

"I remember once I asked my mother if maybe sometimes a person couldn't cry first—I meant pay for one's happiness before it came. Mother looked at me for a moment and her face was full of sadness. 'Why should we have to cry at all?' she asked me."

The unhappiness of Liza's life gave her a philosophical resignation rare in a girl so young: "I knew when I was thirteen that life was not going to be easy. I realized that I had to be ready for those times when I wanted sympathy and there would be none, when I would want love and there would be none for me, when I would want to be happy and have nothing to be happy about."

Rather than getting love, reassurance, and a feeling of safety from her mother, it was Liza's lot in life to provide it *for* her mother.

Her role in Judy's life had by now been transformed in many ways from that of child to that of a parent. Judy often leaned on Liza for emotional strength; Vincente Minnelli has said that "Liza was actually a very calming influence on her mother. Their roles were reversed; Judy had some very childlike traits, while Liza was grown-up."

Often, Judy would come into Liza's room in the middle of the night, wake her up, and want to talk. She couldn't sleep, she'd explain to her groggy daughter, and was upset that Sid was away for so long, or that someone had done her some injustice, real or imagined. "Mama and I talked a lot," Liza says. "She'd put too much trust in somebody, then they'd do something slight, and she'd take it as a slap in the face. The thing I tried to get through to her was that none of it really mattered. Of course people were going to let her down. They couldn't help it."

The next day, after having been kept up until dawn before her mother could get to sleep, Liza would find it very difficult to function in school. As bright a young girl as she was, she hated school.

It was made particularly difficult for her not only because she often got no sleep, but because, by the time she was sixteen, she had attended at least a dozen schools in various cities, both in the United States and abroad. Judy had a penchant for taking her children with her when she traveled; but even when she remained in one city, Liza—and later Lorna and Joey—would be moved from school to school for a variety of reasons. Often, it was because Judy was broke; when her career was on a downslide, she might not be able to afford the private school Liza was attending, so she'd be enrolled in a public school. Then, Judy might have to move because of a foreclosure on an unpaid mortgage; again Liza would have to change schools.

The loneliest times of her life, Liza has said, were the first few weeks she spent in a new school. She didn't have time to make too many friends. "I moved in and worked fast. I had to. I didn't have much time to warm up to people before we pulled out again."

There were other problems for Liza in school as well—mainly the cruelty of other children. Liza has called herself, at the time, "the queen of Ugly." Her unusual looks were sometimes ridiculed; she wore braces, and things weren't made any better by what Judy often insisted she wear: brown oxfords and the same dress she'd bought for little Lorna. Judy began to regularly dress Liza and Lorna alike—which Liza hated. "I was big then, nearly eleven. Lorna was only four. I felt ridiculous wearing the same things a little kid did."

The tauntings Liza endured were bad enough when directed at her—but then they turned against her mother. Many of Judy's travails made the newspapers, and there was a lot of Hollywood gossip about her. When Liza was twelve, Judy gained a great deal of weight, appearing in public grotesquely, almost unrecognizably, fat. Liza was in the Hawthorne School in

94

Beverly Hills when she first heard other children saying hurtful things about her mother. Once a movie star's child said to her, "Your mother's a big, fat pig." Liza cried all the way home from school. Judy told her how to respond to this child: "The next time that boy says your mother's fat, look him dead in the eye and say, 'My mother can get thin any time she wants to, but your father couldn't get talent if he took twenty years of private lessons from Sir Laurence Olivier.'"

There were happy times for Judy and Liza, too. When Judy was in a good mood, when things were going well, she was a funny, warm companion to her children and her friends. She would sing for her children's parties, and, as she had with Vincente, occasionally decide to "get domestic." Liza recalled for *Good Housekeeping* one instance when Judy decided to bake a cake. "I was enchanted with the sight of her in the kitchen, bustling about like any other mother." Their dog Sam and Liza sat on the floor while Judy sang and baked.

But Judy's culinary talents hadn't improved since her days as Mrs. Minnelli. When the cake was done, she took it out of the oven and immediately dropped it on the floor. "Mama and the dog and I all burst out crying," Liza reports. "But then Mama pasted the cake back together again with frosting and all three of us ate it there on the floor, laughing and kissing each other."

Such good times were short-lived, though, during the middle and late 1950s. Judy's inability to get another film deal off the ground left her with but one option: touring in concert. It was a grueling life; a series of week-long stands in a number of cities. Sometimes she would be brilliant, sometimes awful; always she would be taking various pills to get her through the ordeal.

At her return to the Palace in September 1956, Judy inaugurated a new element into her act, an element she would call upon again and again, especially when she felt she needed help with a show: her children. Their appearances on stage with her warmed audiences' hearts, and often gave Judy a respite from the demands of the show. Having them appear with her was a natural extension of her desire that they be with her: she was depressed by the fact that her two babies, Lorna and Joey, would have to be left behind so much of the time.

Liza was given the option of joining her mother, but there was school to consider: Liza was scheduled to begin fifth grade. But she took time off to fly to New York and appear with Judy. During a typical show—audiences always believed such things were totally spontaneous, but they rarely were—Judy brought eighteen-month-old Joey onstage and sang "Happiness Is Just a Thing Called Joe" to him. (On one occasion, something unplanned did happen—Joey began to bawl in his seat as his mother sang "Over the Rainbow." She stopped the song long enough to lean over toward him and say, "Don't cry, my love—this is a *happy* song.")

After singing to Joey, Judy brought him back to his seat and told the audience, "I have two other children and if I don't bring them up here they'll be terribly jealous." Lorna followed, and as Judy began singing "Rock-a-Bye Your Baby," Lorna motioned to Judy to pick her up and hold her in her arms as she had Joey. Judy did so, and when the song was finished, told Lorna to curtsy. The audience was charmed.

Liza was next, and though terribly nervous at first, she took to the stage like a pro; while Judy sang "Swanee," Liza danced. It was her first taste of mass audience approval. "I danced my heart out," she recalls. "We tore the house down. I remember hearing the waves and waves of applause washing over us and also I remember wondering whether my pants had shown while I was dancing."

Judy's fans were delighted by Liza's naturalness: she seemed completely free of stage fright—and pretension. On another occasion, after Judy had had some tea and eaten a piece of licorice onstage, she called Liza to join her from backstage. When Liza came out, Judy put her arm around her to give her a hug. Liza made a face and pulled away. "Mama, that stuff you have in your mouth smells awful!" Again, the audience loved it.

Liza's persona was being shaped more and more by the fact that she was "Judy Garland's

Judy, Liza, Joey, Lorna (partially hidden), and Johnny Luft frolic in the yard

of the Mapleton Drive house early in 1957.

Daughter." Later, she would attempt to ignore the fact, even conceal it, but now, at just ten, all the exciting things in her life were a result of that rarefied position. On November 3, 1956, while Judy was still appearing at the Palace, Liza made her second television appearance (her first had been on the "Art Linkletter Show" in 1955) during the first telecast of *The Wizard of Oz*.

At the CBS-TV studios with Lorna, and dressed identically with her little sister, Liza was brought before the TV cameras—and the nation—by host Bert Lahr. Their exchange had the cutesy, forced sweetness of bad television writing, and absolutely no spontaneity.

Liza, even more than most children of Hollywood, was learning that there is a distinct difference between fantasy and reality; first on the sets of her parents' pictures, then in her everyday life. In public, a sweet, happy, loving image must always be conveyed, no matter what was actually happening behind the scenes.

One of the things that was happening was that Liza had been forced, when Sid was away, to take on the responsibility of saving Judy's life. Getting into the bathroom to talk her out of a suicidal depression was only part of it. When Judy's doctor told Sid that she was taking far too much medication, Liza was given a specific job when Sid was away: find Judy's pills, empty half of their contents down the toilet, and fill them up again with sugar. Judy would think she was taking her usual doses, but the levels would not be dangerous. This became a normal household routine for Liza.

Still, Judy's pill use would far too often result in harrowing, irrational acts. Once, Sid returned home to find everyone gone. The servants had no idea where they were. Sid called everyone he knew, but no one had seen Judy or the children. He spent a sleepless, terrified night. The next day, Sid was notified that Judy had filed for divorce. The story made the papers, but just a few days later, Judy dropped the action and brought the brood home. Sid never found out where she had taken Liza and his children. Judy talked to Louella Parsons about the incident: "We didn't even have a fight," she said. "I was gone exactly eight hours. We had a silly misunderstanding. I thought something that wasn't true. I love Sid and he loves me and I don't think we were ever so glad to see each other in our lives."

Like Liza, Sid Luft never knew what to expect from Judy—but he was always prepared for the worst. After another fight between them, Judy called a mutual friend, told him she had taken "something" and was going to kill herself. The friend, although having been through this before, was concerned—but he became terrified when Judy, with slurred words, told him: "I've got Joey here with me and I may take him with me."

An emergency call was put in to Sid at a local racetrack, and he sped home. The police were called—one couldn't try to avoid scandal in a case like this—and Sid arrived at the house a few minutes before they did. He broke down Judy's bedroom door, and found Judy and Joey lying together on her bed. Judy was drugged and groggy, but Joey was unhurt. Again, Judy was calling out for attention, doing something dramatic to make whatever point she was trying to make to her husband. From this point on, Sid never trusted her fully with his children—and later, their custody battles would be furiously and bitterly fought.

Judy's life with Sid Luft had become an emotional roller coaster. At times, their love and their passion matched what they had felt at the very beginning of their relationship. At other times, they fought bitterly and vindictively, sometimes publicly. In the late 1950s, with Liza just entering her teens, Judy and Sid sometimes saw little of each other for extended periods of time. Sid was frequently away, making arrangements for a new tour; booking Judy was becoming more difficult because word was out that she couldn't always be relied upon to complete an engagement. Her no-shows usually created furious demands for refunds from audiences. And once Judy began a tour, Sid would frequently not accompany her.

Which was all the more reason for Judy to insist that her children accompany her.

Bringing them onstage in what seemed an impromptu manner was in the great tradition of vaudeville (and was, of course, how she had gotten her own start in show business). When things were going well during a concert, Judy would bring Joey, then Lorna, then Liza—if she were present—onstage to sing to, or with. At one point, when Judy wasn't in good voice, and her full concert was too much for her to handle alone, she had Liza take over a section of her show.

It was December 1957. Judy was set to open at the Flamingo Hotel in Las Vegas on the day after Christmas. She had been back in the United States just two weeks after a difficult four-week concert tour in England. Judy wasn't up to the rigors of performing, but finances forced her into it: the English tour had left them with fourteen hundred dollars to spare, and they were fifty thousand dollars in debt—not including unpaid taxes and old debts.

So Judy agreed to appear at the Flamingo. On the third night, her audience—eating, drinking, there more to gamble than to see a concert—was noisy and inattentive, even more so than most Vegas audiences. It didn't help, either, that Judy wasn't in particularly good voice.

Liza had come along—her school was in Christmas recess—and each night watched the show from the audience or backstage. This night, as Liza watched from the sidelines, Judy simply stopped singing, came over to her behind the curtain and pulled her onstage. This time, it *was* unrehearsed. And where before Judy had always introduced Liza as her daughter, this time she simply said, "Ladies and Gentlemen, Liza Minnelli" and walked offstage.

Three months short of her twelfth birthday, Liza stood before the crowd tentatively, told the conductor what she'd like to sing, and began. She sang five numbers that night—including "The Man That Got Away," which must have been incongruous coming from a child—and performed as if it were the most important thing she'd ever done.

The audience was less attentive to Liza than they'd been to Judy; some were angry—they had, after all, paid to see Judy Garland, not her daughter. When she was through, greeted by mild applause, she went offstage to see her mother standing off to the side: she had watched her the whole time. "You were terrific," Judy said, and hugged her. Liza recalls, "I couldn't sing worth a damn then, but it was nice of Mama to say that to me."

At this point, Judy encouraged Liza's ambitions, was grateful for the respite Liza's abilities sometimes afforded her. But later, she would attempt to tear down her daughter's self-confidence as often as she went out of her way to praise her and attempt to help her career. As with so many other aspects of Judy's life, she was capable of completely contradictory emotions and actions toward Liza, sometimes within hours of each other.

Despite the fact that Judy went through several grueling tours in the late fifties, and appeared in Las Vegas, at Los Angeles' Cocoanut Grove, and at the Metropolitan Opera House in New York, she was often completely broke. She owed tens of thousands of dollars in back income taxes, and her salary was sometimes attached by the IRS. And her lifestyle was very expensive: the house in Los Angeles cost one hundred thousand dollars a year just to maintain; travel expenses could be enormous; and, since Judy and Sid were producing her concerts, all the expenses had to be paid by them. Often, a tour would end with almost no profit.

Judy had some imaginative ways of getting around paying bills when she was broke. Liza recalls having had to sneak out of hotels with her mother more than once, because there was no money to pay the bill. Pretending to be going out for the evening, Judy and the kids would put on all the clothes they could possibly wear, sometimes five layers, so they would not be carrying luggage as they left. Whatever they couldn't take with them, they'd leave behind. "I didn't mind," says Liza, "because Mama always made it fun. You know? She was truly one of the funniest people I've ever known! Mama'd say, 'Oh, hell, I needed a new wardrobe anyway.' Descending in the elevator, she would assume her very imperious air; she'd whisper, 'No problem, always keep in mind, *I am Judy Garland . . .* '"

Needless to say, her ruse worked only as long as it took the hotel to bill her. And then there would be thousands more dollars in debts which ate up her earnings far faster than she could make them.

Although Liza most often recounts tales of her life with Judy with humor, the stress she was under was considerable. She constantly felt herself on thin ice, unable to completely enjoy the happy times for fear they would turn ugly. Her comments about her youth, made from the perspective of adulthood, indicate a desire to summon up the least unhappy memories and downplay the others. But her reaction to these events when they were happening may well be imagined. Liza alternates between downplaying the ugly times—calling her childhood "terrific"—and admitting, if only between the lines, the strain she was under. "Nobody had a happy childhood," she has said. "I was really reassured when I found that out. Everything became exaggerated because it was Judy doing it. I was not the only child who was yelled at. I was not an experiment, not a freak. Mama was always there. I got a tremendous amount of love from my parents . . . and a tremendous amount of garbage. It was—how can I say?—crazy. But basically sane. Before Mama did something she knew would drive me nuts, she'd warn me. 'Watch this,' she'd say. 'I'm going to have to do something crazy.' "

But at other times, Liza is less flip in her recollections. "I worried about Mama," she says, "but not in certain ways. I never saw her in a situation she couldn't handle, even if she was having a tantrum or hysterical crying. But when she'd get in a temper, it was frightening, because she'd yell a lot and I'd freeze. Lots of yelling. Now I avoid people who are screaming at all costs."

10

In the spring of 1958, Judy was booked into the Town and Country Club, a night spot in Brooklyn. Her appearance was a disaster. She had not wanted to appear, she was not feeling well, but she was committed. Her first few performances were fine, but her condition worsened, and finally, she was fired. She went before the audience, apologized, and explained that she had laryngitis. In the middle of her talk, her mike was shut off.

It was an awful period for Judy: she had gained a great deal of weight and was bloated almost beyond recognition; her voice, sometimes fine, at other times could not be summoned; the state of New York was attaching her Town and Country salary for unpaid taxes. When the Town and Country Club refused to pay her, the state put her under technical arrest: she could not leave New York until her debt was paid.

To make matters worse, Judy and Sid were once again badly estranged. He had moved out of the Los Angeles house, and she had forbidden him to be around her while she stayed on Long Island, hiring guards to keep him away from her and the children. Sid flew to New York, but Judy refused to allow him near her. Sid telephoned the owner of the club and told him, "I don't want to harass Judy. But she's not too well. I'm at the Warwick, in case you need me."

Judy had brought Joey, Lorna and Liza with her on the trip, and she relied heavily on Liza for myriad assistances. Liza functioned as a companion, nurse, seamstress, masseuse, cleaning person, psychiatrist, errand girl. People around Judy remember Liza as a shy, quiet twelve-year-old, with a pony tail and braces, tentatively off to the side, not speaking unless spoken to, extremely polite when introduced to anyone, and always on call to do her mother's bidding.

Liza knew that Judy was ill during her Town and Country engagement, but Judy was always quite vague about what was troubling her. Many of the people around her—Liza sometimes included—assumed that much of it was psychosomatic, or associated with her "medication."

One day, about a week into the Town and Country engagement, Liza heard her mother crying in the bathroom. She entered, against Judy's wishes, and offered to help. It was then that Judy told her of the terrible intestinal pain she had been suffering for weeks: she had colitis, and was too embarrassed by it to tell anyone. Liza then functioned primarily as a nurse, getting the medicine her mother needed from the drugstore.

Judy's illness, and her troubles with the State of New York, hastened a reconciliation with Sid. He borrowed various amounts of money from several friends, paid the taxes, and brought Judy and the children back to Los Angeles. Before she left for New York, Judy had filed a divorce action against Sid, charging that he had tried to strangle her; once the family returned to Los Angeles, she dropped the suit.

Judy spent several months at home while her colitis improved. Her spirits were low, she was short-tempered. She grew fatter and fatter, despite the fact that she wasn't eating very much at all, she was getting bored. She had recorded a good album, *Judy in Love,* in the spring, but Sid knew that she had to do something on a stage, and in July he booked her into Los Angeles' famed Cocoanut Grove. Her opening night was a smash—all her Hollywood friends were there, she was in great voice, the children came on stage, Liza sang and danced to "Swanee."

But Judy's stamina had left her. Within a few nights, she was losing her voice. The opening had been such a success that a contract was signed to record the show. On the album, recorded toward the end of the engagement, Judy does not sound good—causing listeners who had not been there the first few nights to wonder what all the shouting was about.

The Luft family, minus one, arrives at Grand Central station for Judy's first nightclub engagement in New York, March 14, 1958.

And those who attended her performances after the first few nights were sorely disappointed—as well as shocked by her appearance. "My ankles were so swollen," Judy remembered, "and my face, as if I'd been pumped up with a bicycle pump."

After the Cocoanut Grove, Judy made appearances in various cities across the country, sometimes with Sid along, most of the time without; Liza and Lorna would come along when school was in recess, and sometimes when it wasn't. (Liza missed so much school traveling with Judy that when the family lived in England two years later, she had to take tutorial classes to be admitted to the correct grade for her age group.) Joey, just over three, almost always went along with his mother.

Her 1958 tour, although there were some highlights and resulting rave reviews, impressed only her most ardent fans. There was talk that Judy Garland was a has-been, was unreliable, couldn't sing well any longer. Back in Los Angeles in late 1958 and early 1959, Judy sat around the house, waiting for the phone to ring with job offers. It rarely did.

When Judy was at home for extended periods of time, the best and worst of her personality was revealed to her children. At the beginning of such a layoff, Judy enjoyed the rest, enjoyed living like "a normal person." It was at times like this that her mothering could become exemplary.

She took great interest in her children, when she was not preoccupied with herself. She helped Liza and Lorna with their homework, gave Liza advice on problems at school, tended to all three of her children—sometimes sitting up with them all night—when they were ill. But best of all, both Lorna and Liza have recalled, Judy was their best friend. Not like a parent at all, but a buddy—someone to confide in, giggle with, talk about even forbidden things with.

Even the birds and the bees—a subject most parents either avoid or mishandle badly—was treated with openness, beauty, and delicacy by Judy when the time came to let Liza in on the secret. She explained to her daughter that she would "become a woman" when her menstruation started. Liza was fearful, but Judy told her it would be "a wonderful day" and that, when it came, they should toast the event with sherry.

Very typically for Judy, though, when the day came she discovered that Sid had locked the liquor cabinet to keep her from drinking too much and she could not get to the sherry. Undeterred, she and Liza drank to Liza's emerging womanhood with cooking wine.

But, too, the dark side of Judy would reveal itself with more and more frequency the longer she remained inactive. Just as she had as a child, Liza could never know how long a happy period was going to last, or when her mother might fly into an irrational rage. The entire household—Sid, the children, the servants—often had to walk on eggshells around Judy, fearful of setting her off. Liza and Lorna would return from school, and the first question they would ask the butler or the cook was, "What kind of mood is Mama in?" If the answer was negative, they would avoid her. But often, that was impossible.

Judy was never off pills during this period; she simply took more at certain times than at others. Her mood in late 1958 was dark from inactivity and her chagrin over her bloated condition. She was emotionally frail, her marriage a weak vestige of what it had been, her career in the doldrums when compared to her former triumphs. She became increasingly difficult to live with. Her demands on Liza were often overwhelming; demands on her time, her emotions. And Liza was now leaving childhood, becoming a young woman; before long, she would be entering high school.

Liza's responsibilities around the house, usually considerable, increased while Judy was recuperating. She would help Lorna get ready for school; she would later report that she often drove both Lorna and Joey to school, despite the fact that she didn't have a driver's license, because, although the chauffeur was always drunk, Judy was too fond of him to fire him.

She would make out shopping lists, answer Judy's fan mail, act as her mother's personal secretary; and whenever her mother needed her, for some assistance perhaps too personal to ask of a servant, Liza was there to help. The relationship became highly symbiotic: Judy needing Liza as a companion, helper and friend; Liza idolizing her famous mother, happy to help in whatever way possible, but always afraid that whatever happiness or stability they were sharing would evaporate before long.

At school, Liza was becoming more and more involved in the performing arts. She still studied dancing, and was working on her singing, although she felt she didn't have much of a voice. Before long, though, she would have an opportunity to sing on national television.

Gene Kelly, who had remained friends with both Judy and Vincente Minnelli, was at a party at Lee and Ira Gershwin's when Vincente arrived with Liza in tow. She was not yet thirteen.

As usual, a crowd gathered around the Gershwin piano, and as someone plunked out the tune, Kelly began to sing "For Me and My Gal." Liza sang along, but toward the end of the song Kelly stopped and let her finish it alone. He was impressed by her youthful enthusiasm and the strong urgency of her singing. He thought it would be fun to have her on a television special he was planning, "singing the song her mother sang in my first movie."

Kelly asked Liza and Vincente if she could be a part of the show. Liza was thrilled, and Vincente thought it was a wonderful idea. Judy, too, gave her approval.

The preparations for Liza's appearance resulted in newspaper reports headlined, typically, "Judy Garland's daughter gets chance on TV show." One article, after reporting that Liza "has a strong resemblance to her singing mama," quoted Liza on her career ambitions. "I'd like to sing and dance. I guess I'd like to do that the rest of my life."

Kelly gave his opinions on Liza: "Her voice makes you think of Judy when you hear it," he said. "She's got that same kind of pathos. She is sweet and charming, with a lot of her mother's qualities. This is a great lark to her. She's a bright girl and a quick student, and she could certainly go professional if she wants to. I think she has inherited both her parents' aptitude."

As exciting as it must have been for Liza to be the object of a news story, the article's author did something which would vex Liza throughout her early career: she referred to her as "Lisa," even going so far as to quote Kelly calling her "Lisa." Later, Liza would do a TV special called "Liza with a Z" and sing a song in which she lamented the mispronunciation of her name.

The special, aired on April 24, 1959, featured a self-possessed Liza wearing a well-tailored suit and a bow in her hair. Kelly gave her an affectionate introduction, telling the story of hearing her sing at the Gershwins'. With Kelly, she sang and danced to "For Me and My Gal," in a little-girl voice highly reminiscent of Judy's.

Variety reviewed the show, describing Liza's appearance but not characterizing it beyond saying, "Liza, incidentally, is a vocal and physical ringer for her mother."

While Liza's first major television appearance was being aired, Judy was preparing to make her debut at the Metropolitan Opera House. It had been a brainstorm of Sid's—he thought of Judy as a prima donna, anyway—and it was arranged as a charity affair. Her opening on May 11, 1959, was a fabulous success; but as with the Cocoanut Grove, she was not able to maintain the magic of opening night. She began a tour which took her to opera houses and other large auditoriums in cities like San Francisco, Chicago, and finally Los Angeles.

It was a wonder she was able to do it. Sid never ceased marveling at her recuperative powers. No matter how sick she was, how tired, usually she was able to get her adrenalin flowing and give a great performance on the first few nights, even if she had to be pushed out onto the stage. Once she heard those waves of applause, that thundering love from the audience, she shone. But when she had proven yet again that she could wow a city, give a black-tie audience the best show it had ever seen, she weakened, her illness and fatigue getting the better of her. When she was strong, all her shows were good; when she was weak and sick and exhausted, she could bring herself only so far up, keep her magic up only so long.

The maturing Liza, age twelve, 1958.

Liza on stage with Judy at the Cocoanut Grove in Los Angeles, July 1958.

The dashing Tony Curtis dances with an awestruck Liza after Mama's Cocoanut Grove performance.

Vincente and Liza dance at a Hollywood party, early 1959.

John Bubbles backstage with Judy after appearing with her at New York's Metropolitan Opera House, May 11, 1959.

Liza, finishing the seventh grade at an exclusive private school and, unable to take any more time off from her education, stayed behind until summer recess, when she joined Judy for a couple of performances. By the time Liza was in the eighth grade, in the fall of 1959, Judy was again in a career slump, waddling around the house more bloated than ever. Sid realized that there was something wrong other than a tendency toward overweight, when he took the entire family to a ranch specializing in weight loss.

Sid dropped ten pounds, Liza fifteen; but Judy, on the same diet, shed not a pound. Very worried, Sid knew Judy would never admit she was ill, would never let herself be hospitalized. He had two friends, both doctors, come to the house incognito to play the piano and sing.

Judy joined them, and they were shocked. It was not fat under her skin but water. Something was seriously wrong, and they both told Sid Judy should be in a hospital.

Sid, fearful now, tricked Judy into going to New York, closer to Doctors Hospital, the one medical facility he knew she trusted. Finally, she admitted that she was very ill, and allowed Sid to take her to the hospital. There, the doctors discovered that she had a liver disease, which Judy always referred to as hepatitis but which is now believed to have been cirrhosis. Her liver was swollen to four times its normal size; there were twenty quarts of excess, poisonous fluid in her body. She was on the verge of a coma, and the doctors told Sid she might not pull through.

Luft called Liza in Los Angeles, to give her the news. He broke it to her as gently as possible, but she knew instinctively that if Mama was in the hospital, something was awfully wrong. She thought of Mr. Mayer and her grandfather, and wondered if Mama was going to die, too.

Sid assured her that Judy would pull through—he had convinced himself she would, with her indomitable spirit—but Liza was a deeply troubled girl when her stepfather rang off.

Judy remained in the hospital for seven weeks, and was discharged on January 5, 1960. Almost as a present to her Mama, Liza appeared on the "Hedda Hopper's Hollywood" TV show on January 10 to sing "Over the Rainbow." Seeing her daughter perform that particular song gave Judy mixed emotions. She was proud of Liza, but her daughter's energy and verve made her own condition seem even worse. The doctors had told her she would be a semi-invalid for the rest of her life, that she must not drink any liquor or take excessive pills. Worst of all, she was told that she would never work again.

In some respects, Judy was relieved. It might be wonderful to be finished for good. The past two years had been a nightmare. She talked about it two years later: "I had so many fears, so many anxieties. I'd had them as a child and I guess they just grow worse as you grow older and more self-centered. The fear of failure. The fear of ridicule. I hated the way I looked.

"I cried for no reason, laughed hysterically, made stupid decisions, couldn't tell a kind word from an insult. All the brain boilers gave me up. I staggered along in a nightmare, knowing something was vitally wrong, but what? It got to the point where I was a virtual automaton—with no memory! I played some very big dates in 1958 and 1959. I don't remember any of it. I didn't know what I was doing."

Judy recovered from her illness and her nightmare, and she did work again—making the greatest comeback of her career and returning to films. But the nightmare eventually returned, and there was no illness to blame it on—just "medication." Judy was never able to escape the clutches of drugs. Whether it was because of her psychic demons, or because of the enormous pressures on her to raise her children, pay her bills and keep herself functioning, she continually returned to pill and alcohol use in spite of the most determined efforts on her part—and on the part of those around her—to get her off them for good.

For the next few years, as so often before, there were terrific highs and abysmal lows. And Liza Minnelli, entering adolescence mature beyond her years, began to carve out a life—and a career—of her own. But it would take great strength for her to cut herself off from Judy, and independence bordering on rebellion.

THREE

"You're an admirable young woman, but you exasperate me."

—*Judy to Liza, 1964*

Judy rehearses a "Born in a Trunk" segment for "The Judy Garland Show," 1963.

11

For more than five months, Judy recuperated at home. She was confined to bed for weeks, and thereafter was indeed a semi-invalid. She had been weaned from all medication while in the hospital, except for a mild energizer, Ritalin; and, of course, there was no liquor.

Thus, Judy was herself—not the product of her medication—for the longest sustained period since she was a girl. She did a few benefits at the end of her recuperation, and recorded an album. Although she was subject to depressions—she wondered whether she would ever get well, felt lonely for her gay social whirl, and missed working—she was most often warm and chatty with Sid and the children, talking to them about school and what was happening in the outside world. It was one of the longest periods of stability in Liza's life.

In the spring of 1960, Liza was completing eighth grade; she had turned fourteen in March. If her precociousness had evolved into remarkable maturity for a girl so young, her physical bearing more than matched her intellectual savvy. She was lanky and tall—already half a foot taller than Judy—and her training as a dancer gave her a command of her body, a grace, which most women do not attain until their early twenties.

And she was beginning to be striking. Gone were the braces, the schoolgirl bows. Although many would consider her homely—herself included—others thought that Liza Minnelli was becoming an attractive—if somewhat unorthodox-looking—young woman.

Judy felt, just months before her daughter would enter high school, that Liza needed experiences outside the realm of show business, away from Hollywood and New York. Judy also thought it would be nice for Liza to learn French, so it was decided that Liza would spend the summer of 1960 in a town called Annecy, in southeastern France, with six other girls and one of their mothers as a chaperone.

Liza left Hollywood in June, and by the end of July, Judy was in London. She had wanted a change, a chance "to get off by myself and think about the future," so she had gone alone. London was Judy's favorite city in the world, the place she considered her last refuge. Sid knew it would be therapeutic for her to leave Hollywood, where she was constantly reminded of her lack of professional activity; and although they had been getting along relatively well, he agreed with Judy's assessment that "we've been joined at the hip so long—I just have to get away."

With Judy in London, accompanied by friends Kay Thompson and Ethel Merman; Liza in France; and Sid, Lorna, and Joey in Los Angeles, the Luft family was spread as thin as it would ever be. Lorna and Joey were cared for primarily by their governess; Joey had yet to begin school, Lorna was completing second grade.

Liza was the loneliest of the group, living in a strange country, knowing only the girls she had traveled with (and not friendly with all of them), and studying a foreign language. She learned to speak French fluently ("if grammatically imperfectly," she admits) and developed her first "big crush on an older man": singer Bobby Darin, whom she had seen at a local concert.

She wrote letters to Judy and Sid, telling of her activities and her loneliness. Far too often, Judy would not reply. On August 4, Liza sent off a letter to London: "I wrote almost three weeks ago and still haven't gotten any answer . . . am dying for some response." Later in the letter, she tells her mother, "I am still madly in love with Bobby Darin."

Late in the summer, while Liza was in the French Alps with her companions, Judy and Sid came to visit her. Sid had been in London several weeks, and Judy wanted them both to talk to Liza about something very important: coming to London to live with her, Sid, Joey, and

Lorna. "She wanted to leave all the unhappiness behind in America and live in the city she dearly loved," Liza recalled in the *Good Housekeeping* interview. "She was wonderfully funny and whimsical about it and she made me roar with laughter. I told her that I would love to live in London."

The Lufts rented a "lovely old house" which had belonged, at different times, to Somerset Maugham and Sir Carol Reed. At first, it was just Judy, Liza and Sid; Lorna and Joey joined them later. Liza had a wonderful time in London. She loved the city as much as her mother, absorbing its culture, and its accent, as only a budding actress could. (When she returned to the States, she would respond to comments about her accent by throwing her head back and exclaiming "Blimey!" in her best cockney.)

In London, life with Judy continued to be as good as it had been during her recuperation earlier in the year. She was almost completely well again, off medication and liquor, and she and Liza had great fun shopping, seeing the sights, haunting Piccadilly Circus, talking to the streetwalkers who worked there—they fascinated Judy—and simply being each other's friend.

If Liza had been like a parent to Judy before, now she was an equal. They were so much alike; their intuition, taste, sense of humor jelled in a way only best friends usually experience— rarely are they shared to this extent by a parent and an adolescent child.

That fall in London with Judy was the happiest time of Liza's life. For all the problems being Judy Garland's daughter had created, for all the ugliness and unhappiness Judy was capable of creating for her daughter, Liza idolized her. She saw the effect her mother had on people: the adulation, the love she generated among millions. One of Liza's duties back home had been to answer Judy's fan mail, and so many of the writers spoke of how much Judy meant to them, how she had made their lives better, what a wonderful woman she was. One is reminded of Liza's quote, "Millions of people adored my mother, and they never even met her. Can you imagine how *I* felt?"

In her own way, Liza was a Judy Garland fan, too. She was fascinated by her mother's celebrity, and saved mounds of press clippings about her theatrical triumphs in Hollywood and New York. When she attended a Garland concert, she was awe-inspired by what her mother could do with a song, with her own and the audience's emotions. More so than others, perhaps, because she had usually seen her mother, moments before, trembling, overcome with fear, unsure whether she could even face the audience, much less entertain them.

And she would get caught up in the adoring hysteria rampant in most Garland audiences. Later in the fall, Judy felt physically able to resume her career. Sid was worried, but it was something Judy at least had to try. She returned to the London Palladium for two concerts a week apart. At the first, Liza sat next to the Duke of Windsor, a friend of her mother's. She was amazed to hear the Duke humming along with the overture, and singing along with Judy— with every lyric correct. Princes adored her mother; surely she was truly someone special. Judy's shows were triumphs; she *would* be able to work again.

For Liza to have this woman as her best friend, even for short, tentative periods of time, was tremendously important during this, her most formative time. Judy's wit, her joy in making puns, sharpened Liza's intellect. They were forever amazed at how each would think the same thought at the same time; once, dining in Judy's suite during one of Liza's earlier visits to London, they watched a turgidly acted scene on television. Neither Judy nor Liza said anything as the scene progressed, but all at once, at exactly the same time, they each reached for the breadbasket, picked up a roll, and hurled it at the TV screen. Then they threw the remainder of their meal at the set.

Other times, both Judy and Liza would begin to giggle at the absurdity of something or someone; in the middle of what might be a very serious conversation, they would titter for reasons known only to them; "a private joke," it would be explained—and later, when they were alone, they would laugh uproariously at how ridiculous it had all been.

Liza was set to enroll in an English school, but because of her many absences from classes in the United States, and because the American educational system is behind the English, she had to go to a tutorial school ("Miss Dickson's and Miss Wolf's School for Young Ladies") before an institution in London would accept her. Lorna and Joey enrolled in the Eden School, and Judy would walk them to classes almost every morning.

The first week of November, though, was a bad one: Lorna underwent an emergency appendectomy on a Friday, while Judy sobbed in the hospital corridor. When she and Sid were told that everything was going to be all right, they went out with friends for a late meal. Early Saturday morning, all four of them were wretchedly sick with food poisoning. By Monday, Sid was feeling better, and so were their friends, but Judy, as Sid put it, was "still feeling pretty rocky."

As happy as the Lufts were in London, it was a financial hardship to stay there. Sid had had to borrow twenty-five thousand dollars for the move to London, and their financial problems had never been resolved. Judy's success at the Palladium, and shortly thereafter with one-night stands in Paris, Great Britain, and Amsterdam, made her anxious to revive her full-time career. The doctors had underestimated Judy. Not only was she not an invalid, but her voice was better than ever; she felt more confident and "together" than she had in years.

She and Sid decided to return to the United States. Judy now had new management, Freddie Fields and David Begelman, and they wanted to re-establish Judy as a potent concert attraction and as a motion picture actress. Sid had become involved in several other potential ventures, trying to carve out a professional niche for himself as something other than Judy Garland's husband/manager; he thus welcomed the transfer of the burdens of managing Judy's career from himself to Fields and Begelman.

Three weeks before she left London, Judy appeared in concert at the Free Trade Hall in Manchester. Brian Sales of the London *Daily Express* described part of the evening: "Judy Garland brought the family into the limelight last night. And as she sang with her fourteen-year-old daughter Liza, it could almost have been the Garland sisters.

"Off stage, they look like mother and daughter. But on stage with the new slim Judy dancing around in drain pipe slacks, they look like sisters . . . Judy and Liza sang 'After You've Gone' . . . A start in show business for Liza, who looks so like her mother did twenty years ago? 'Perhaps,' said Liza afterward. 'I would like to go on the stage, but as a dancer. I've just tried and tried and tried to sing but I can't. But I'm taking dancing lessons. I'd love to dance in musicals.' "

On December 31, the Lufts returned to New York, staying at the Carlyle Hotel. The next night, Vincente Minnelli married for the third time, his marriage to Georgette having ended in divorce early in 1959. Liza phoned him to offer her best wishes to her father and his bride, Denise Giganti.

Now, as 1961 began, the family settled into a new city. Lorna and Joey were enrolled in Public School 6. Liza auditioned for admittance to the High School of Performing Arts, the school upon which the movie and TV series *Fame* are based.

Later, Liza would realize that many of her opportunities had come about because of her family ties, but at her audition—she danced and sang, did some improvisation—it is highly unlikely that her name was any factor at all in her being accepted to the school, something doubly difficult when you're asking to be admitted at midyear. The panel Liza performed before was impressed by her dance technique, her enthusiasm, her poise. Judy wasn't surprised that Liza's audition was successful; she told an interviewer a few months later, "Liza I'm not so worried about. She's practically a pro already. Very hip to show business. She's in the New York School for the Performing Arts, where she's majoring in the dance. She'll do well."

Liza worked hard at Performing Arts, and soaked in the New York theatrical world around her. She went to Broadway and off-Broadway shows almost every night, sometimes with Judy, sometimes alone or with friends. By February, Judy had embarked on a nationwide concert tour that would culminate in her greatest triumph, the Carnegie Hall concert in April. Once again, Liza was alone in a new city—Judy on the road, Sid working on his projects. The Broadway shows offered her a distraction, as well as inspiration.

It was one show in particular that Liza credits with convincing her that show business was indeed the life for her—*Bye Bye Birdie.* "It wasn't that tedious process I saw at Metro," she says. "I could see it happening before my eyes." And, more important, "The chorus of *Bye Bye Birdie* fascinated me. It had kids in it, and a camaraderie that I recognized. It seemed like an answer to the kind of loneliness I felt. Just friends kidding around, with lots of laughter."

While Liza studied show business, Judy was making history with it. Her concerts in the late winter and spring of 1961 were among the best of her career. She was in terrific voice, she was reasonably slim. She had worked out her show in a series of concerts throughout Europe and the southern United States, and when she sang at Carnegie Hall—for the first time—on April 23, it was the greatest night of her life.

And the ultimate comeback. Judy's friends and fans knew what she'd been through, knew how spotty her performances had been in the late 1950s, how fat she'd become. Now, they heard she was singing wonderfully again, was healthy, slimmer, and lovely. They came to cheer her, to see for themselves that she had once again risen from the depths.

And they were not disappointed. The concert was a wonder, probably the best of Judy's life (the album *Judy at Carnegie Hall* was her best-selling LP and won an unprecedented five Grammy Awards in 1962, including Album of the Year and Best Female Vocalist.) It ended in an orgy of adulation unparalleled in theatrical history: her friends in the audience hugged each other, tears streaming down their faces; Henry Fonda yelled "Bravo!"; the entire front portion of the audience moved up to the stage, reaching to touch Judy, give her flowers and shout "Bravo!" themselves.

Judy touched all the hands she could, kissed and hugged her children, brought them up on stage to meet the audience.

For Judy, this was life. She knew now she still had it—better than ever, in fact. She had vowed to set New York on its ear again. "A really good reception makes me feel like I have a great big warm heating pad all over me," she said. "I truly have a great love for an audience and I used to want to prove it to them by giving them blood. But I have a funny new thing now, a real determination to *make* people enjoy the show. I want to give them two hours of just POW!"

That she had done. She repeated her triumph a month later, to meet the demands of people who'd missed a performance that became instantly legendary. Shana Alexander wrote in *Life:* "Judy Garland is not only the most electrifying entertainer to watch on stage since Al Jolson, she has moved beyond talent and beyond fame to become the rarest phenomenon in all show business. Part bluebird, part Phoenix, she is a legend in her own time."

Judy was thrilled to be back in New York with her children. During her southern tour prior to Carnegie Hall, she had missed them dreadfully. A week before she opened in New York, staying in a hotel in Charlotte, back on "medication" to help her with the rigors of the tour, she fell into a deep depression, telling her traveling companion she wanted her children brought to her. He tried to explain that it was the last stop before New York, that it would disrupt their schooling, that if she could just wait a few days she'd see them.

She began to talk under her breath. "Can't even have my own children . . . Goddammit, I work my ass off, making money for everybody, can't even have my own children with me."

Now, they were back with her, and there were good times. In June, Judy, Liza, and Kay Thompson got together at the piano; Kay had brought over a new song for Judy to hear. She and Liza sang it, then Judy joined them for a special Thompson arrangement of "The Thrill Is Gone." They went on to "Great Day," Liza squealing with delight at "Lift up your head and shout" and "It's not far away . . ."

Kay's version of "On the Atchison, Topeka and the Santa Fe" led to a series of MGM

Judy leans over to kiss Liza after her historic Carnegie Hall return, May 21, 1961.

stories; Kay then asked Liza to sing "Jamboree Jones" and when that was over, all three joined in for "Bob White."

Liza was singing, and her voice was getting better, but her ambition still was to dance. She got a chance to do it professionally in July. Judy had brought the family up to stay in the Kennedy compound in Hyannis Port, Massachusetts; President Kennedy had been a fan and became a friend when Judy made several appearances on his behalf at American military bases in Germany during the 1960 campaign.

Liza had been apprenticing at the Cape Cod Melody Tent, doing the menial chores required of all such positions, and got a chance to dance in the chorus of "Wish You Were Here."

Judy and Kay Thompson attended Liza's first performance, and Judy cried. As she watched her daughter, moving self-assuredly on stage, she sniffled to Kay, "Remember how tiny she was when she was christened?"

Later, Judy told an interviewer, "The only reason I'm letting Liza do this now is because she has been longing to do summer stock. When summer's over, she'll go back to school. I think it robs a youngster of too many things. It's too competitive. I don't think children should be thrown into that at all. They should have proms and football games and all the fun of growing up . . . I missed a lot. It's a very lonesome life."

It was in part these feelings of Judy's which prompted her to uproot the family once again, moving them to the wealthy, conservative New York suburb of Scarsdale. At this point in her life, she wanted the children to have some traditional stability, good schooling; and she wanted Liza to at least experience the other side of life. She feared she was leaving her daughter no choice but to pursue "life upon the wicked stage"; living in Scarsdale might at least let her know that a choice was available.

Judy and Sid were again estranged. She had told him, coldly this time, with no emotion and an unmistakable finality, that she would divorce him. He had sold the Mapleton Drive house for $225,000; after all the mortgages and liens were paid, and several personal loans, Sid was left with $10,000. He was no longer acting as Judy's manager, his business ventures were failing to ignite, and he was in bad financial straits.

Back on pills, Judy was again prone to irrational fears and paranoia. She hired guards to protect her and the children from Sid; she was convinced he was going to kidnap them. On one occasion, she called the police to have him forcibly evicted from her apartment. That night, they went out to dinner. The relationship was more volatile than ever, but with far more downs than ups now; it was the beginning of the end.

Judy had worked hard during all of 1961. She filmed a brief but brilliant performance as a German hausfrau testifying at the Nuremberg trials for Stanley Kramer's film *Judgment at Nuremberg,* her first film in six years. Before and after Carnegie Hall, she sang in forty-two cities—a staggering burden, but one she bore with new strength. Except for episodes brought on by abuse of her medication, she was relatively happy and her career was as strong as it had ever been.

On Halloween 1961, Judy returned to Scarsdale and went trick-or-treating with her three children, dressed as a clown and spraying shaving cream on the windows of the stuffy citizens of Scarsdale.

This stuffiness, and the insular snobbishness of the town, made Liza's life at Scarsdale High School less than ideal. At this point in her life, Liza had adopted a bohemian New York theater look and attitude. When her classmates learned that Judy Garland's daughter was going to go to school with them, they visualized a glamorous young lady; what they got was a disheveled, gum-chewing, sweat-shirted "beatnik," someone they would never associate with under normal circumstances. Liza and her classmates were immediately wary of each other; Liza knew they looked down on her, and she attempted to compensate for that by impressing them with stories of her friendship with Marilyn Monroe and her "adult relationship" with George Hamilton.

Judy and the kids harmonize on the stairs of their London house, late 1960.

Her classmates looked at Liza and didn't believe a word of it. She became a loner, and adopted an I-don't-care attitude as a defense: "I couldn't find anyone who was as bright as I was. I guess it was because I grew up with adults . . . kids just weren't into adult conversation, like philosophy or literature or anything like that. I'd start a conversation, and nobody would join in."

If Judy had indeed hoped to tempt Liza away from show business, enrolling her in Scarsdale High had exactly the opposite effect. Liza took the only action possible if she was to function in that alien environment: she joined the Drama Club.

She was given the lead in that semester's production: *The Diary of Anne Frank.* Many of her classmates were resentful, sure she'd been given the plum role simply because of whose daughter she was, but Liza didn't care; she was going to make the best of her first real *dramatic* opportunity.

She gave a touching, realistic portrayal of the young girl fighting the horrors of Nazi terrorism, and Judy, there with Sid during a brief reconciliation, cried throughout the performance, weeping into her powder puff because she had no tissues. Surprised and delighted by her daughter's acting strength, she went backstage, hugged Liza and exclaimed, "My God, I've got an annuity!" Later, Judy added, "I've always known she was a marvelous dancer, but she dazzled Sid and me with her performance . . . She was very professional about rehearsals, took direction only from her director and wouldn't let Mama butt in with free advice."

So impressed was Judy that she offered to finance sending the entire production to Israel and Greece to perform the play there. The cast went the following summer.

The sojourn in Scarsdale, however, was short-lived. Judy's performance in *Judgment at Nuremberg* was the talk of Hollywood (she would go on to win an Oscar nomination as Best Supporting Actress) and director Stanley Kramer offered her another film, this time with a starring role opposite Burt Lancaster in *A Child Is Waiting,* a drama about a teacher in a school for mentally retarded youngsters.

It was a role she dearly wanted to play; not only would it re-establish her as a movie star, but she had cared about such impaired young people since her experience with the mute little girl at Peter Bent Brigham Hospital in Boston.

She would have to go back to California to make the film, and she decided once again to move the children with her. "My children are the most special thing in my life," she told an interviewer. "They are very portable. I've uprooted them, dragged them from one country to another, because I'll never leave them in the care of servants. They are happy only as long as their mother and daddy are with them. You try to keep them as long as you can and prepare for the day when they'll leave. You have to be ready not to be an idiot about it when they do leave, because they will. They must have a life of their own."

The day Liza would leave would come sooner than anyone thought—and it would be a direct result of her mother's irrational behavior.

12

The Lufts were back in California, Judy and Sid shakily reconciled, and they moved into a palatial rented home in Bel Air, the most expensive area of Beverly Hills.

Financial problems were, for now, a thing of the past: Judy had been making excellent money from her concert tour, the sales of her Carnegie Hall album, her work in *Judgment at Nuremberg*, on a TV special with Frank Sinatra and Dean Martin, as the voice of a cat in *Gay Purr-ee*, and in *A Child Is Waiting*. Her career was stronger than ever, and so were her finances.

Liza, back in a Beverly Hills private school, completing the tenth grade, was now totally enamored of the performing life. Her experiences at the Cape Cod Melody Tent, at the High School of the Performing Arts, and as Anne Frank, had solidified her interest until it started to become an obsession; clearly, show business was in her blood.

For as far back as she could remember, Liza's principal identity had been as Judy Garland's daughter. It was something she could accept less and less as she grew older and became more her own person. But now, planning to follow in her mother's footsteps, she realized that she would be more than ever compared to her mother, called Judy's little girl, thought a cute replica of young Judy or resented for being given opportunities other aspiring performers might not have.

And so Liza tried to put as much distance between Judy and herself as possible. By dancing, she felt she might be able to be different enough not to generate constant comparisons; but her performing opportunities so far, with few exceptions, had been as a singer, and almost purely because she was Judy's daughter.

It was impossible for Liza to avoid singing; her household was much too musical, and she discovered that although her voice might not be beautiful, it was big; she had good range; and singing a powerful number while dancing could be a dramatic entertainment. She realized she would *have* to sing, and she began working on it.

There was always singing in the Luft household: Judy would often sing to herself, and so would Liza and Lorna. Lorna recalls, "We always sang everything around the house and suddenly you'd hear Mama yelling 'Wrong lyrics!' from the bathroom, or 'Flat! You're singing flat!' from the kitchen. Liza and I grew up listening to that incredible, really fantastic voice every day and it just had to rub off somehow."

But Liza didn't want it to rub off too much. After she started being conscious of her voice, she realized she sounded a lot like her mother—too much so, for her taste. She began to work at changing her vocal sound and style by singing in the bathroom. "There's an echo in the bathroom that makes it possible to hear yourself wonderfully," she explained. "So I trained myself in there—I had to find out what was really me. It meant changing the breathing patterns I'd grown up with."

Liza was to find it very difficult to separate herself from her mother while still trying to gain experience as a performer. Almost all her show business opportunities so far had come to her only because of Judy. Her second television appearance had been as co-host of *The Wizard of Oz*; she had sung "Over the Rainbow" on the Hedda Hopper program, her appearance on the Kelly special had been to sing another song her mother made famous; her concert performances had all been with Mama; and now, she had an opportunity to work on a motion picture.

But again, there was no escaping it: she was wanted as the voice of Dorothy in an animated "sequel" to *The Wizard of Oz*, called *Return to the Land of Oz*. Liza wanted to do it; it was professional experience, she would be required to sing, and she would be paid. Judy was skeptical. "I thought they were just exploiting Liza to use my name," she said. "But when I finally read the contract, it stated that she was to be billed under her own name. They wanted Liza, not Garland. I was out—and I didn't mind!"

Judy also wanted to make sure Liza would be good, and she asked that a demo record of Liza singing her songs be sent to her first. When she heard that, Judy gave her final okay, as did Vincente.

The film, a two-hour, $2.2 million production, featured the voices of Ethel Merman as the Wicked Witch, Danny Thomas as the Tin Man, Peter Lawford as the Scarecrow, Milton Berle as the Cowardly Lion, Margaret Hamilton as Aunt Em and Herschel Bernardi as the wooden horse.

Despite this talent, the film remained unreleased until the early 1970s, when it played in Australia and England; it wasn't seen in America until 1974. The film never made money, and Liza has since expressed regret at ever having been involved in it. The songs were unmemorable and, as one British trade paper said in reviewing the film, "the action . . . is rather unimaginative and repetitive." Liza, though, received some positive critical notices: " . . . [Her] quiet, intelligent reading of Dorothy strikes just the right note."

Since, as a budding performer, Liza couldn't avoid having her identity so caught up in Judy's, she tried desperately to separate herself from her mother on a social level. She became so sensitive, in fact, about being known only as Judy Garland's daughter that she tried, whenever possible, to keep the fact from new acquaintances. One young friend was to find out who Liza's mother was in a rather singular way.

Judy and Sid allowed Liza to date, despite the fact that she was not yet sixteen, because of her maturity and sense of responsibility. A young man over eighteen began squiring her around town, occasionally taking her to a nightclub where she would play the sophisticate role with great glee.

The young man had known Liza for quite some time, and was completely unaware that Judy Garland was her mother. One night, he took Liza to the Pink Pussycat, the top burlesque nightclub in Hollywood. Sid Luft was there and saw them. He didn't say anything to them but told Judy, who did not like the idea.

The next day, the young man received a telephone call. "Judy Garland wants to see you. A car will be over." He was amazed and puzzled: why should Judy Garland want to see *him*? He walked through the huge front door of the house to see one of the most famous women in the world standing before him with her hands on her hips. "How dare you take my daughter to a place like that?" she asked him.

Nearly overwhelmed, the young man put things together, realized what Judy was talking about, and tried to come up with an apologetic explanation.

Those friends around Liza who knew who she was often had to stifle their natural curiosity about Judy; Liza did not like being asked about her mother. Tom Cooper was a twenty-one-year-old aspiring singer and Garland fan who had met Judy, Sid, and Liza in 1959 in Las Vegas, then ran into Sid again this January of 1962 at a press party announcing the Golden Globe nominations for 1961. (Judy was their Cecil B. DeMille Award for her "outstanding contributions to the field of entertainment throughout the world.")

Sid remembered Tom, and they talked. "Incidentally," Tom said during the conversation, "I can't believe how Liza's changed—I saw a photo of her in a fan magazine and she's really grown up since I last saw her. She's really a nice-looking young lady."

"Really?" Luft replied. "Why don't you take her out? You're a nice guy—I trust you. Liza is lonely, she doesn't have many friends here. Why don't you date her?"

Tom called her, told her the story, and she laughed. "He's always trying to fix me up with guys." Tom suggested they get together sometime for lunch.

"What are you doing tonight?" Liza asked. Tom went over, and Liza was fascinated by the fact that he was a singer, performing at the Statler Hilton Hotel in downtown Los Angeles. "I'd love to get your opinion," Liza told him. "I've cut a couple of demos with my vocal teacher and I'd like you to hear them."

Liza and Tom hit it off immediately—not romantically, but as friends. "For a fifteen-year-old girl she had such maturity. She wasn't a giggly young girl at all—but she still had a playfulness and was great fun," Tom says.

Liza sang "The Travelin' Life" for Tom—she would later record it on one of her first albums—and he was impressed. "She really belted it out. She said, 'Do you really like it? I'm trying to improve as a singer.' But she was mainly interested in dancing."

For a period of several months, the two were practically inseparable. But Tom knew there were certain things he needed to be careful about. "Liza was very sensitive about being known as Judy's daughter. She was very eager to make new friends and in many cases met my friends. Almost without exception, she wouldn't want them to know she was Judy's daughter. She was very touchy about that because she wanted to be accepted on her own. The more she got to know me, and when she found out how much I loved her mother, that sometimes caused a little bit of a problem with our relationship. Whenever I would ask questions about Judy, she would get very touchy. She was afraid that someone would want her as a friend just because she was Judy Garland's daughter."

Tom was an amateur film maker—he had made an 8 mm version of *A Star Is Born* as a teenager—and he asked Liza if she would like to appear in one of his films. She excitedly said yes, studied the script, rehearsed with Tom and two other cast members and shot the film in his apartment.

Called—pretentiously, Tom admits—*An Incidence of Seeking,* the eight-minute film features Liza as a young girl driven to insanity by her boyfriend and his new love. "The high point of the film," Tom relates, "is when she goes crazy and lets out a blood-curdling scream. It was eleven at night and I had these two old-fogy landlords and one was always trying to peer in. Liza lets out this incredible scream for the movie and the landlord was peering through the blinds and then started pounding on the door yelling, 'What's going on in there?' I told him we were just filming a movie but I don't think they ever trusted me after that."

After Tom had processed the film, he ran it for Liza. She was a little skeptical. "I don't understand this movie at all, Tom," she said. "And is that the way I look? I'm so ugly!"

"I think she felt she wasn't pretty," Tom understates. "But I think she looks good in the film."

Judy never did see the movie, but she saw some still photographs taken during the filming, at Liza's sixteenth-birthday party. Liza, Tom, and a few of Liza's other friends were around the piano, singing, when the photographer gave Liza the photos. Judy and Sid came into the den and Liza jumped up. "Look, Mama, these are from the movie we did."

Judy looked at the photos. "Gee, you look like a beatnik. Like Paul Newman in drag!"

Tom and Liza remained close until Liza joined her mother in New York on the first leg of a trip to London for the filming of *I Could Go On Singing.* Before Judy left—alone—for New York, she moved Lorna and Joey out of the rented house into the Beverly Hills Hotel with her and asked Sid for a legal separation. He refused to sign any papers, thinking that Judy's mood would change, as it had so often before.

When Judy went to New York, she left the children in the care of their governess. A few days later, she was admitted to the hospital with a throat infection and laryngitis. Luft flew to New York with all three children, checked into the Stanhope Hotel, and called Judy. She was bitter and told him he'd better get out of town because he had failed to file income tax returns for 1958, 1959 and 1960. She told him again she wanted a divorce.

Judy was discharged from the hospital on April 22. On April 27, she was getting ready to take the children with her to London. Luft told her he wouldn't allow it. What followed

Judy performs the climactic musical number in *I Could Go On Singing*, 1962.

during the next twenty-four hours might have been reminiscent of a Mack Sennett comedy if it hadn't been so sad.

Judy was staying on the eleventh floor of the Stanhope with the children; Sid was on the sixth. On Saturday, April 28, Lorna and Joey's nurse took them across the street from the hotel to play in Central Park. Liza was staying with friends a few blocks away.

Judy was afraid that Sid would take the children from her to prevent them from going to London. She had Stevie Dumler, assistant to her agent, Freddie Fields, accompany them and their nurse to the park. Stevie took the time to call Judy to tell her everything was okay, but by the time she returned to where they were playing, they were gone.

Judy was frantic, and Stevie went down to Sid's room, heard the children's voices, and asked to be let in. Sid opened the door, refused to let her bring the children back to Judy, and slammed the door shut.

Beside herself, Judy wondered what to do. She called Liza and asked her to come over immediately. Liza could talk to Sid, mediate the matter. If not, her ingenuity might come up with a plan of action. Liza threw on some clothes and rushed over to the Stanhope. She found two policeman standing guard in front of Judy's suite, and several of her mother's associates, including her lawyer, with Judy.

"He's got the kids," Judy told Liza—and Liza recalls feeling that her mother was laying it on pretty thick for the benefit of those around her. She tried to cheer the room up. "Well, let me go down and see them," she said.

Judy told her Sid wouldn't let her in his room; she couldn't get in. "Of course I can," Liza retorted, and went downstairs.

Sid let her in, and told her he didn't want his children going to London, and that they didn't want to go either. "Well, look, Pop," Liza said. "I don't really want to go either. But isn't there a way we can do it without the whole New York police force in the lobby?"

Sid told her *he* hadn't called them, and Liza left a few minutes later, nothing resolved. She told Judy the kids were okay, and that Sid simply did not want them going to England.

"Liza," Judy said gravely, "he is not going to take them from me."

After a while, Judy was informed that the children were back in Central Park with their nurse. Judy told Liza to go down and get them and bring them to the side entrance of the hotel, where four bodyguards would spirit them into Judy's car.

Liza went down, spotted her brother and sister, and began running toward them. She then heard someone else running behind her. It was Sid. She at first tried to dodge him, then caught herself, realizing how absurd the whole thing was. She stopped. "Wait a minute, Pop! What are we doing?" she exclaimed.

Sid wanted to know what *she* was doing. She lied, telling him she just wanted to be with Lorna and Joey. She and Sid stayed with them for a while, then all returned to Luft's suite. Before long, Judy called and demanded that Liza come up to her suite. When Liza told her the effort hadn't been successful, she added, "Look, Mama, I'll go to Europe with you."

Judy told her to get her clothes, and Liza went to where she was staying, grabbed a few things, and returned. A guard was waiting for her, and whisked her into a limousine. Moments later, Judy, Lorna and Joey flew out of the hotel, barely put together, and ran into the limo, which sped off.

Liza was amazed. "How'd you do it, Mama? Tell me! Tell me!"

Judy explained that she had gotten Sid to let her into his suite, then screamed that he was hitting her. Her bodyguards burst in, pinned his arms behind him while Judy rounded up the children. With Luft cursing and struggling, Judy thumbed her nose at him and left.

So Liza, Judy, Lorna, and Joey took up residence once again in London. Sid followed, and several times Judy allowed him to see the children. But she had them made wards of the English courts, which meant they could not be taken out of the country by either parent without the

Judy and the children pose for a press photographer at New York's Idlewild Airport after fleeing Sid Luft, April 28, 1962.

court's approval. Over the next year, there would be bitter fights, bodyguards, kidnap attempts, brief reconciliations—all leading up to an acrimonious public divorce trial and custody fight in 1963 and 1964, at which Luft would give evidence to support his contention that Judy was an unfit mother.

Judy plunged herself into work on *I Could Go On Singing,* which would become her final film. It was almost autobiographical, the script dealing with an emotionally unstable singing star who has an illegitimate son by a lover (played by Dirk Bogarde), is forced to give up custody at the start, and returns fourteen years later, attempting to win back her son. Ultimately, he decides to stay with his father and not disrupt his life to become a part of hers.

It was an extremely difficult movie for Judy to do, and her personal problems didn't help matters. Dirk Bogarde commented after filming was completed, that in the beginning of production the crew referred to Judy as "Miss Garland," but by the end were calling her "it."

Judy was as difficult as she had ever been, sometimes keeping the crew waiting for hours. She could not have looked forward to playing scenes that often hit so painfully close to home.

One scene, in which Bogarde explains to his son why he shouldn't disrupt his life and become a part of his mother's, might have been written about Judy and Liza: "I know what fun she's been to be with," Bogarde's character tells the boy, "and how kind she is, and good, and wise, too, sometimes. And it would be exciting; you'd see places you've never seen before, you'd fly; you'd catch boats; and you'd laugh a lot. I know her, Matt. I loved her—I still do love her. But mark this: Jenny gives more love than anyone. But she takes more love than anyone can possibly give."

Liza visited the set several times, and had a few "dates" with Gregory Phillips, the young man playing Judy's son. They were photographed at an amusement park, and in Judy's London flat, clowning, dancing, studying the movie's script.

Early in July, Liza left for Israel with the cast of *Anne Frank,* and when that tour was over in early August, she enrolled at the Sorbonne in Paris; Judy once again felt her daughter would be well served by a strict, classical education. But sixteen-year-old Liza was not very impressed by the august reputation of that renowned school. She found life there boring. "I wanted to live in New York on my own and take lessons in singing and dancing and acting and see if I could *do* anything."

Judy had returned to the States with Lorna and Joey in August, and was preparing for a nightclub stint in Las Vegas. Liza decided to leave the Sorbonne, return home, and tell Judy she had decided to go into show business. She feared the worst in her mother's reaction; she knew how much Judy wanted her to get a good education. She flew first to New York, to discuss her decision over breakfast with her father. "Daddy, I want to come back here to New York and go on the stage."

Vincente was philosophical. "Yes, I think it's about time," he told Liza. "You have so much energy you might as well start using it."

Liza expressed her fear of Judy's reaction. "Well, I'm all for it, if that helps," Vincente said. "Just tell her as you told me."

There are three distinctly different versions of what ensued when Liza told Judy of her decision. One is Judy's, the other two were told by Liza at different times. The disparities result less from a *Rashomon*-like difference in recall than from a penchant of both Judy's and Liza's for revising the facts to create just the right image of themselves or their family life. Early in her career, Liza's stories of life with Judy were always sugar-coated, and not until later did she let some of the truth out, let some of the hurt show.

Judy's version is all sweetness and light. While appearing in Vegas, she received a telegram from Liza: "DEAR MAMA: I'M COMING HOME. I WANT TO TALK TO YOU."

"I knew what it was immediately," Judy related to an interviewer. "I think she decided to go into show business when she was an embryo. But I wanted her so much to get the best education. When the wire arrived, all I could think about was this child flying half the way around the world, all of the time rehearsing what she would say. Then I started rehearsing what I would say, all sorts of motherly things about going back to school. Liza was off the plane practically before the door was opened. She charged right up to me; I shot the works: 'Liza, darling,' I said, 'why don't you go into show business?' Then we both started crying right there at the airport and it got very messy and happy."

It's difficult to imagine Judy going to the airport to meet Liza, especially considering how much the family flew and the fact that Judy was in the middle of a Vegas act. Liza's first version of the events, takes place in Judy's dressing room, with Liza tentatively beginning her pitch. "I think it's really time. Daddy is all for it, I really want to study, I want to be very good—"

Before Liza could utter another word, she related, Judy said simply, "I think it's wonderful." Liza was stunned. But then Judy added, "But if you do it, you're going to do it on your own. Not one penny from me."

"That's what I wanted to do," Liza said she replied.

Judy then went on to caution her daughter about the pitfalls of stardom. "You've *seen* what's going to happen to you."

"And I had," Liza reflected. "But I'd also seen a little bit how to avoid them [the pitfalls]".

After Judy's death, Liza perhaps felt a little freer to present a less flattering picture of her mother. In a 1970 interview, she described Judy's reaction to her announcement quite differently:

She got that cold, dispassionate look in her eyes that told me she knew, though she was against it, there was nothing she could do about it. "All right," she said, "you do as you please. I can't stop you. I won't try. But you're going to have to make it on your own. I know it's been bothering you for a long time. I hope you make it, baby, I really hope you do. But you might as well know something else now, so you won't expect it later. There will be no money from me. When you leave, you leave me and everything I have. It's got to be that way. You can't have me to fall back on every time you fail or you'll do nothing *but* fail, knowing I'm waiting. Do you understand what I mean?"

I don't think I did. I was sure she'd soften up sooner or later. That time I was wrong.

If Judy was indeed opposed to Liza's entering show business—and she never helped her daughter financially—she did assist her in ways only Judy Garland could have. With Liza's career still a far-off, wistful ambition, Judy was quite willing to share with her daughter everything she had learned in almost four decades of performing.

In a New York *Times* interview by Tom Burke in 1969, Liza recalled one instance in particular when Judy gave her tremendous insight into the art of acting:

I was up for a television show, *Ben Casey* or something, and the part was a pregnant girl who had had an abortion that had gone wrong and she's in the hospital. I knew how I wanted to see it, but not how to *be* it. So I sort of gingerly took the script to Mom, and said, you know, "Mama, help me." We sat down on the floor, and she said, "Now, read me your lines, and the doctor's lines, both." His line was, "Did you want to have the baby?" I read it and Mama said, "All right, he's a doctor, he isn't getting personal—but how *dare* he intrude on you, how *dare* he ask you that, how *dare* you be in the hospital, if

One of Liza's first professional composites, 1963.

only you could have married the father, if only he'd loved you, which he *didn't.* Now, *did you want to have the baby?!!"*

All I had to say was "No," but it came out right. Because she had given me the thoughts—the pause, not the line. Then she said, "Read me his line again," and I did, and she said, "Now this time you are going to concentrate on *not crying.* That's all you have to worry about, not letting him see you cry. Your baby is dead, your life is ruined, but you're not gonna cry, you're a strong girl, your parents have told you, your teachers have told you, *you know it, you know it, you're not going to cry!"*

And my "No" came out even better. She taught me how to—fill in the pauses. And if there's a way I act, that's the way. From that one day on the floor. And now, if maybe another actor will say, "What are you using in that scene?," I'll say, "Well, I'm playing that I'm not gonna cry." They'll say, "Whaaat?" But *I* know!

Judy also taught Liza invaluable lessons about singing, instilling in her the realization that singing a song is acting, too, and a lyric needs to be approached much as a script would be. "Just because you're holding a note," she told her, "don't think the emotion of the word is over. You never lose the thought behind the word; you are not just singing a note."

But for all of Judy's help, there were times—increasingly frequent as Liza's career took off and Judy's disintegrated—when her mother attempted to hinder Liza's career. Sometimes these attempts were unconscious, couched in a desire to protect or publicly "assist" Liza. Other times, there were blatant indignities visited upon Liza.

As with so many other aspects of Judy's life, how she treated Liza's budding show business career depended much on her condition, on how medicated she was, on how her own life was progressing. But Liza's decision to go into show business, to be an independent young woman wanting a little bit of the spotlight for herself, seriously altered the relationship between Judy and Liza. No longer was Liza Mama's little girl. And when Judy feared that Liza was becoming a threat to her stardom, was a younger, fresher, more desirable, more dependable version of herself, it was often nearly impossible for her to bear along with her own increasingly frequent professional failures.

During the next few years, being Judy Garland's daughter would make all that had gone before seem like an Andy Hardy picture.

13

The autumn of 1962 was a hellish period for Judy, and, by extension, for Liza. Much of Judy's time was spent arguing bitterly on the phone with Sid, making plans to hide Lorna and Joey from him, or making depositions to contest his claim to their custody.

The custody battle had turned ugly, with charges and countercharges back and forth between these two people who had once loved each other. Over the next eighteen months, depositions and in-person testimony by Judy, Sid, household servants, doctors, and friends would paint Judy as a woman who had attempted suicide twenty-three times, was "mentally unbalanced" and "emotionally disturbed," would speak to her children in a "loud and intoxicated voice."

Vernon Alves, Sid's business partner and a former assistant to Judy, testified that Judy had tried to jump out of a window of a Philadelphia hotel in 1961. "She was running around without any clothes on . . . from room to room," he said. "I spent most of my time trying to catch her and she was bouncing off the wall. The last thing I did was catch her before she got out the window, and threw her down on the couch."

Luft accused Judy of taking the children away whenever he had visitation rights, and of keeping them out of school for her own professional benefit, to appear with her while she performed. "Lorna and Joe have attended at least eight different schools," he told the court. "Because they have been shunted from one place to another they are scholastically behind other children the same age."

Judy countered that it had been her money which had paid for the children's upbringing for most of the marriage, that she had had to pay many of Sid's debts, that Sid had sold her professional services without her knowledge, that the children were so frightened of their father that she was forced to seek psychiatric treatment for them, that when Luft did have the children he "has gone directly to his hotel and never taken them anywhere else. At the hotel he drinks intoxicating liquor in their presence. He takes their allowance from them and does not return it."

At one hearing at which both Judy and Sid were present, Luft submitted to the court a list of items he said were his and that he wished removed from Judy's house on Rockingham Road. The list was shown to Judy, who checked off items she requested not be removed from the house. Among these were two beds, several paintings, drapes, and a Meissen rooster.

Asked why she wished to keep the beds, Judy replied quietly, "Because my children are sleeping in them."

The effect all of this acrimony—and the court's decision to award half of the children's custody to Luft—had on Judy can only be imagined. She was drinking heavily, relying more and more on pills. Her personality was more than ever subject to radical changes. Daily life with her was becoming untenable. Liza was unable to cater to Judy's every whim as she had before; she was becoming her own person now. And she knew her mother so well, knew when she was bluffing, knew when to avoid her.

Judy was no longer able to elicit sympathy from her daughter whenever she needed it. Once, Liza had asked her mother why her fans would send her get-well cards, even when she wasn't ill. "Darling," Judy replied, "sympathy is my *business*."

Liza began to avoid her mother whenever it was clear that she was "not herself." Coming home from school, Liza would question the cook or the butler. "How's Mama today?" If the answer was negative, Liza would go out, or ask the staff not to tell her mother she had come home.

Judy's drug-induced paranoia, while in the past directed at her mother, her sisters, her husbands or co-workers, now began to be turned on Liza. Resentful of her daughter's newfound independence from her, embarrassed by the fact that Liza clearly was on to her, Judy would have bitter fights with Liza, which usually culminated in an hysterical command to "get your fat ass out of my house!"

Liza, in her characteristic soft-pedaling way, has described the situation like this: "Mama went on a kick now and then where she used to kick me out of the house. Usually I'd stand outside the door, and pretty soon she'd open it and we'd fall into each other's arms, crying and carrying on. But one day she did it and I took her up on it. I went to New York."

What happened was this: after a particularly bad argument, Judy threw Liza out, and did not open the door a few minutes later. Liza pleaded to be let back in, but Judy refused. After spending the night in the poolhouse, Liza was still not allowed into the house. The family cook drove her to Vincente's house, where she stayed for several weeks before leaving for New York.

Why did Judy take such a drastic step? Alma Cousteline, Judy's maid for four years, joined the household a few months after this incident and relates that the staff told her that Judy, in a drugged state, convinced herself that Liza, young, vibrant and attractive, would, consciously or unconsciously, lure away from Judy any man she might be romantically involved with. "Liza was young and Liza was attractive," Alma says, "and Judy had begun to get kind of down during that period. She'd get to looking bad, and Liza was peppy and full of life, and Judy was jealous.

"There wasn't any truth to it," Alma adds. "Judy just had that kind of mind."

Liza May Minnelli, the daughter of Judy Garland and Vincente Minnelli, was sleeping in New York's Central Park on a cold late-fall night.

She had been thrown out of the Barbizon Hotel for women, and most of her clothes confiscated, when she couldn't pay her bill.

She had stayed with family friends for a few weeks when she first arrived in New York with a hundred dollars in her pocket. She hadn't asked her father for any money, and she certainly wasn't going to get any from Mama.

Proving that she could make it in show business to Mama was the most important thing of all. For all the support Judy could give Liza's ambitions at times, at other times she was able to, perhaps unwittingly, diminish her daughter publicly. Often, when she spoke of her children, Liza would come in a poor second to Lorna in Judy's estimation. Sometimes, the implication would be vague—speaking matter-of-factly about Liza, rapturously of Lorna—other times, it was much more direct: "What I live for is to see that my children grow up to be honest, hardworking people. I don't care if they go into show business, but Liza is already on her way and if that's what she wants, super. Lorna, however, has a much better voice than Liza and will probably overtake her if she decides to get into the business."

If that wasn't enough to foster sibling rivalry, nothing would be. Liza's determination to succeed, to *show Mama*, became obsessive. She lived from day to day, sometimes staying with friends, once sleeping on the steps of the fountain in front of the Plaza Hotel, sometimes able to afford a cheap room.

She did some modeling of teenage fashions for *Seventeen* magazine (tall and with the grace of a dancer, she was an ideal model) and that gave her enough income to study acting at the Herbert Berghof Studio in Greenwich Village and singing with David Soren Collyer.

She began the sometimes dehumanizing process of "making the rounds"—attending every audition one could find in the hope of landing a job. It didn't take her long to discover that, though she might have cut the apron strings, Mama was still her constant companion.

The fact hit home when she walked into one theater, gave her name to the casting director, and heard one of her rivals pipe up, "Gawd, that's just what we need—Judy Garland's daughter!"

Whether the implication concerned talent or favoritism, it was not a pleasant position for Liza to be in—especially among her peers. She found that casting directors were unable to separate Liza Minnelli from what she would later somewhat derisively call *la famille.* Some of them would pass her over for fear of seeming influenced by whose daughter she was, others latched onto her for the very same reason.

The realization that theater people were looking upon her as "a novelty," says Liza, "nearly killed me. Man, I was down about that for weeks. I thought, God, I can't go on playing *that* part for the rest of my life. Then an older actor I met at an audition said something that changed my outlook. And just in time, too.

"He told me not to hesitate a moment if being Judy Garland's daughter could get me in the door. 'But when you go out on that stage,' he said, 'from the first moment they see you, let them know you're Liza Minnelli.' "

It was advice that helped Liza's self-image, but it wasn't that easy to follow. She got roles—in productions like *The Fantasticks*—but always she was Judy Garland's daughter. "With each review," says Liza, "I could have written the beginning: 'Judy Garland's daughter, Liza Minnelli, has certainly inherited her mother's talent . . .' I tried not to care too terribly much."

The nadir for Liza in this respect had to be the review which called her Judy Garland, Jr. But if Liza had determined to grit her teeth and seize what opportunity her unique position offered, she couldn't have asked for a more fortuitous event: she was given the chance to make her off-Broadway debut precisely because Judy Garland was her mother.

A group of young producers was putting together a revival of the 1941 musical *Best Foot Forward* in a rather seedy 100-seat theater built into the back room of a Seventy-third Street bar in Manhattan. A show like that, in a place like that, almost never gets much attention and is quickly assigned to oblivion—unless, somehow, the producers can get a name or two to agree to appear in it.

That was impossible—but they might be able to get the next-best thing. The show's director-choreographer, Danny Daniels, was aware that Judy Garland's daughter had been appearing in stock, and he asked one of his talent scouts to try and locate her. As Liza tells the story, "I was on my way to class when a little man stopped me right on the corner of Forty-sixth Street and Broadway. He said, 'Danny Daniels is looking for you for a show.' I thought he was just kidding because nobody comes up to you on the street and says a thing like that. Except in a bad movie."

Finally convinced that it was all quite serious, Liza was persuaded to audition. But first, she had to call Mama. They had been in touch by phone, and with all of Liza's independence, she still felt constrained to get Judy's permission. "She got so nervous, and she started telling *me* to relax and remember my poise and not get nervous and what was I going to sing and should she fly out special arrangements . . . Wow, she was funny. She was a nervous wreck!"

Liza herself was a nervous wreck at the audition, but the show's producers were delighted—not only would they have Judy Garland's daughter in the show, but a talented, fascinating performer as well. They signed her up—at the Actors Equity minimum of forty-five dollars per week. Liza was part of a New York show—off Broadway, to be sure, but that, after all, was only one word away from the big time. Liza was ecstatic.

She began rehearsals of the show, a piece of fluff about a boys' prep school, a group of girls who come up for a weekend dance, and a fading movie queen who makes an appearance.

134

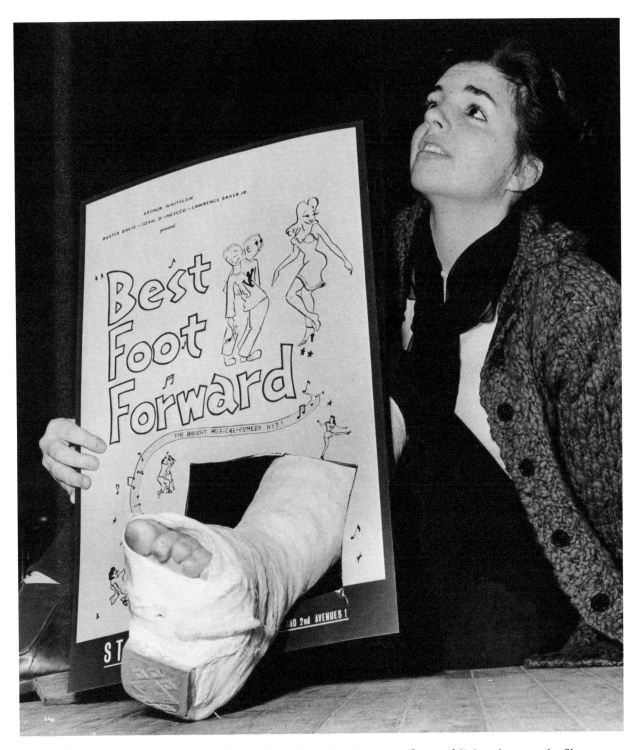

After breaking a bone in her foot during rehearsals, Liza poses for a publicity photograph. She opened in the show April 2, 1963, but confined her performance to singing.

Liza was to dance in most of the numbers, and sing several songs, including a lonely ballad, "You Are For Loving."

Rehearsals went well until the night of the first run-through. In the middle of a dance number, Liza caught her foot on a loose floor board, and broke a bone. She spent her seventeenth birthday in a hospital, and the rest of the rehearsal period with her foot in a cast. The show's publicity director played up the "best foot forward" angle, sending out photos of Liza in her cast, gamely carrying on.

Liza's presence in *Best Foot Forward* had exactly the effect its producers desired. One of them exclaimed, "It got the most publicity of any off-Broadway show in history." The public was consumed with curiosity about Judy Garland's daughter, and on opening night, police had to set up barricades to keep in line the crowds who had come to see Liza and, they hoped, Judy—surely she wouldn't miss her daughter's first night, April 2, 1963.

Judy had assured Liza that she would attend, and several seats in the first row were set aside for Judy and Sid, who had again reconciled. As the curtain went up, and Liza came out on stage, she saw that her father, and many of her friends were in the audience. But Judy's seats were empty. All through the first act, those vacant seats stared back at Liza, and her performance that night came from somewhere amid the anger, embarrassment and bewilderment she felt at her mother not being there for her most important professional milestone.

At intermission, the show's stage manager, Tony Manzi, recalls a frantic Liza on the telephone to her mother's hotel suite. "But Mama," she was saying, almost in tears, "I *told* you it was tonight. How could you have thought it was *tomorrow* night?"

The next day, the United Press International review was headlined, "Judy Foregoes Liza's Triumph." The article went on, "Judy Garland stayed away from the theater last night and let daughter Liza Minnelli take the bows for a well-deserved personal success in her New York stage debut . . . 'My wife decided it was best not to let anything detract from the girl's debut,' explained agent Sid Luft, husband of the screen and television star . . . 'actually, we didn't get back until this evening,' Luft said by telephone from their suite in the St. Regis Hotel. 'We missed a plane connection in Florida. In a sense, we are delighted that we weren't there in view of all the excitement stirred up about this. We wanted Liza to have her own big night without any distraction.' "

Liza has said she believes her mother didn't attend for just that reason, but the question must be asked: why didn't Judy tell Liza she didn't want to steal any of her thunder, rather than letting her daughter expect her to be there and wonder where she was?

The next night, Judy did attend, with Sid, Lorna, and Joey. "Oh, did I cry," Judy recalled. "I cried and cried. I was so proud of my baby. She had worked so hard and done it all alone. And you know Liza's the first one to do this. I never had a Broadway show. All I had were variety shows."

Liza's appearance in *Best Foot Forward* received national press attention. *Look* magazine wrote of her, ". . . a new star was born. Liza brought the house down. She has everything—a big voice with the faintly mournful catch, and a wealth of musical-comedy talent that is more unique than reminiscent. Where did the vivacious 17-year-old daughter of Judy Garland and film director Vincente Minnelli get the talent that aroused unanimous praise? Perhaps it was born in her, and nurtured during years on the periphery of her mother's spotlight."

Best Foot Forward became the hottest ticket in town, and Liza Minnelli was very much in demand for national television spots. Ed Sullivan caught the show and booked Liza for an appearance on his enormously popular Sunday night variety program. It gave the show a million dollars in free publicity. "The producers were real shrewd in hiring Liza," Tony Manzi says. "What other tacky off-Broadway show gets one of its songs performed on the 'Ed Sullivan Show'?"

A portent of what was to come might have been Liza's appearance on "The Jack Paar

A scene from *Best Foot Forward*.

A publicity pose for *Best Foot Forward*.

Vincente congratulates Liza after the opening.

The next night, the Lufts came to see Liza.

.Show," for which she had taken some time off from rehearsals to do before *Best Foot Forward* opened. Judy had arranged the stint with a phone call to Paar, a friend of hers.

Talking to Liza about it the day of the taping, Judy advised, "Make sure the audience sees your cast. They'll love that!"

Probably because she was somewhat awestruck Liza agreed to a cute little gimmick by Paar: he introduced Liza as Dyju Langard, a new sensation from Armenia. Only after she had given her game performance, hobbling on her cast, did Paar reveal her name as an acronym for Judy Garland. It was another of Liza's low points.

None of that was necessary after *Best Foot Forward;* people knew who she was, and she was getting booked as much because of her talent as because of her mother. Still, she would get irritable walking near the theater, when fans would whisper, "There's Judy Garland's daughter!"

The success of *Best Foot Forward* could be attributed almost solely to public interest in Liza. The producers encouraged her to accept outside bookings for television, and as a result she missed an inordinate number of performances. Because she was officially not the star of the show (no one was billed above the title), the producers didn't feel constrained to refund money to irate customers who had come to see Liza and didn't.

Liza's replacement was Marcia Levant, daughter of Oscar Levant, but the family connections here weren't strong enough (as one newspaper put it, "Oscar wasn't Judy"), and attendance dropped off. When Liza left the show for good in early September, the producers brought in Veronica Lake for one of the roles in a last-ditch attempt at saving it, but to no avail. The show closed on October 13, 1963, after a fair-to-respectable seven-month run.

Producer Arthur Whitelaw was somewhat bitter at Liza: "The show was a success. It was selling out. We could have run for two years. But it only ran seven months because without Liza it didn't sell out."

Ironically, Liza left the show because of Judy. Mama wanted her daughter back home. On the phone, she pleaded for Liza to come back. "Oh, no, Mama, I really can't." There was the show to do, she explained, and besides that, she was in love with a young man she had met in New York, a dancer named Tracy Everitt.

But Judy would have her way. She called Everitt and offered him a job dancing on her new television series, "The Judy Garland Show," which had gone into production in Hollywood the month before. It was not something an aspiring young dancer could say no to. Everitt quit the chorus of *How to Succeed in Business Without Really Trying,* Liza quit *Best Foot Forward,* and Liza and Judy were reunited.

14

During the spring and early summer of 1963, Judy had been preparing, then taping, the first few segments of "The Judy Garland Show." It was an ambitious project, an expensive one, and one that Judy felt confident would keep her financially secure for the rest of her life.

For the third show, taped in July, Judy's main guest star was Liza Minnelli. Liza's success in *Best Foot Forward*, her other national TV guest stints, and a moderately selling 45 r.p.m. version of her solo "You Are for Loving" made Liza's choice as an early guest star more than just an exercise in nepotism.

Mel Tormé, in his book about his experiences as the show's director of special material *The Other Side of the Rainbow*, describes his first meeting with Liza: "Judy's eyes sparkled as she introduced her pride and joy to us. Liza was a walking caricature of both her mother and her father . . . She also had inherited a great amount of talent and seemed overwhelmed at the thought of appearing on the show alongside her mother, whom she openly adored."

Judy was not in a happy frame of mind at this time. CBS-TV executives had criticized her first two shows: the skits didn't work, Judy didn't sing enough; Judy touched her guests too much; she sometimes seemed neurotic and edgy. Never one to take criticism well, she was preoccupied and uptight during Liza's rehearsals. Trying to keep slim, she was also using amphetamines heavily, but Tormé reports no ugliness while Liza was around. "After the taping," he wrote, "Judy disappeared. There was no little gathering in her trailer, no drinks with the cast or crew, no good-night kisses. No Judy. It was perfectly understandable. She had been a good soldier that whole week. She had kept up her spirits for the sake of Liza, and it had no doubt been quite a strain."

During a run-through of the opening spot, Judy became quite emotional. She was to sing "Liza," the Gershwin tune which gave Liza her name, with special lyrics by Tormé, while walking among huge photo blowups of Liza in various stages of her life, from lying naked as an infant on a bearskin rug to the present.

Tormé reports: "She wept openly as she sang . . . looking at the pictures all the while and shaking her head from side to side emotionally. Liza ran up on stage at the finish of the song and embraced her mother tearfully. There was nothing phony about this overt display of affection. Judy loved her kids actively and passionately and her devotion was returned in kind."

The "Liza Show" in the Judy series was aired on November 17, 1963. It turned out as a charming hour, with Judy and Liza playfully dueting on "Together," "We Could Make Such Beautiful Music Together," "Bob White," "The Best Is Yet To Come," "Bye Bye Baby," "Let Me Entertain You," "Two Lost Souls," and "I Will Come Back."

Liza pulled Judy down into her lap for several of the songs ("I feel real dumb when you do that," Judy said to her daughter, who was about half a foot taller than she) and they donned tramp outfits for the last two numbers.

Liza sang "You Are for Loving," in a tender, vulnerable performance in which her voice was highlighted for the first time; singing with Judy, Liza tended to be overwhelmed.

"The Judy Garland Show" was not a success. Scheduled opposite the phenomenally popular "Bonanza," it would have been difficult for any show to carve out a share of the national audience. But Judy's show faltered, changed personnel, changed formats, and never was able to catch the public's imagination. By the last few shows, concerts in which Judy simply sang— wonderfully and touchingly—it was too late, the show had been canceled.

Judy was devastated by her show's failure.

Judy and Liza tape Liza's first appearance on her mother's show, July 1963.

Judy in rehearsal for the series, 1963.

Judy and Liza singing "I Will Come Back" at the conclusion of Liza's appearance.

It was supposed to be her crowning career achievement, and her financial security, and now there was nothing. Her reconciliation with Sid, such as it was, had lasted but a short time, and a brief affair with Glenn Ford had ended.

At eleven in the morning on November 22, Judy heard the terrible news from Dallas: her friend the President, a man she would call several times a month and who would ask her to sing "Over the Rainbow" to him over the phone, had been shot and killed.

Judy was inconsolable, crumpled hysterically on the floor, Liza trying to comfort her but having nothing to guide her this time in how to deal with Mama. She wasn't acting, wasn't just seeking sympathy. She got up, tried to throw herself against the wall, crying out "What are we going to do?" Liza followed her, shook her shoulders, pleaded "Stop it, Mama, stop it, please!"

Finally, Judy lay spent on the floor, Liza hugging her mother to her breast, Judy talking about hopelessness, Liza calming her. "I know, Mama, I know . . . "

The country recovered from the trauma of those four days. But for Judy, John Kennedy's death was but another body blow to a woman who was approaching the final round. Her life, beginning late in 1963, would contain too many desperate comeback attempts, soaring triumphs followed by canceled concerts or poor performances, failed marriages, ugly, hurtful actions against her servants, her friends, and her family. Before long, Judy Garland would drive away from her almost everyone who cared about her—including the one person who loved her the most, Liza.

Shortly after Kennedy's assassination, Liza fell ill. Her temperature was dangerously high, and she couldn't get out of bed. A frantic Judy called the doctor, who diagnosed her problem as a kidney stone and put her in the hospital. She spent a painful month there, and just before she was released, her agent (she had signed with Creative Management Associates in September) came to her room and asked if she would like to star in *Carnival,* a successful Broadway show which was being produced in stock. "I grabbed a pen and signed the contract right there."

Judy wasn't happy about Liza leaving for New York to rehearse the show. She wanted Liza with her, as an emotional buffer against the depressions that were more and more frequently coming over her. But Liza left and went to work in Mineola, Long Island, where the first *Carnival* production would be presented.

Just two months after her initial kidney problem, Liza had a relapse and was hospitalized again. Judy flew in from California and insisted that Liza return home: she was too ill to go on tour. Liza tried to explain that she had signed a contract, that she was committed to appear in the show—she *couldn't* just walk out.

"I shall do everything in my power to stop you," Judy told her, coldly furious.

"Mama went into a rage at my refusal," Liza said later. "I was so frightened. I knew Mama could pull a lot of strings against me—regardless of everything, Mama's power is considerable."

Judy indeed pulled out all the stops. She called the newspapers, telling them that Liza was forbidden to do *Carnival* and if the producers insisted that her contract was unbreakable, she would sue them.

Liza spent every night of the ensuing two weeks crying herself to sleep. "I loved my mother, I wanted to make her happy, but everything went wrong."

Liza went forward with the *Carnival* rehearsals, and Judy continued trying to disrupt her daughter's activities. On opening night, the show had just begun, and Liza was onstage. Bob VanderGriff, *Carnival's* stage manager, remembers being shocked to hear the backstage telephone ring. "It should not have been ringing," he says, "because it can be heard in the audience."

One of the stagehands picked the phone up quickly. The caller asked to speak to Liza.

Liza rehearses her appearance in *Carnival*, despite her mother's objections, January 24, 1964.

The stagehand explained that she was in the middle of a performance. The caller asked that a message be left: Judy Garland had just tried to commit suicide.

The producers debated whether to tell Liza immediately, or wait until after the performance was over. They decided to wait.

But as Liza was leaving the stage at intermission, the phone rang again, and this time she picked it up. VanderGriff heard her ask into the phone, "Is she going to be okay?" The answer was evidently positive. "Tell her I'll see her after the show," Liza said.

"She went out and gave a terrific second-act performance," VanderGriff recalls.

By now, Liza was convinced that Judy's suicide attempts were never really serious—she never actually intended to kill herself. She was crying out for attention, trying to make her point—and, in this case, trying to show Liza just how angry she was about her defiance. Liza, however, was no longer impressed with such histrionics. If Mama was okay, what reason was there to interrupt the show?

The next day, with Judy already out of the hospital, Liza spoke to her on the phone. She returned to a group of friends awaiting that night's Garland show and happily reported, "Mama says this is one of the good ones."

Carnival spent several weeks in Mineola, then moved to the Paper Mill Playhouse in New Jersey; Judy's efforts to have her way with Liza did not cease. Pat Hipp, a press agent for the theater, wrote an article for the Asbury Park *Press* about the trials and tribulations of having Liza Minnelli as your star.

She recalled sending out press releases with only veiled references to Judy, so as not to offend Liza. "We were selling a lot of tickets for the month's run," Pat wrote. "And then, whammo! Judy Garland's lawyer called. She was pulling Liza out of the show. 'Too young,' Judy was quoted as saying. 'Much too young to be in the theater. Not now—and maybe never!'

"Then began the coast-to-coast phone calls. The begging, the hysterics. We didn't know from minute to minute if we had a show."

Liza was completely exasperated, embarrassed, fearful. "She seemed to be held together by snapping rubber bands, rather than cartilage," Pat remarked. "I had certainly noted her intensity. Her concentration during rehearsals was spooky. But a star? All I knew was that she was hyperkinetic and that Judy Garland had left us all wringing wet with nerves.

"Rehearsals were going badly, and the cast's morale was shot. Judy was pulling the rug out from under us—then just as suddenly as Judy had started making trouble, she was stopped. Vincente Minnelli, we were told, persuaded her that Liza should have her chance."

The show opened, and Pat Hipp recalls vividly the opening night. "Liza walked on; how truly a waif she was. She'd been crying backstage before the performance. She was gorgeous. Not in the sense of beautiful, but of real, of lost, of heartbreaking, of needing. And her voice reached out and loved us. It was beautiful."

The show was a hit, and Liza's reviews were good. Mike McGrady of *Newsday* wrote, "The comparisons to Judy Garland are inevitable—the tremulous voice, the respect for the lyric, the wide eyes, the clenching hands, the eyebrows never still. Yet, by the time she sings her second number, 'Yes, My Heart,' the applause belongs to her alone; from that point on forget to make the comparisons."

Judy was no longer directly hassling Liza, but indirectly there was no way for the girl to escape her mother. Bob VanderGriff recalls an incident in which he was trying to get Liza from the theater to a restaurant for a press interview and back in time for the second show. Time was short, and Bob wanted to avoid leaving by the stage door because there was a group of fans waiting outside for Liza's autograph, and if she were to stop and accommodate them, there would not be enough time left.

VanderGriff asked the limousine to pick them up in the front of the theater, but as he and Liza walked to the car, a few fans spotted them, and within seconds most of the people had come around the front and up to the car, asking for autographs.

Liza wanted to oblige the fans, but Bob insisted that there wasn't any time. He said, "No, Liza cannot sign any autographs today," and closed the door.

The crowd got angry, and assumed that it was Liza who was refusing to sign their autograph books, photos and programs. Several of the fans began yelling at her. "You're so stuck up! Who do you think you are? You're just Judy Garland's daughter, not some big shot!"

The car pulled away and Liza crumpled into the back seat, crying. "She was miserable," VanderGriff recalls. "She was sure everyone was coming to see her just because she was Judy Garland's daughter."

The *Carnival* tour was a success, but there was more bad news for Liza. She had not been managing her money well at all; she was five thousand dollars in debt. She was told that if she didn't pay her creditors, she would have to declare bankruptcy. "Seventeen years old and bankrupt!" Liza later exclaimed. "That would have set some kind of record."

A Surrogate Court judge in New York ordered that all of Liza's earnings would have to be turned over to Judy, who would then be required to deposit the money in New York banks in Liza's name. Liza would not be able to get any of her money without the court's permission.

Liza had asked the court to allow her to control 50 percent of her earnings, but she was turned down. She gave a lawyer power of attorney to pay off her debts, and they were eventually cleared up. The financial arrangement remained in effect until Liza turned twenty-one in 1967.

15

With Judy out of the country, Liza was left to her own devices throughout the spring and early summer of 1964. She was living in New York again, no longer romantically involved with Tracy Everitt, sharing an apartment with a girlfriend, and actively pursuing her career. She did a couple of shows, including a tour of *The Fantasticks* with Elliott Gould, a dramatic TV appearance on "Mr. Broadway," and began work on her first album for Capitol Records.

Her voice was no longer like chalk on a blackboard. She had worked determinedly to improve it, and it now possessed a melodic sweetness to go along with its vulnerability in a ballad; and there was still, of course, the power of the Broadway belter. It no longer mattered that Liza's voice wasn't as good as her mother's in its prime, or even that, as an instrument, it was inferior to that of the country's new singing sensation, Barbra Streisand. It was a good, interesting, idiosyncratic voice, with yearning and charisma and a desire to please. People began to listen to Liza Minnelli.

Judy's preoccupation was with Mark Herron, an actor ten years her junior who had been a Judy Garland fan most of his life and to whom Judy gravitated when they were introduced at a party by costume designer Ray Aghayan.

Judy was at a low point—her show canceled, rumors of her difficulty and temperament spread all over Hollywood, her custody battle with Sid in full swing, her reliance on pills and alcohol stronger than ever, Liza declaring her independence. Herron was both awestruck at meeting one of his idols and moved by her clear need for protection and love. Judy responded to his good looks, his youth, and his obvious caring, and they became inseparable companions.

Mark accompanied her on a trip to Australia, where she was to give concerts in Sydney and Melbourne. The Australian press, as sensationalistic as some of its British counterparts, swarmed all over Judy the minute she arrived. One reporter asked, "Is it true, Miss Garland? What Sid Luft said? That you tried to commit suicide twenty-two times?"

Shocked, Judy passed the buck. "Why don't you ask Mr. Herron that question?"

Mark, at a loss, relied on his wit. "Who's counting?" he replied. Judy roared with laughter.

The press didn't know what to make of Mark Herron. Newspaper reports referred to him as everything from Judy's traveling companion to a homosexual, a male nurse, and a gigolo. Herron tried to laugh it off.

Entering Australia, Judy had her drugs confiscated by customs officials. She was panic-stricken; she would never have been able to function with absolutely no pills. She obtained new drugs from an abortionist with black-market connections.

Her concert in Sydney was a huge success; she won the audience over despite the fact that her voice left her entirely several times. But they had never seen Judy Garland live, and that ineffable magic she could create on stage was very much in evidence.

Melbourne was another matter. Her appearance in that city may well remain one of the low points of her entire life. Perhaps because her new pills were from Europe and contained unfamiliar dosages, Judy was not functioning well the night of the show. She arrived on stage an hour late, helped by Mark. She stumbled over her microphone cord, forgot lyrics, sang off-key. She tried to charm the audience with banter, then completely forgot the lyrics to her next song; she was unable to pick the song up at any point.

Mark Herron helps Judy through a crowd in Melbourne during her Australia tour.

There was shocked silence from the audience, then someone yelled out, "Have another brandy!" Judy tried to continue; but when she knocked over a chair, more in the audience started to heckle her, and others began to leave.

"Where are you going?" Judy cried out.

"Home," someone replied. "And that's where you should go!"

Judy was devastated, tried to begin another song, then put her microphone down and walked off the stage.

The next day, the newspapers had a field day, with blazing headlines about the "drunk" Judy Garland's dreadful display. She and Mark quickly left Melbourne, but not before a crowd of people had gathered at the airport to boo her as she boarded her plane. She nearly collapsed from shock when she realized what was happening. The following week, *Variety* reported, "The legend of Judy Garland was sadly and brutally shattered . . . "

Unable to face the press in the United States, Judy convinced Mark that they should fly to Hong Kong. There, in a hotel room, Judy read *Time* magazine's account of the Melbourne disaster and became very depressed. That same night, one of the worst typhoons in Hong Kong history, with ninety-mile-per-hour winds, struck the city. Judy was terrified; Mark held her close in their bed as the hotel building swayed back and forth and the violent winds buffeted the windows.

In New York, Liza read of her mother's troubles in Melbourne, but there was nothing she could do; she wasn't even sure at this point where Judy was.

The next day, in Los Angeles, Mrs. Chapman, Joey and Lorna's governess, was driving Lorna to school. The car radio was on. The announcer broke in: "Judy Garland is dead . . ." Mrs. Chapman quickly turned off the radio.

"What did that man say about Mama?" Lorna asked. "Did he say she died?"

Judy had taken so many pills to calm her fear of the storm that she had lapsed into a coma and was rushed to the hospital. Stomach pumping did little good, and Judy was pronounced dead. A nurse made an official announcement. Hearing this, Mark Herron, on the verge of hysteria, refused to acknowledge that Judy was gone, and insisted that Judy's oxygen line be adjusted, that efforts to keep her alive continue. Before long, signs of life returned.

Judy's personal physician, his wife, and Judy's secretary flew to Hong Kong, thinking Judy was dead. When they arrived, they discovered she was not dead but was still in a coma, and that there was little hope for a full recovery: there might have been brain damage, her doctor warned; and she would be susceptible to pneumonia.

Although Liza was not there, she tells a story probably related to her by Herron as if she had been present, preferring to have the harrowing vigil at Judy's bedside remembered with humor. She told the New York *Times* in 1969, "She had a crazy sense of humor. I remember once, she was in the hospital, she was very ill, and we were standing around her bed. She was asleep. She opened her eyes. Everybody was tense. She sat straight up and said, 'Spyros Skouras choreographs the Rockettes.' And lay right back down and went right back to sleep. *What?* I mean, what kind of crazy imagination did that come from?"

Actually, Judy was not just awakening from sleep, she was coming out of her coma. Mark, who had just helped Judy avoid the grave, now had to tell her that her sister Suzy was dead. A second suicide attempt had succeeded. "Poor Suzy" is all that Judy said, and never spoke to Mark about it.

A few weeks later, on June 11, Judy was well enough to announce to the press that she and Mark had been married aboard a ship on June 6. The press was skeptical, especially since Judy was still legally married to Sid Luft. Luft mocked the whole thing, and used it in his custody fight as further proof of Judy's unstable mental condition. She had made the entire story up. But she assured everyone that she and Mark would eventually wed.

152

While in Hong Kong, Mark, then Judy, caught the nightclub show of two young Australian singers billing themselves as the Allen Brothers. They weren't brothers at all, but close friends Peter Allen and Chris Bell, and Judy took an immediate liking to them. So impressed was she with their talent that she decided, almost on the spot, to manage their careers and make stars of them.

She particularly liked Peter, who was good-looking, witty, bright, and completely adoring of Judy. Her motherly mind began turning: Peter was just a few years older than Liza. Surely they'd like each other . . . There and then, Judy determined to introduce the two young people at the earliest opportunity.

Judy and Mark traveled to London from Hong Kong, visiting Tokyo and Alaska along the way. Once in London, Judy had Peter and Chris join them, and began seeking bookings for them in local night spots.

It was the fall of 1964. Liza's first album had been completed and pressed, and was scheduled for release that December. Liza had been working on her voice, but hadn't said much about her efforts to her mother. As far as Judy knew, Liza was still primarily interested in dancing. Once Liza had copies of the finished album, she sent Judy one.

Mama was impressed. "Where did she get that voice?" Judy asked wonderingly. "Oh, my God, she must have worked her little old ass off!"

Judy was very proud of her daughter. She admired Liza's fighting spirit, even when it was directed at her: after the *Carnival* standoff, Judy admitted to Liza, "You know, that was the first time you defied me, and it infuriated me—but God, how I admired you for doing it!"

Now, Judy started to get ideas. Despite a one-night triumph as one of a score of stars at the Palladium in July, Judy was worried about her voice. Her throat had reportedly been damaged during the stomach pumping in Hong Kong, and she despaired of carrying a two-hour concert all by herself. But she needed to work, and wanted to play the Palladium again.

But what if Liza joined her, this time for an entire show? *Judy and Liza at the Palladium!* The more she thought about it, the better she liked the idea. It was perfect: it would give Liza's career a boost, and take half the burden of carrying a two-hour show off Judy.

She called Liza in New York, told her how impressed she was with the *Liza! Liza!* album, then brought up her idea. To Judy's surprise, Liza wasn't receptive. "Oh no, Mama, why? It's too much, Judy and her kid. Why don't you do it yourself?"

Perhaps Liza thought it frightening—it was, after all, the Palladium, which could have been rechristened the Judy Garland Theater—or it may have seemed to her just another example of her status as Judy Garland, Jr.

But Judy, as always, would have her way. She left Liza thinking she had accepted her refusal, then called the British press and announced the concert. Word spread so fast that the show was sold out by the next day, unadvertised. Judy called Liza back and exclaimed, "We're sold out, isn't it great!"

Liza knew she was helpless to resist, but quickly her doubts turned to excitement. She was thrilled that her mother had asked her to share the spotlight in a hall so important to her. "It was her first acknowledgment that I might really be talented," Liza has said. She called a friend, composer Marvin Hamlisch, and asked him to arrange several numbers for her.

Liza arrived in London two weeks before the scheduled November 8 concert. There was a great deal of pre-publicity, and much excitement among Garland fans. Liza's inclusion in the program was greeted with mild interest by Judy's fans; few in Britain had ever seen or heard Liza, and no one knew quite what to expect. But seeing Judy again was enough for them: there was such a clamor for tickets that another show was scheduled for November 16.

The day of the show, a rehearsal and last-minute preparations were in progress. Mark Herron, who had worked with Judy on the show and convinced her to learn several new songs,

153

kept a close eye on things. Judy's British fan club secretary was there, along with representatives of the theater and Judy's record label, and dozens of others. Judy was calling the shots, and conferred with the orchestra while Liza chatted in the seats with Mark and several of Judy's fans.

She told them how nervous she was working in such a big theater, and when someone suggested that working with Mama might be calming for her, she replied, "The trouble is, we've never performed together before and we sing in different keys. It's difficult to blend." A comment was made that Liza had had a good teacher in Judy. "But Mama's not my teacher," Liza replied.

Every so often Judy would call out her name and Liza would run up on stage with a quick, "Yes, Mama?"

The performance of Judy Garland and Liza Minnelli at the London Palladium on November 8, 1964, is a milestone in show business history, and a fascinating exercise in psycho-dynamics. For whatever Judy's motives were in sharing the Palladium stage with Liza, she was not prepared for what happened.

It was a Garland audience. They had paid money to see Judy, and if Liza came along in the bargain, fine. But it was going to be Judy's night.

As it turned out, it almost wasn't. Judy sang several numbers to enthusiastic applause, then introduced her daughter—"Ladies and Gentlemen, Liza Minnelli." The audience applauded politely, but without undue enthusiasm. Liza walked down a ramp to the center of the stage, bowed to Judy, then stood alone as her mother walked off stage. She ripped into an exuberant number, "The Travelin' Life," with enough energy and youthful joy to take the audience's breath away. She then performed "Pass That Peace Pipe" and "Gypsy in My Soul" in a lovely voice. When she had finished the numbers, the audience erupted into rapturous applause and "Bravos!" They were delighted to see that Judy Garland's daughter was not only talented, but had an exciting stage presence too. The reception the audience gave Liza after her two numbers was more enthusiastic than it had given Judy before that.

Judy was stunned. She was not in particularly good voice that night, and as the evening progressed, it became clearer and clearer that Liza was giving a more exciting performance. It was the first time that Liza had ever given her all while performing with Judy, had held nothing back. On Judy's TV show, Liza's shyness and inexperience had resulted in her voice's being barely audible over Judy's; this night, the opposite was true: Liza's voice was the dominant one when they sang in duet.

Perhaps to save her voice and her energy, Judy had elected to sing mostly ballads as solos, leaving Liza's repertoire to consist mainly of up-tempo numbers. It was, as the concert unfolded, to prove a bad decision, no matter how necessary. Liza's youthful energy combined with jazzy musical numbers to thrill the audience, and her applause was frequently filled with cheers and "Bravos!" Several of Judy's quieter numbers, sung poorly with a wavering vibrato and cracking high notes, were sometimes greeted perfunctorily. While Judy's performance was not terrible, it wasn't on a par with what her audiences expected of her.

Liza was threatening to steal Judy's audience from right under her nose. And there was nothing that Judy could do. She tried to put Liza in her place; repeatedly throughout the concert she reached out and pushed Liza's arm down to adjust the mike she was holding. It was her way of telling the audience, "Liza's just a novice. I'm the pro. I have to show her how to hold a microphone properly."

Some observers interpreted Judy's action as one of motherly concern; trouble was, Liza was having no problem being heard; her microphone was picking her voice up perfectly well from where it was.

Judy's struggle to keep up with Liza in their duets resulted in her voice's fading more and more during the second half. At a repeat performance a week later, she kept missing notes; at one point, after a moving ballad performance, Liza said to her, "How can I follow that?"

Judy and Liza rehearse their Palladium Concert, November 8, 1964.

Judy replied, in her self-deprecating way, "By hitting better notes." In the second show, by the time, in curtain call, Judy was to sing "Over the Rainbow," she was not up to it. She asked the audience to sing it to her—"You know it better than me."

During the curtain calls, it was reported, Judy pushed Liza off the stage so that she could take a bow by herself.

Later, Liza spoke of that night in her *Good Housekeeping* interview. "When I was a little girl and had jumped up onstage to dance while she sang, it was an unrehearsed, amateurish, spontaneous thing. *Working* with her was something else. I'll never be afraid to perform with anyone ever again after that terrifying experience. She became very competitive with me. I wasn't Liza. I was another woman in the same spotlight. It was just too hard for me to try to cope. And it was *her* night. I *wanted* it to be her night."

The experience left Judy exhausted, and with widely conflicting emotions. Professionally, the concerts were hardly triumphs for Judy; Liza's vibrant performance had seemed mostly to make Judy's ebbing abilities seem all the weaker by comparison.

Liza could have toned herself down; she could have let Judy's energy level set the pace for the evening. That would have been a very daughterly thing to do. But Judy of all people knew that that wouldn't have been a very *professional* thing to do; Liza was there to give the audience their money's worth. Her stock in trade was her energy and her exuberance; to have clamped a lid on them would have been to cheat her audience, herself and Judy.

So while Judy might have been furious at Liza for her actions—some observers feel Liza even *overdid* things to score points—she had to admire her for giving the kind of performance she would have if her mother had not been on the stage with her. Judy's comment a year before was again apropos: "You are an admirable young woman, but you exasperate me."

According to Liza, Judy's competitiveness ended after the Palladium, and she began a period of "unparalleled motherhood." Part of her mothering was playing matchmaker for Liza and Peter; she told each about the other in the clichéd "have I got a girl/boy for you" manner, and made sure that they met in London. "Mother kept on so about how handsome and exciting he was and insisted I meet him," said Liza.

Both of them had a "sure, Judy" attitude. "I kept stalling," Liza says. "Like, how *square* can a song-and-dance act be?" But when they met, there was an instant attraction, and Judy's fondest wish came true: within a month, they became engaged.

Peter and Liza had joined Judy, Mark, and Chris Bell for dinner at Trader Vic's restaurant in London. The talk had been about marriage, and Peter said he'd like to go steady with Liza. Judy was in the powder room, and Mark, acting fatherly, said, "You'll have to be engaged to do that."

"All right," Peter said, "let's be engaged, then." He took a diamond ring off his little finger and put it on Liza's ring finger. Flabbergasted, Liza heard Peter say, "Liza, if you'll marry me I'll never stop trying to make you happy."

"Yes, Peter, I want that," Liza replied.

Judy returned to the table and Liza exclaimed, "Mama, we're engaged!" Judy started to cry, and the rest of the night was spent in celebration.

Returning to New York on November 26 to audition for the lead in a Broadway show, Liza showed off her engagement ring to reporters at Kennedy Airport. "He's as nutty and crazy as I am," Liza said of Peter. "I mean by that he is funny. We kick up our heels, run around, laugh, and talk to strangers. We're uninhibited."

It would be more than two years before Liza and Peter were married, partly because of parental opposition: this time, though, it wasn't Judy throwing roadblocks up in front of Liza, but Vincente. He felt that both of them were much too young to take such a step, and because both he and Judy had suffered through several failed marriages, he was particularly protective of Liza: he told her she would have to wait.

Judy, Mark, and Liza greet Peter Allen and Chris Bell on their arrival in London, 1964.

Liza was stunned, especially since Vincente had always been her strongest ally. "It scared me," she said. "My father is not a man to object without reasons. I loved Peter. I *loved* him. What was more important than that?"

Still, Liza and Peter made no definite wedding plans. And, despite Judy's initial match-making, she too convinced Liza again and again to postpone setting the date. Ostensibly, she needed Peter and Chris to open for her when she was on the road. But she, too, thought they were too young: "I want Liza and Peter to have their professional ambitions either realized or out of their systems entirely, before they marry," she said.

They would have the opportunity. Judy took Peter and Chris with her to several cities for many of her concerts, and Liza was about to embark on her most important career move: she would star in a full-fledged Broadway production, *Flora, The Red Menace,* playing a naïve young woman who, through romance, gets caught up in Communist intrigue.

Liza had wanted the part ever since Fred Ebb, the show's lyricist, played her some of the songs he and his partner, John Kander, had written. Ebb had met Liza shortly after *Best Foot Forward,* and he remembers vividly the first impression she made: "I remember this shy, awkward girl coming into the room. She looked awful, like Raggedy Ann. Everything was just a little torn and a little soiled. She just sat there and stared at me, and I stared back."

Despite this, Ebb was captivated by Liza's eccentric energy, and it was he who worked with her on the voice and the delivery that had wowed the Palladium audience.

Now, she was auditioning for Ebb's show, but it wasn't his decision to make. The producer was Hal Prince, the director George Abbott. Abbott had seen Liza in *Best Foot Forward,* a show he had directed in its original 1941 run. He had not been impressed with Liza.

Dreadfully nervous, her nails chewed down to their nubs, Liza waited to come out before the assembled production team and prove that she *was* Flora. It seemed like an eternity before she was announced: "Liza Minnelli, *Best Foot Forward,* 'The Ed Sullivan Show,' Judy Garland and Vincente Minnelli's daughter."

Liza was in the middle of her first song when she heard Abbott mutter, "This is a waste of time." He was convinced Liza was not right for the part. "She's not what I had in mind. I don't think she'll be able to carry it."

He listened to the rest of Liza's audition halfheartedly, and she was thanked and dismissed. She was discouraged, but she wasn't going to give up. "Whenever there's something I want, really want, I persevere until I get it," Liza said. "I wanted to do *Flora* so badly that I just kept auditioning. I kept going back until they couldn't get rid of me."

Finally, after Eydie Gorme, Abbott's first choice, was unavailable, there was no one but Liza; everyone else wanted her, and Abbott relented.

Before long, Liza had won Abbott over completely: "I think she is the most wonderful girl, very vital and devoid of any pettiness. She's always on the job, she has an unerring instinct for what's true and right, and she's a quick study. I find her a delight."

The rest of the cast—including her leading man, Bob Dishy—shared Abbott's estimation of Liza. Fearful at first that Liza would throw her mother's weight around, they were relieved to discover that Liza was very much like them: nervous, unsure, working hard to make a good impression. But Liza did feel extra pressure on herself to be good, because of who she was: "Of course I've had to prove myself to some extent," she told Joanne Stang in The New York *Times* on May 9, 1965, "and that's kind of rough. People keep expecting you to live up to a legend, but if you keep thinking about that, you're dead. You can't put that responsibility on yourself. Anyway, your famous parents can open a lot of doors for you, but between 8 and 11 P.M. there's no pull. First of all, people aren't going to put $40,000 behind a name if there's nothing to back it up, if it's just a curiosity thing. Mr. Prince was not *about* to do anything like that. And Mr. Abbott has never once referred to my family. He's never once referred to . . . you know . . . to my mother. He's always respected me for myself."

Returning from a prolonged trip, a joyous Judy hugs Lorna and Joey as Mark Herron looks on, January 1965.

Liza rehearses her Broadway debut in *Flora, the Red Menace* with (left to right) producer Harold Prince, director George Abbott, co-star Bob Dishy, composer John Kander, and lyricist Fred Ebb.

A scene from *Flora*.

A scene from *Flora*.

Backstage after the show, Judy congratulates Liza on her performance.

Once *Flora, The Red Menace* opened at the Alvin Theater in New York on May 11, 1965, the critics began to respect Liza Minnelli for herself, too. Walter Kerr began his New York *Herald Tribune* Review, "Liza Minnelli, who no longer needs to be identified as Judy Garland's daughter and I apologize for just having done so, has many a fetching way about her. Her smile, for instance, is marvelously unsteady, always eager to shoot for the moon, always on the verge of wrinkling down to half-mast . . . she acts lyrics extremely well."

Variety's reviewer commented, "(Audiences) who expect just to ogle 'Judy Garland's daughter' should leave applauding an excellent on-her-own performance by the girl. Miss Minnelli has intriguing stage presence, a good voice, and a captivating manner . . . "

This time, Judy appeared for Liza's opening-night performance, and she and Mark attended the cast party afterwards (as did Vincente). Judy had not interfered in any way with Liza during rehearsals, but at one point in the run Liza received a call at the theater from a frantic New York hotel manager; Judy had locked Joey and Lorna out onto the hotel room terrace in freezing February weather. Would Liza come and help them? Liza was forced to interrupt a run-through to go to her siblings' aid; her feelings about the matter can well be imagined.

Ln June, Liza received one of Broadway's highest accolades: the Tony Award as Best Actress in a Musical. She was the youngest woman to ever receive the award. Judy Garland's daughter was well on her way to a brilliant show business career of her own.

On June 12, Judy was taken to the hospital by ambulance from her Brentwood home, suffering, it was reported, an "emotional upset" after "an allergic reaction" to a drug. In reality, she was attempting to withdraw once again from her dependence on pills, fearful that she would lose Mark Herron unless she did so. She remained in the hospital twelve days, then left to return to work because of the ever-increasing pile of debts which faced her.

Such attempts at detoxification were futile; Judy always returned to drug use. Now, her Jekyll and Hyde personality, her paranoia, her abusiveness with the people around her, increased. The ascent of Liza's show business star seemed directly the reverse of her own disintegration as a performer. Her concerts were too often canceled, her performances too often poor; there were instances of audience vitriol almost as bad as in Melbourne. She was still capable of a moving, toughed-out kind of concert, but her voice was not what it had been just two years before.

Her personal life became a series of failed relationships, bizarre events, court appearances. She married Mark Herron on November 14, 1965, but within six months they were separated; in her divorce deposition she claimed the marriage had never been consummated. She then became "engaged" to Tom Green, a young publicist whom she ultimately had arrested for stealing jewelry from her; the truth was that she had given two rings to Green to hock in order to raise money to pay her hotel bill; the management was threatening to lock Joey and Lorna out of their rooms. The case was thrown out of court but received a great deal of press attention.

Judy's unpredictability, the abuse and accusations she could heap on someone who had incurred her wrath, drove away from her most of the people who truly loved her. Old friends who had always been there for her before, no longer were; it was a form of masochism to try to help her, to care about her; and a form of self-defense to say to oneself, "I've done all I can. There's no more I can do for Judy." It would not be long before Liza would be forced to adopt this attitude herself.

To understand just how difficult it could be to be around Judy Garland during the middle and late 1960s, one need only talk to Alma Cousteline, Judy's maid from 1963 to 1967. A pleasant, loving woman in her seventies now, she takes in young children and cares for them in her home while their mothers are at work.

Alma recalls vividly Judy's treatment of Mark Herron. "Mark tried so hard to make a go with Judy. I like him very much. But she didn't want him to go after his own career. She didn't want him to get ahead of her. She felt that she wasn't working and she didn't want him to be the' man to make the money, so she would have to be under him."

Herron was rehearsing a play, and the prospect of it succeeding frightened Judy. "Judy would nag and bug him when he wanted to rehearse his lines, so finally Mark rented an apartment in the Hollywood area so he could be by himself, and she still wouldn't leave him alone."

Herron, too, came to be accused of stealing by Judy. She had a bag of money, amounting to twenty-eight thousand dollars, and one day she couldn't find it. "She accused everybody of stealing it," Alma says, "Mark, everybody." There was a great deal of tension in the household for several days. Then Alma had a rare opportunity to clean Judy's bedroom. "Her dressing room

Liza accepts her *Flora* Tony Award from Bert Lahr, 1965.

was in bad shape, because Judy couldn't stand to hear a carpet sweeper. The only way you could run a vacuum would be if Judy had to go to a doctor, or if someone took her for a ride. So her dressing room would get in such a shape. She would throw her nightgowns, everything she had on the floor, when she was up at night rambling, playing her records. I guess she must have been going through her act onstage—you know, dressing and redressing. She stayed in her room two or three days and you couldn't get in there. I'd spend hours and hang up her clothes and on Sunday I'd say, 'If she will sleep long enough for me to get into this room, then I could clean it up, vacuum it.'

"So finally I got my chance and I was cleaning her bathroom and I got under the sink and the money fell out so I went to Mr. Herron and I said, 'You know all that money that was lost that she was accusing everyone of taking—well, here it is.'"

Alma isn't sure why Judy had so much cash, but it wasn't unusual for her. "She would come out sometimes with great big handfuls of money. She would pay us in cash. She'd pay us by throwing the money at us and say, 'All you want is my money.' She wouldn't pay you like a person usually would get paid."

Alma recalls a particularly horrifying moment when she ran into Judy in the hall. "She was standing in front of the mirror with a razor blade in her hand, and she was cutting her face with it. And she says, 'Just look what that thing did to me,' and I said, 'What thing?' and she said 'Mark Herron' and cut herself again. I said, 'Oh, Miss Garland, don't do that, give me that razor blade.' And she said, 'Look, he cut me here, he cut me there.'

"Mr. Herron was in the bedroom and I ran to him and I said, 'Mr. Herron, get up and come out here because Miss Garland is standing in front of the mirror cutting her face.' He ran into the hallway and said to her, 'Judy, darling, just look what you're doing. Don't do that.' And the blood was just dripping down from these little cuts all over her face. He said, 'Just look what you've done to your beautiful face,' and she said, 'You did that,' and he looked so pathetic and said, 'Darling, I haven't done that.'"

Herron finally got Judy to stop what she was doing, but she began calling people—Tom Green, her friend John Carlyle, Peter Lawford, and telling them to come over. When they arrived, she showed them her cuts and said that Herron had done this to her. In each case, Alma had to tell them that it was not Herron's doing.

When Alma speaks of some of the things Judy would do to her servants, it seems incredible that they remained with her, in some cases for years. Lionel Doman, Judy's butler, while confirming Alma's stories, speaks with great affection for Judy. "The bad things she did, that was her head, not her heart. It was the drugs. At heart she was a wonderful woman, like a child, really, and very much in need of loving. I loved her very much."

Alma agrees. "I took her to heart," Alma says, "because in her condition she had no control over her life. It was really sad. I remember one time I took her down a tray of shrimp creole—she loved that—and she said, 'Oh, dear, you fix my tray so pretty.' I did it because I had respect for her. To make her feel good. And no sooner had I put the tray on the bed than she took all the food and threw it on the floor. Everything—peas, shrimp, rice. I attempted to clean it up and she said 'Get out!' So Lionel said, 'Let's go home,' and we went home.

"And Mrs. Chapman [the children's governess] called and said she had torn up everything in the living room—pictures of Kennedy—she idolized him—pictures of Joey, Lorna, Liza were all torn up. She tore up pillows, everything she could get her hands on. Joey called us, too. He, Mrs. Chapman and the rest hid in the hedge and Lionel and I came back and you never saw such a mess in your life. Dishes, pictures and everything out of the kitchen cupboards—she broke a gorgeous vase, silver and crystal. Lionel took pictures, because he didn't want her to accuse him of stealing what she broke."

All of Judy's servants took a great deal of abuse from her, and their duties were always far greater than their jobs should have entailed. But most of them stuck it out until Judy made it

167

impossible for them. Alma recalls the day Mrs. Chapman left. "I was in the back of the house doing some mending on the machine for the children and she came back and called us names and wanted to know what we were doing sitting on our fat behinds and I said 'I'm mending' and she looked at Mrs. Chapman and said, 'Well, what is that Texas bitch doing?' and Mrs. Chapman said, 'Miss Garland, I'm not a Texas bitch,' and Judy grabbed the hot iron and came after Mrs. Chapman with it and Mrs. Chapman said, 'Miss Garland, if you put that iron to me I swear I'll put it in your face.' I said, 'Miss Garland, don't do that, baby, give me the iron.' I got the iron from her and Judy told Mrs. Chapman to get out and Mrs. Chapman went to her room to pack and Judy was trying to get into the room. There was no reason for what Judy did. Mrs. Chapman left and she never did come back."

Mrs. Chapman wasn't replaced, and Alma recalls that Joey and Lorna suffered for it. "Those children were well cared for when Mrs. Chapman was there. She was like a mother. She saw to the clothes, food, recreation. She saw to them having a good time. They had a good life with her. That was the sad part. They didn't have a mother at all after she left. Mrs. Chapman used to get beautiful clothes for the children—after she left, the children went down, they grew out of their clothes, and so it got to the point where it was pathetic. I tried, I did the best I could for them—I cooked, washed, and ironed for them—but I couldn't be a mother to them. I had my own home and my husband to take care of. I couldn't do it."

Finally, things became untenable for Alma, too. "I remember that last day I worked for Judy. It was so hard to deal with her personality changes. I had brought some food down to her and she told me to have Lorna come to her bedroom and she was as sweet as pie. I told Lorna that her mother wanted to see her, and she didn't want to go. She was frightened and trembling and she said to me, 'Come with me, please' and I said, 'Okay, I'll go with you' and I said 'Miss Garland, Lorna is here and may we open the door please' and she said 'Yes' and Lorna went in and put on an act, saying, 'Hello, Mama. I'm so happy to see you. Oh, you look gorgeous' and her mother greeted her beautifully and I went up to get a vodka and tonic that Judy had asked me for and the minute I got back down to the room she said 'You big fat woman, get out of here' and I said 'You wanted the drink and here is your extra glass of ice' and I gave her that glass of vodka and she threw it on me—ice and all—and then she got up and ran into the dressing room and began banging on the doors and saying, 'Get out, get out of my house.'

"I had gotten sick of Judy—I thought, I'm not getting paid enough to go through this—so I left. And I didn't look back."

No matter how much one loved Judy at this point, it was often necessary—for one's sanity if nothing else—to separate oneself from her. Liza attempted to do this whenever possible. "When she's in a low period," Liza said, "I don't answer the telephone. Peter does . . . and keeps me from going off the deep end."

Despite Judy's proviso to Liza that her career goals would have to be accomplished with no money from Judy, Liza came to Judy's financial aid several times in the late sixties. But there had to be a cut-off point. John Carlyle recalls a telephone conversation in which Judy asked Liza for money, and Liza refused. Alma recalls another phone call: "Judy didn't hear from Liza much at all. She always avoided talking to her mother. Christina Smith, Liza's make-up lady, told Judy she would have Liza call her which Liza did and Judy was happy as can be. But from then on she didn't hear from her again until Liza was in Las Vegas and every time Judy tried to contact her, Liza would try to avoid her, so Judy would cry, cry, cry and say, 'Oh, my baby, how I love her' and said how she had brought her up and helped her start out on her own career. She said, 'I've done so much for her and she shouldn't put me down. Now I need her, I'm broke, I don't have anything. She should appreciate me, I'm her mother.'"

Another time, angry with Liza for refusing her money, Judy threatened to sue her for a million dollars, which was the amount of money she felt it had cost her to raise Liza. Nothing came of the threat.

Liza marries Peter Allen, March 3, 1967.

There were brief reunions, most notably for Liza's wedding to Peter Allen on March 3, 1967. Judy's airfare was paid for by Twentieth-Century Fox, since Judy would be doing publicity for her signing to do *Valley of the Dolls*. Liza sent Judy money for Joey and Lorna's passage, but Judy didn't have enough money to buy Liza a wedding present. With John Carlyle's help, Judy managed to come up with eighty-eight dollars between them, borrowing some cash from Alma and Lionel. They went to a Beverly Hills shop and picked out an Irish linen tablecloth they could afford, although it wasn't their first choice. The saleslady, aware of the dilemma, said, "But Miss Garland, you have a charge account with us."

Judy replied, "I do? How marvelous! All right, let's have the one you showed us first. And charge it!"

As they left the store, package in hand, Judy turned to John and giggled. "My God, when will they get their money? How will they get it?"

Judy and Joey flew to New York, followed by Lorna and Sid. The morning of the wedding, Judy called over to Vincente Minnelli's hotel room. They had not spoken in years ("Judy hated Vincente Minnelli," Alma says), and all Judy said to him when he answered the phone was, "If you had any class, you'd escort me to our daughter's wedding." And so they appeared together for the first time in sixteen years.

Peter and Liza set themselves up in Liza's New York apartment, and shared with Judy a brief happy period in her life. She was thrilled to be a mother-in-law, it was such a "normal" thing to be. And her career seemed to be on the verge of a new resurrection: she had been cast as Helen Lawson in the screen version of Jacqueline Susann's huge best seller, *Valley of the Dolls*.

Liza didn't want her mother to do it. Another character, Neely O'Hara, a drug-addicted cinema bitch goddess, was rumored to have been modeled after Judy, and the whole project just seemed sleazy to Liza. "Do you think the public would like to see you in that role?" she asked.

Judy reminded Liza that Louis B. Mayer didn't want her to do *A Star Is Born* because she would be playing the wife of an alcoholic, and when she produced the movie herself later, it became her greatest film triumph. She wanted the part, the challenge, the income and the comeback. She would do it.

But she couldn't. The pressures, the fears, were too much for her, and she realized that the film was going to be dreadful. She was in such a state during rehearsals that Lorna called Judy's doctor to say there was no food in the house and Mama needed medication and they were hungry and could he come over? On the set, a week's filming produced no usable footage. Finally, the producers had no recourse: they fired Judy and replaced her with Susan Hayward.

It was another defeat for Judy, and a very public humiliation. The press accounts said nothing about why Judy didn't want to do the film, just that she had been "unprofessional." Her nights became more sleepless, her demons more haunting. She wanted to prove to the world that she could still entertain; and she made another Palace comeback in late July, appearing with Lorna and Joey in a vaudeville turn that was astoundingly successful. Vincent Canby in the New York *Times* wrote, "The show that will occupy the Palace for the next four weeks is a top-notch vaudeville presentation, touched by the pathos of real-life soap opera . . . Her presence dominates the proceedings from the first note of the overture. That is, her presence and those sad and forlorn tales of her personal life that we all know so well and that inevitably color our reaction to her actual performances for better or for worse. Aside from the problems with her voice—and, let's face it, there are thousands of singers with voices, if that's all you want—Miss Garland was in fine fettle last night."

But she wasn't always in fine fettle; sometimes she would give good performances, sometimes poor ones. Other times, she wouldn't show up at all, prompting audience demands for refunds. Still, she completed 120 concerts between June 1967 and June 1969, the last two years of her life. Her financial problems were worse than ever; it was later charged that she had been swindled out of a great deal of money owed to her. She needed to work as often as possible,

Judy and Vincente attend Liza's wedding.

Lorna, Joey, and Judy in a publicity still for her final Palace engagement, July 1967.

both to support her children and pay her staggering bills, including the back taxes that always seemed to haunt her.

Sick or well, in good voice or bad voice, Judy Garland *had* to work. And her resiliency, her ability to perform well under the most adverse conditions, was truly amazing. Usually, her audiences were enraptured, either because she was giving a brilliant performance or because by sheer guts she was getting through a concert when she was obviously not up to being on that stage.

The grind was a terrible one, grueling and debilitating for her. She should have retired, or at least have worked a great deal less. But that was something she couldn't even consider.

For the next two years, Judy and Liza saw each other only intermittently. Sometimes, when Mama was in one of her "high" periods, they would socialize together; other times Liza would go to great lengths to avoid Judy.

Tom Green recalls pleasant evenings at Liza and Peter's New York apartment. "We'd all get together and there was a piano and they would all just sing and have a good time. It was very easygoing, there were no tensions, no problems. Liza cooked dinner and it was just like normal people getting together with their relatives for an evening."

Other times, though, Judy would pull her "stunts," the kinds of things Liza had referred to as "something she knew would make me nuts." Tom recalls the three of them attending a performance of *Mame,* then the biggest hit on Broadway. "The seats we got were not the best, and we were crowded into an extra row of seats. Judy didn't like that, so after intermission we tried to sit in the aisle and we got one of those uppity ladies who objected and the usherette said, 'You can't do that.'

"So we left. We didn't have a chance to tell Liza that we were leaving. And just to get back at the theater, Judy called the police while I was in the bathroom and told them that she had heard someone had planted a bomb in the theater and she was concerned because her daughter Liza was in there and would be killed. It was such a blatant bullshit story, they paid no attention to it. But just to make sure, when she went in the other room, I called the police back and told them it was just Judy being strange.

"But I was impressed that for her own personal reasons she was willing to say something that would be very embarrassing to Liza. She just didn't think before she did it. It would have been very embarrassing if the theater had been cleared and there was a big story in the newspapers and it was an obvious prank."

With Liza and Peter living in New York, Judy spent as much time in that city as she could, sometimes in hotel rooms, sometimes in a rented townhouse. Having her mother so near to her put tremendous strain on Liza; Judy's demands, her stunts, her need for constant attention were making it almost impossible for Liza to lead her life.

It got so bad at one point that Liza left instructions with the doorman of her building that Judy was not to be let up to see her unless Liza had left word in advance that she was expecting a visit from her.

Judy's life was clearly coming to an end. How, those around her wondered, could she have survived even this long? She worked herself to near exhaustion week after week. She was surrounded by sycophants and leeches, people who used her to make money for themselves. She continued to be battered by terrible financial news: the IRS was after her for over half a million dollars in back taxes, money she thought her "business managers" had paid.

She would set unrealistic goals for herself; she decided she wanted to replace Angela Lansbury in *Mame* on Broadway, and made a real effort to get the part, going so far as to audition in her townhouse for the producers. There was a great deal of interest on the part of the producers, but it was impossible: Judy Garland, having to function night after night in a book show, needing to remember lines and show up on time for the curtain? Her doctor and lawyer intervened and convinced the producers she could not handle the strain.

Liza in the TV presentation of "The Dangerous Christmas of Little Red Riding Hood," November 1965.

She was crushed by the clear implications. Her rages and irrationalities got worse. Once, she screamed at Lorna to make her bed. She did. A half hour later, an enraged Judy called Lorna back into the room. "I told you to make your bed. Why didn't you?" Dumbfounded, Lorna saw that Judy had torn the bed apart again. "Mama!" she cried out, unbelieving. But she made the bed again, as her mother watched.

Another time, at night, when Judy's demons were raging inside her, she rampaged around the house, breaking mirrors and vases, throwing things. Finally, she threw Lorna and Joey out of the house.

They went to Liza's apartment at two in the morning, ringing her doorbell until a barely awake Liza answered. "I expected this," she told them. "It's happened to me."

They talked about what was wrong with Mama. Joey piped up, "Maybe she's just lonely." All three of them, the children of Judy Garland, tried to understand this woman, tried to temper their hurt and anger with sympathy.

At 3 A.M., Judy called. Liza asked her what was happening. Judy accused her of stealing the children away from her, of turning their minds against her. "Mama, how can you say something like that?" Liza asked.

"That's right," Judy answered, "stay together, all three of you. Leave me all by myself here, I don't care." She hung up.

A few minutes later, she called back. This time, Joey answered, and Judy threatened to spank him if he and Lorna didn't come right home. By now, they were terrified. What would Judy do if they did go home? Peter took them over to Judy's by cab. When she came to the door, she hugged and kissed them as if they had been kidnapped and released, then turned on Peter. "Get out of my sight!" she raged at him, and slammed the door.

There were times, when Judy was in New York, that she would stay in one hotel and the children in another. Alma came to New York with Judy several times when her stay would be protracted, and she recalls nights when Judy called at three in the morning from her hotel room and asked that Joey be brought over to her. "She never asked for Lorna, but she wanted Joey to be with her. It was snowy and cold sometimes, and we'd have to bundle this sleepy little child up . . . and Joey would cry, 'Why do I have to go? I'm afraid.' And we would say, 'You know your mother isn't going to hurt you—go and be a little man and console your mother. That's what your mother wants you there for.' But he was scared to death. He was afraid of her behavior. But she did not abuse them, never. And I don't think she would have stood for anyone else abusing them."

Liza's star at this point was steadily ascending. She had four albums in release, selling well; she had played Little Red Riding Hood in a television special, "The Dangerous Christmas of Little Red Riding Hood," and she was becoming a much in-demand nightclub performer.

The contrasts between Judy and Liza were becoming starker and starker. Liza was wowing audiences with her energy and vocal power. Judy, while singing "What Now, My Love" at the Garden State Arts Center in Holmdel, New Jersey, in June 1968, slumped over from her sitting position and passed out, microphone still in her hand. Unable to waken her, the staff called an ambulance, and her fans watched as Judy was carried off on a stretcher.

After *Valley of the Dolls*, no one would hire Judy Garland for a motion picture again; she had made her last film in 1962. Liza's motion-picture career was just beginning. She had played a small role in the Albert Finney film *Charlie Bubbles*, and was now set to begin filming her first starring role, as Pookie Adams in *The Sterile Cuckoo*. It was a straight dramatic role, with no singing, despite the fact that Liza's reputation was being made as a singer and nightclub performer.

Her performance in *The Sterile Cuckoo* would make Liza Minnelli a major star, and win her an Academy Award nomination.

Judy Garland did not live to see the movie.

17

In June 1969, Liza was in New York, filming her second starring role, in Otto Preminger's *Tell Me That You Love Me, Junie Moon.* She had completed *The Sterile Cuckoo,* but it was not scheduled for release until the end of the year.

Liza had seen nothing of Judy for over six months; Judy had been in Europe until late May, when she returned to New York for a visit. She wanted to see Liza. Wendell Burton, Liza's costar in *Cuckoo,* recalls an evening in Liza's off-the-set apartment during which Judy called. "Liza's mood had been quite up and happy, but when Judy called, it changed. She got a little down. She said her mother wanted to come and visit her on the set, but she had asked her not to. She was afraid that having Judy around would ruin her concentration."

Judy was now living in London with her fifth husband, Mickey Deans. They had been married in March. Judy had met Deans, owner of the "in" New York discotheque Arthur, during a night out at his club. Judy had called Liza to invite her to the wedding. When she had extended a similar invitation to her wedding to Mark Herron, Liza had replied, "I can't come to your wedding, Mama. But I promise I'll come to the next one." But she didn't make it to this one either.

A lot of people couldn't make it to Judy's wedding. Out of a guest list of several hundred prominent people—a list released to the press—only fifty came to the reception, over half of those newsmen. Judy now had few people she could truly call friends, and many of them objected to her marriage to Deans, thinking him opportunistic and her foolish.

She and Deans set up house in London, and he began acting as her "manager," getting various bookings for her. He also hit upon the idea of allowing a Swedish documentary team to film Judy, almost around the clock, for a film about her Scandinavian tour. Judy did not like the idea, but both she and Deans were broke and needed the 50 percent of the film's earnings they had been promised.

It was a terribly ill-conceived plan, especially since Judy was in an increasingly desperate state. She was painfully thin, appearing corpselike; she was often so drugged she was unable to function; her concerts, while well-received by the Scandinavians, who had never seen her before, were more and more difficult for her to get through.

The film, Deans discovered, contained footage of Judy nude, as well as drugged and intoxicated. Deans realized he had made a mistake, and asked a court for an injunction against the film. He got it, but later the case was decided against him, and he and Judy were slapped with court costs. Only a little used copyright law prevented the film from being shown.

Deans had dozens of ideas for exploiting the fame of Judy Garland; he convinced her to fly to New York with him in June to discuss a chain of Judy Garland cinemas. He was not able to put the deal together, and Judy spent her forty-seventh birthday in a stranger's apartment, in bed most of the day. Joey and Lorna were in California. Liza was busy making a movie, unwilling to allow her to visit the set.

Liza did see her in Manhattan during this stay, and she was shocked not only by her appearance, but by her bearing: she seemed like an entirely different woman, a little old lady resigned to a life of quiet rest rather than the vibrant, partying-all-night Mama she had known. For the first time in Liza's life, Mama seemed defeated.

176

Judy marries Mickey Deans in London, March 15, 1969.

Mickey and Judy returned to London on June 14. In the early morning hours of June 22, Judy's friend John Carlyle decided to give her a call. It was 10 o'clock Sunday morning in London, and Mickey Deans answered the phone. John asked for Judy, and Mickey replied that he didn't know where she was, she might be in the bathroom. He would have her call John back.

Mickey got up, and saw that the bathroom door was closed. He called Judy's name, but got no answer. The door was locked, and no response came to his pounding and shouting.

He went outside, climbed onto a section of roof from which he could look in the window, and saw her. She was sitting on the toilet, her head down on her chest. He climbed through the window and tried to rouse Judy. It was then that he knew she was dead. He unlocked the door, called an ambulance, then returned John Carlyle's call. "John," Mickey said into the phone. "Judy's dead."

Liza was in Southampton, Long Island, that Sunday, taking a weekend vacation from filming. Peter, his sister, and a friend were with her. A phone call came, Peter took it. He then walked into their bedroom and told Liza she should wake up, there was something he had to tell her.

She knew something was dreadfully wrong, and she blurted out, "My father's dead." To her, Judy dying was inconceivable. She had too much resiliency, had bounced back too many times, had been pronounced dead and survived.

When Peter told her the news, she began to hyperventilate, feeling as though she had just done a grinding dance number on stage. She thought immediately of Joey and Lorna, tried to call them, but got no reply. Then she thought to herself that she must have an autopsy done, so the world—and Joey and Lorna—would know that Mama hadn't killed herself. She couldn't have done that, Liza knew, in spite of all the attempts and all the phony attempts.

Everyone had to get back to New York. Liza knew that she would have to be the person to keep everything together with Mama dead, just as she had so often kept everything together while Mama lived. She stole a few minutes alone, sitting on the lawn of the house at which she was a guest.

Her mind was a jumble, thinking about Mama and all the craziness, all the fun, all the laughing, all the amazing things that had happened to them, all the love they felt, in spite of everything. She remembered only the good times; she didn't want to dwell on the bad. *Mama was always there,* she thought to herself. She was always there for me. *And she loved all of us so much.* Now, she was gone forever.

Liza almost broke down, and she would come close again and again over the next few days. But she vowed to herself that she would be strong for Mama. She would do this right. Judy Garland would be laid to rest with dignity. The world would know that her children loved her, that she deserved to be honored in death for the woman she was. Liza would not allow any negatives.

Liza spoke to Mickey Deans in London, and it seemed as though that he was so devastated by Judy's death that he could not be relied upon to make any arrangements. Liza knew she would have to be in charge. She got through to Sid, Joey, and Lorna, who had already heard the news. She told them, "Mama wanted to be cremated." But Sid was aghast at the idea, and Joey and Lorna began to cry. Liza felt that her mother, knowing the reaction of her children, would have agreed to a traditional funeral. And there was by now a great outpouring of public sympathy for Judy. There would have to be a service, a chance for her fans to pay their last respects to Judy. "I can't let people not see her," Liza told the press. "But I intend that it be done with dignity."

Liza then called her father in Los Angeles. He greeted her happily, pleased to be hearing from his now very busy daughter. There was silence on the other end, then Liza managed to say, "Daddy, Mama died today."

Kay Thompson, Lorna, Liza, and Peter Allen leave the New York funeral parlor where Judy's services have just taken place.

Vincente replied, "Oh, darling . . . I'm so sorry." Minnelli recalled being impressed with Liza's stoicism. "Liza was in total control, almost philosophical. But she was also concerned about the job that had to be done.

"Over the next day and a half, Liza would periodically call to tell me what she'd arranged," Vincente said, "and to ask if I thought it was right. 'Are you coming to the funeral?' she asked.

" 'Darling . . . I can't.' Liza sensed how awkward I would feel with news photographers around, trying to maneuver all of Judy's ex-husbands so that they could be photographed together. She allowed me to grieve in my own way."

Judy's funeral was held in Manhattan, at the Frank E. Campbell funeral home, at Madison Avenue and Eighty-first Street. Over a twenty-four-hour period, twenty-two thousand people filed past Judy's open coffin, some weeping, others gently touching the mahogany casket, others laying flowers.

James Mason delivered the eulogy, and the mourners banded together to sing "Battle Hymn of the Republic," the song Judy had sung on TV in tribute to John F. Kennedy after his assassination.

While the public paid its respects to Judy, Liza's wish was realized: a London coroner ruled that Judy's death was not a suicide, but an "incautious self-overdosage of Seconal" which had raised the barbiturate level in her body beyond its tolerance.

On June 27, the funeral was over. Judy Garland's family dispersed, her fans went back to their normal routine. But for Liza, things would never be the same. "When Mama died," she said later, "I first went through shock. Then I felt a strange exultation . . . as if Mama's death had suddenly freed her spirit, and her spirit was really with me."

Perhaps Liza's own spirit, too, had been freed. Now, at last, she could truly become her own woman. But in the strange way things have of coming full circle, she could now finally accept with gratitude the reality she had sometimes fought so hard against.

"I know my mother was a great star and a great talent," she said shortly after Judy's death. "But I am not thinking about those things today. What I am thinking about is the woman, my mother, and what a lovely, vital and extraordinary woman she was.

"It is because of my memory of that woman that all my life I will be proud to say, 'I am Judy Garland's daughter.' "

EPILOGUE:
AFTER JUDY

"It never crossed my mind that I would grow up to 'be' my mother till people told me so and made me afraid of it."

—Liza Minnelli

Liza in *New York, New York*, 1977.

18

If Liza had expected that with Judy's passing she would be able to become her own woman, she soon realized that she would never be able to erase completely from the public's mind her identification as Judy Garland's daughter. For even as she was becoming a superstar in her own right, developing a strong, trend-setting public image, winning Tonys, an Emmy, and an Oscar, still her mother was never far from her side.

Magazine and newspaper profiles of Liza throughout the early seventies always made reference to Judy, usually in their headlines: "Liza: 'Some people will always look for Mama in me,' " "Liza Minnelli: Winning Garlands on Her Own," "Liza Minnelli: The Lies About Mama and Me."

Once Liza had established herself as a major public personality in her own right, however, she was less concerned about constant references to her mother. She had discovered who she was, and part of who she was was Judy Garland's daughter: "At one point in my life it really bothered me when they compared me to my mother, when people were reliving their youth through me and were not getting what I was trying to get across," Liza told Craig Zadan for *After Dark*. "I could always tell, there'd be a room full of 150 people and there would be one person who just didn't want to know what I had to offer, but was there to recapture that moment of their childhood. But then I realized, well, why not? My job is to give pleasure and I had no right to let that kind of person upset me. I'm very fulfilled in what I'm doing. When people tell me that my performing is so much like my mom's I don't get upset. I'm proud. My God, there was nobody on earth like Mama."

Over the course of the fourteen years since Judy died, though, Liza has become more and more like her mother. The similarities, both in their careers and their private lives, are in some cases quite obvious, in others less so—but they are always startling.

The most intriguing career parallel is that both Judy and Liza were unable to follow up their greatest cinema triumph with anything nearly as successful. After *A Star Is Born*, Judy did not make another film for six years, and her last few starring films were not financial winners. Her greatest successes after *A Star Is Born* were on the concert stage.

Liza's dazzling performance in *Cabaret* earned her an Oscar and international superstar status. But her next three films were ignominious failures at the box office and, like her mother, her career at this point consists largely of concert appearances.

In their personal lives, the similarities between Judy and Liza are striking. Like her mother, Liza is highstrung, nervous, full of energy and terrified of being alone. Like Judy, she loves night life and partying.

Both Judy and Liza were very insecure about their looks as young girls; Liza frequently referring to herself as "The Queen of Ugly," and both sought the attentions of attractive men as evidence of their desirability.

Like Judy, Liza is surrounded by gay men while seemingly harboring personal disdain for homosexuality, and married a man rumored to be gay. And, most disturbing, there have been persistent rumors of drug and alcohol problems surrounding Liza, rumors she has consistently denied. In the first several years after Judy's death, Liza's interviews concerning Judy took on the tone of public psychiatric sessions; Liza often appeared to be working out her feelings about her mother as the tape recorder whirled:

"Do I have to talk about her anymore? I don't know what else to say. Can't people accept that? Why do they want me to be the keeper of the flame and the destroyer of the myth at the same time? People are wishing things on me. It never crossed my mind that I would grow up to 'be' my mother till people told me so and made me afraid of it . . . I loved her in so many ways. She was a friend of mine—a trying friend, but a friend . . . This is what I tell myself: She did everything she ever wanted to do. She never really denied herself anything for me. See, I say, she had a wonderful life—she did what she wanted to do. And I have no right to change her fulfillment into my misery. I'm on my own broom now.

"When talking about Mama you have to understand one thing: I'm very sensitive and I'm also fairly intelligent. But if I get into a more sensitive topic, then *that* takes over from the intelligence. I'll be wafting along and everything is fine, then something will click and it's too close to home and it hurts. You can't have a relationship like that with someone and discuss it at length with anybody without it touching you. It's very special to me. It's something that no one will ever understand."

Less than four months after Judy's death, Liza Minnelli finally came into her own professionally with the release of *The Sterile Cuckoo*. The public and critics were enraptured by Liza's touching portrayal of a vulnerable young college girl experiencing her first love affair. She didn't sing a note, and her reviews spoke of a budding *actress:* "The screen has a big and important new star in Liza Minnelli," the *Motion Picture Herald*'s reviewer proclaimed. "She . . . gives a dramatic performance of the sort that wins Academy Awards . . . Here she is wistful; there she is funny; sometimes she is both. At times she is strikingly reminiscent of her mother . . ."

The Los Angeles *Times:* "Her performance is so strong and so compelling that nothing else about *The Sterile Cuckoo* concerns us very much . . . Warmth, vulnerability, resilience and independence, a need to love and also a capacity to love. These qualities cling to Miss Minnelli as cashmere clung to the stars of an earlier day."

Barely had her new film opened than Liza flew to Paris for a triumphant concert appearance at the Olympia. The French loved her, her performing style having taken on new depth and maturity, and they soon dubbed her "la petite Piaf Americaine."

It was heady praise coming from the French, and the first time Liza had been compared to anyone but Judy.

Once she returned to Hollywood, Liza learned she had been nominated for an Oscar for *The Sterile Cuckoo*. She had to share the news with her husband over the phone—he remained in New York, gamely trying to make some career headway on the New York club scene.

A separation for Liza and Peter was close at hand. They no longer moved in the same circles (if indeed they ever really had); each had a difficult time adjusting to the other's group of friends. "I hated Peter's friends and he disliked mine," Liza would say. "The only person I loved and trusted was Fred Ebb. I'm sure Peter misunderstood my devotion to Fred, just as I distrusted his coterie of acquaintances."

Peter's "coterie of acquaintances" was largely gay, and the fact was not unreported. In a *Rolling Stone* profile of Liza, Tom Burke reported the following scene which took place not long after Judy's death: "No one was speaking at all. The radio played an opulent orchestration of 'Sad, Rainy Day.' 'You know,' Peter remarked quietly, to no one, 'that is really *quite* a well-written song.' 'Yeah,' Liza said flatly. 'It's the fags' national anthem.' Nobody laughed."

After their separation, Liza would have a fling with musician Rex Kramer, which made news. Talking about it in *Time* magazine, Peter Allen made an extraordinary comment: "Rex was exactly opposite from me. He was a country boy who hated the city and loved girls."

Later, Liza would describe her marriage to Peter as "horrible"; asked by an interviewer to discuss their sex life, she refused, saying: "That's one of the demons, honey."

Peter's sexuality, though, was only part of the problem. As Liza would admit later, they were living out the script of *A Star Is Born.* "Everything was good for about a year and a half

Liza and Wendell Burton in *The Sterile Cuckoo*.

because we talked to each other all the time. But when my work went up and he was having trouble, the guilt I felt made me terribly unhappy. And the strain he felt trying to make me not unhappy . . . well, it just got so complicated that we suddenly stopped talking. That was the saddest part, losing communication with your best friend."

Breaking up with Peter, Liza feels, freed him to succeed: "The minute I left, he started writing marvelous songs." Today, Peter Allen is a singer-songwriter who recently sold out Radio City Music Hall with a one-man show and won an Oscar in 1982 for co-writing the theme song from Liza's movie *Arthur*, "Best That You Can Do." By all accounts, he and Liza are still friendly, but not close; he told Alan Ebert in *Us* magazine: "A friend is someone you can call up on the phone. You can't call Liza. Liza's a star."

A few days after the 1970 Academy Award ceremonies, Liza officially announced the separation. The Best Actress Oscar that year went to Maggie Smith in *The Prime of Miss Jean Brodie,* and newspaper headlines were not kind: "LIZA LOSES OSCAR, HUSBAND."

It was about this time that rumors of Liza's drug use began surfacing. She had been in a motorcycle accident a few days before the Oscar ceremonies, and despite twenty-nine stitches in her face and a broken tooth, she was determined to attend the event. Her doctor gave her a painkiller which left her glassy-eyed and a little disoriented at the awards, fueling the speculation. "The doctor had given me something," she said later. "He said it was a mild painkiller. But I never take pills—even one aspirin knocks me out. So I sat there not knowing what was going on."

She would frequently have to deny rumors: She got defensive with the New York *Times* sometime later: "Look: I'm *terrified* of any kind of drugs. Why, I don't even enjoy drinking. Oh, I may have one on occasion [but] I don't like anything that screws up my self-control, anything that dulls my senses. I think if God has given you a talent, you have a duty to develop that talent, that it's a crime to do anything which destroys it. You're not *allowed* to do that."

Liza very skillfully told her public exactly what it wanted to hear from Judy Garland's daughter. The rumors subsided, for the time being.

Memories of Judy's death came back rudely in July, when the National *Enquirer* ran a blazing front page headline: "More than a year after her death, Judy Garland is still not buried." The story went on to say that Judy's body had been stored in a temporary crypt, and no one had come forward to pay the expense of moving her to a permanent resting spot at Ferncliff Cemetery in Ardsley, New York. Horrified by the news, Liza said she was under the impression that Judy's husband, Mickey Deans, had made the necessary arrangements. Deans claimed to have no money. After several months, the money was raised and Judy was properly buried.

Deans was quoted in the *Enquirer* as saying that Judy had died a million dollars in debt. Reports were that Liza spent several years helping to pay off her mother's debts.

Liza's next film, Otto Preminger's *Tell Me That You Love Me, Junie Moon,* was not the critical or commercial success that *The Sterile Cuckoo* had been. But Liza had little time to worry: she was about to begin her first musical, playing a part she had wanted to do on Broadway years earlier: Sally Bowles in *Cabaret.*

It was the opportunity of a lifetime, and Liza knew it. The Sally Bowles character had been immortalized in Christopher Isherwood's *Berlin Stories* and the Broadway show had been a big success. But more than that, Liza saw a great deal of herself in Sally, just as she had in Pookie Adams of *The Sterile Cuckoo.* Sally's devil-may-care, one-day-at-a-time attitude, despite the growing menace of Naziism in Germany, appealed to Liza. She understood this character, she liked her: "Sally is a girl who improvises her whole life, and her fantasy of tomorrow is so strong that she really can't take a good look at *now* . . . Sally wanted to be everybody but herself. [But] I think she is eternal. That's what attracted me. There will always be a Sally Bowles somewhere or other. I see her as a reflection of many tragic figures . . . I agree with Mama in one sense. I don't

186

Liza as Sally Bowles in *Cabaret*, 1972.

Cabaret.

Liza and Michael York in *Cabaret*.

think that anybody who's really interesting is problemless. But they try to cope with [their troubles], deal with them, overcome them. That touches me . . . They're the kind of people that I want to do justice to—that I respect."

During the filming of *Cabaret* in Germany, Rex Kramer visited the set until he was barred because he'd become an unwelcome distraction. They had been together a year, but Liza wanted to end the relationship. "He said he'd leave me only if I fell in love with somebody else," she said. So she invented a new lover and told Kramer they were through. He wasn't convinced, and became one of the very few of Liza's ex-beaux to bad-mouth her to the press.

Describing grand tantrums in which Liza would "literally rave, then collapse," the jilted suitor bitterly summoned up demons from Liza's past. "She would worry about not sleeping and would start taking downers to help herself," he said. "The pace she sets for herself is simply terrific, but she just can't slow down."

Soon afterward, Kramer's wife would file a half-million-dollar lawsuit against Liza for "alienation of affections" and "criminal conversation" (adultery). The suit was settled out of court, but Liza was livid. "I knew he was using me," she fumed, suspecting that the suit had been a plot hatched between Mr. and Mrs. Kramer.

Cabaret took six intensive months to film, with brilliant director Bob Fosse pushing Liza to the limit of her talents. When it was over, she was exhausted, and took a vacation with co-star Marisa Berenson at Deauville on the French Riviera. Berenson introduced Liza to cafe society, and made her a part of the jet set, old money, and European royalty. She felt intimidated and inadequate, but the cream of society was charmed by her buoyancy and wit, and were themselves impressed to meet *her;* after all, her family ties made her the closest thing to royalty America would have. Liza became a treasured member of the international set of Beautiful People.

Liza's next romance would bolster her reputation as something of a *Don Juana.* She met and fell in love with the handsome eighteen-year-old son of another show business legend, Lucille Ball. Liza and Desi Arnaz, Jr., shared a desire to be seen as individuals apart from their famous parents; young Desi and his mother were estranged over a series of rebellions on Desi's part, including an affair with actress Patty Duke which produced a child. One of Liza's goals in the first few months of the relationship was to encourage him to patch things up with his mother. "I was raised with so much drama, I don't crave it," she would say.

Lucy, happily, approved of Liza, and the February 1972 premiere of *Cabaret* in Los Angeles found Desi (now Liza's fiancé), Lucy, Lucy's husband Gary Morton, and Liza's father at her side. The evening was a dazzling triumph for Liza. *Cabaret* was acknowledged as one of the best musicals in Hollywood history, and her performance, both musically and dramatically, drew raves the effusiveness of which had rarely been seen in Hollywood before.

The film established Liza as a superstar, and as a fashion trendsetter, a reflection of the youthful dissatisfactions of her time. Sally Bowles, as interpreted by Liza, was not just a character but a symbol, and so did Liza become one. She achieved the rare status of being featured on the covers of *Time* and *Newsweek* in the same week, both headlines alluding to Judy Garland: "A Star Is Born: Liza Minnelli in *Cabaret,*" and "Liza Minnelli: The New Miss Show Biz."

The references to Judy no longer really mattered: Liza was one of the biggest stars in the country, and she *had* done it on her own.

There was never any doubt that Liza would be nominated for an Oscar, but it was far from certain that she would win. As sometimes happens, there were no fewer than four female performances in 1972 worthy of an Oscar: Liza's, Diana Ross's in *Lady Sings the Blues,* Cicely Tyson's in *Sounder* and Liv Ullmann's in *The Emigrants.*

Liza attended the 1973 ceremonies with Desi and her father, wanting the award badly but never able to put far from her mind her memories of how much Judy had deserved an Oscar for *A Star Is Born* and hadn't won it. She was wracked by nerves and a negative attitude.

190

At a party with fiancé Desi Arnaz, Jr., 1972.

Nineteen seventy-two was also the year of *The Godfather,* the critically acclaimed drama that had set a new all-time box-office record, and dramas traditionally do much better at Oscar time than musicals. So it was a great surprise that Academy members voted for *Cabaret* over *The Godfather* in every major category except Best Picture. By the time the Best Actress Oscar was about to be announced, *Cabaret* had won eight Oscars, *The Godfather* just two: Best Screenplay and Best Actor for Marlon Brando. Things looked good for Liza.

But even at her supreme moment of triumph, a little something was taken away from her. Rock Hudson, prompted by cue cards, read off her name as a nominee and added, "This is a horserace, and bloodlines count. Liza's got the bloodlines."

The writers may have been well-meaning, but Liza wasn't happy. "I didn't much like that one thing said last night," Liza told the press. "That performance was *mine.* And when I said to them, 'Thank you for giving *me* this award, you've made *me* very happy,' I meant the emphasis right where I put it."

A star (and award winner) on Broadway and in movies, Liza also scored big on television in her second special, "Liza with a Z," also directed by Bob Fosse. Critically acclaimed, it won Liza an Emmy Award.

Liza's affair with Desi Arnaz ended during the spring of 1972, and she was then linked romantically with Ben Vereen and Edward Albert. But it wasn't until Liza went to London the first week of May, 1973, for concert appearances that her next real romance developed. She had been attracted to men her own age or younger, but this time it was someone quite a few years older: Peter Sellers.

The British press had a field day with the story, hounding the couple to distraction. Liza complained, " . . . So there I'd be in a hotel or something and you hear 'knock, knock' on the door and you say 'Who is it?' And someone says, 'Room service,' and you open the door and—twelve people with cameras flashing in your face. I called up Peter and I said, 'Peter! I can't get out of the *house!*' and Peter said 'Neither can I.' So then I'd go downstairs and they'd all be following me and asking me questions and I'd say, 'Oh, blah blah blah,' and they'd call it a press conference! I was just trying to get them off my back. I would just tell them, 'Look, I fell in love with a lovely man. Now please go away.' And then they'd ask if we were going to get married. Well, that's bloody private!"

Liza did say a while later that she and Peter planned to wed, but a little over a month into the mercurial affair, they decided to call it quits. Liza was clearly a tempestuous young lady, and while the press loved it, her friends wondered about the stability of her emotional life.

Her career, in concerts at least, was in high gear: she won raves wherever she appeared. There were reports that she and her father were planning to film a biography of Zelda Fitzgerald, but Zelda's daughter objected, and the project was dropped. Vincente kept looking for a suitable property in which he could direct his daughter.

While on tour in Canada, Liza received a telephone call from producer/director Jack Haley, Jr., whose father had been the Tin Man in *The Wizard of Oz.* She vaguely remembered Haley from her teenage years in Hollywood. He was working on a compilation film about the MGM musicals.

In an interview about the movie, *That's Entertainment,* Liza recalled, "I was working in Toronto when [Jack] called me. He had been going through some of Mama's films and, at the end of *In the Good Old Summertime,* had come across a frame of me being held up by Mama and Van Johnson. He said, 'Why don't you come down and see it and the rest of the picture?'

"I didn't want to do it at first, because I hate anything that smacks of exploitation of my family. [And I thought] I really couldn't handle all that tribute stuff about Mama. But then my father told me, 'This guy is good and you should at least look at what he's done.' So I did. I went to Metro and Jack met me and said, very blasé, 'I've got something to show you.' What a con

Vincente congratulates Liza on her Best Actress Oscar, 1973.

man! . . . I saw the shot with me in it. Then he showed me the rest of *That's Entertainment*, with Mama dancing and singing in all those films. Well, of course, I'd seen a lot of them already, but all together like that . . . it was too much. I couldn't handle it at first. I just howled. They had to stop the film, and I went outside with Jack.

"We'd walk and talk and then go back and see some more clips. And then I'd have to stop again, so we'd walk around for a while and then I'd go back for more. It was just so damn sensitive. . . . It was like watching my parents' lives go by up there on the screen. I'd never seen my mother singing with her sisters before and then there was all my dad's work . . . and at the end, me, as a baby. It just broke me up. I cried and cried."

Liza was impressed with the care and taste that Haley had used to re-create the MGM years, and she agreed to narrate one of the segments of the film.

She and Haley began dating, but Liza was too busy for the romance to get very serious at first. In January 1974, she broke Broadway records with a three-week stand at the Winter Garden Theater in New York, a one-woman show which won her a special Tony Award. After the show closed in New York, Liza took it to Las Vegas and four other cities, appeared at the 1974 Academy Awards, then returned to Vegas. There, her pace caught up with her: her doctor ordered her confined to bed. She stayed there one day, then was off on a cross-country tour, a trip to Spain, and then back to perform in Toronto.

Liza Minnelli was becoming known as one of the most successful—and certainly the most indefatigable—concert performers in history.

Liza's romance with Jack Haley, twelve years her senior, heated up. She found him sensitive, caring, mature, *settled*. Like Judy, Liza craved domesticity, "normalcy" as much as she desired night life and the spotlight. At this point in her life, the desire to settle down was predominant. She was twenty-eight years old, one of the world's biggest stars, but she had not experienced lasting love. She and Haley decided to be married.

She was still not divorced from Peter Allen. They'd been married seven years, separated for four. Peter commented, "When you've been separated longer than you were married, it's time to get a divorce."

The knowledge that Dorothy's little girl was going to marry the Tin Man's son garnered snickers in some of the more cynical Hollywood corners, but to Liza and Jack it was a beautiful thing. His engagement ring to her was a five-carat emerald; her wedding dress was a bright yellow. They might as well have some of the magic for themselves, and follow their own Yellow Brick Road to the wonderful Emerald City.

They were married on September 15, 1974, in Santa Barbara, California. Sammy Davis, Jr., was the best man and his wife, Altovise, the matron of honor. Fred Ebb gave the bride away. The couple's parents remained in Los Angeles preparing for the reception.

When Liza emerged from her limousine after the ninety-minute ride back to Los Angeles, the first glimpse many people would get was of her ruby red shoes. Liza's favorite designer, Halston, had recreated the famed jeweled slippers from *The Wizard of Oz*. Clearly, any aversion Liza once had to being compared to her mother was disappearing.

Haley was an emotional refuge for Liza. "Jack is so big," Liza said. "He's a corner I can hide in . . . He's a joy to live with . . . When I wake up alone in a strange city and Jack's not in bed to hold on to, I get terrified. I'm frozen when I'm not with somebody I know and love . . . It's nice to have someone to take the hurt away."

Seemingly, Liza's success had not driven away her "demons." She needed protection, and she found it with Haley. That he was a father figure to her can be surmised by a magazine interview published in 1975. The author reported that during her visit with Liza, she referred to Haley twice as "Daddy" and several times as "Vincente."

The latter term may have been an in joke for the couple, since Haley had once said he was

194

Liza with Peter Sellers in London as they make their romance public, May 1973.

Liza and Jack Haley, Jr., are married in Santa Barbara, September 15, 1974.

Liza in *Lucky Lady*, 1975.

unconcerned with being overshadowed by his wife's career: "If somebody ever said to me, 'Mr. Minnelli, could I have your autograph?', I'd sign *Vincente* and be proud."

Liza's reaction? "Isn't that gorgeous?"

In terms of cinema, Liza Minnelli's career began to fade with her next picture, *Lucky Lady,* co-starring Gene Hackman and Burt Reynolds. The filming, in an underdeveloped area of Mexico, was a nightmare for the entire crew. And despite the fact that Liza was a newlywed, rumors began appearing in print that she was having an affair with her playboy leading man, Reynolds. Liza was frustrated and annoyed.

"Burt was going with *Lorna,* and when he said to me 'Look, Dinah [Shore] and I are breaking up,' I went, 'Oh, no! Couldn't you wait until after the movie, Burt? *Please.* Because I'm gonna get the rap, I *know* it.' Because I get blamed for *everything!* So Jack came down every single weekend. We were trying to counteract what we knew would inevitably happen. And it did, sure enough . . . Taking the rap for my sister—I kept saying to her, 'Lorna, will you please come out of the closet with this thing?' I could have *killed* her. Do other people know it's not the truth? I don't want people to think I'm cheating on my husband."

Lucky Lady was a box-office failure, an especially ignominious one, since it was Liza's first film since *Cabaret.* But Liza wasn't too worried; no one can have a hit every time out, and besides, she and her father had finally found the right vehicle in which to team for the very first time.

It was something of a dream come true for Liza to work with Vincente, and she was excited about the project: she and Ingrid Bergman would co-star in *A Matter of Time,* the story of a young servant girl who meets an aged contessa and relives her glamorous life as the contessa recounts it.

There was another reason Liza wanted to do the film: to prove that her father still had what it takes. He hadn't made a film for six years (Barbra Streisand's *On a Clear Day You Can See Forever*) and there was some concern that his faculties weren't as sharp as they had been. Indeed, a journalist visiting the set in Italy wrote that Minnelli was "one of those people who gives the impression of being there, but is not actually present."

Publicly, Liza came to her father's defense, but privately she was very worried. The film did not seem to be coming out well; she feared he was losing control of the production. In tearful transatlantic phone calls she would tell friends she thought her father was becoming senile.

When American International Pictures saw Minnelli's version of the film, executives were not pleased. They significantly re-edited the movie, but it did little good. The reviews were scathing: The Los Angeles *Free Press* review began, "If Liza Minnelli wasn't so talented, I would say in *A Matter of Time* her career could end. This film is such an embarrassment to everyone involved (except Bergman) that it makes *Lucky Lady* seem like *Gone With the Wind.*"

Liza took her frustration out on American International Pictures, enlisting the help of some of Hollywood's biggest creative names especially Martin Scorsese, to take out a full-page ad in the Hollywood trades protesting AIP's wresting of creative control from Minnelli. It was little solace. In a town where the maxim "You're only as good as your last picture" is gospel, Liza Minnelli now had two strikes against her, and her last hit had been almost four years earlier.

Once again, an exciting project took her mind off her disappointment. She signed to make *New York, New York,* a realistic dramatic musical—much like *Cabaret*—with one of Hollywood's hottest young directors, Martin Scorsese. She would play a young big-band singer in the years after World War II, opposite Robert De Niro, one of Hollywood's best young actors. Once again, it was an actress's dream come true.

Judy Garland would be at her daughter's side all through the making of this "film noir" musical. On the surface, Liza's character, Francine Evans, bore little resemblance to her mother; she was closer to Doris Day, in her pre-Hollywood days. But *New York, New York* represented Judy's era, and Liza's characterization would owe much to the essential spirit of her mother.

Ingrid Bergman and Liza in Vincente Minnelli's *A Matter of Time*, 1976.

The filming took place entirely within the confines of the MGM lot, the first time Liza had made a completely "Hollywood" film. Her dressing room had once been her mother's, and her hairdresser had done Judy's coiffures.

On film, Liza looked—and acted—more like Judy than ever before. Martin Scorsese commented, "You put a wig on her and she looks like her mother! What can I tell you?" The period styles did indeed evoke Judy, but it is much to Liza's credit that her vocal renditions were reminiscent more of the typical touring big-band white-girl singer of the late 1940s. Her usual brassy style was considerably toned down for the realities of character and period.

At the end of the film, however, after many years have passed and we are in the fifties, Francine Evans has become a star. She is singing "New York, New York" on a concert stage and it is Judy Garland up there. It is the closest Liza has ever come to giving an *impression* of her mother, and it is almost eerie. *Variety* would comment, "Minnelli is so much like her mother . . . Reincarnation is really the only word."

Liza's dramatic performance in *New York, New York* is among her best; she was caught up in the intense creative energy between close friends De Niro and Scorsese. "It's a whole new way for me," Liza said. "I couldn't get away with a thing. Bobby and Marty are this *force*, this energy. It's watch-out-pal-or-you'll-get-run-over. And this went on for 22 weeks. It's the only film I can remember that I never sat down between shots."

In several important ways, however, *New York, New York* was a production out of control. At the end of filming, Scorsese had over four-and-a-half hours of film; he edited that down to a more manageable 163 minutes, then had to remove another eleven minutes at his studio's request. The film was released in June of 1977, to decidedly mixed reviews. Most audiences did not like the film, or De Niro's considerably unappealing leading man. Even Liza's wonderful performance, and glowing reviews for it, couldn't help the film at the box office. It was her third financial failure in a row.

It would prove the undoing of her film career. Liza did not make another movie until *Arthur,* in 1981, in which she would play a supporting role. But she can be justly proud of her performance in *New York, New York.* She would in fact say that it, more than any other, was the movie she most would have liked her mother to see. "I thought the acting there was my best. It was the first time I got to play the *sane* one. Why wasn't it a great success? Because I honestly think that everyone thought it was going to be something that it wasn't. It's a sub-culture film about musicians, and they advertised it as a big Hollywood musical. And it's a very stylized, very dark film, in that atmosphere where everything was always supposed to be perfect. I admire it greatly."

During the filming, the inevitable romance rumors again swirled, this time linking Liza and Scorsese. They were again vehemently denied, but when Liza began to take a musical production, *The Act,* to Broadway, and Scorsese stepped in as director during out-of-town try-outs, the rumors began again. This time, to the public they appeared to have been true: Scorsese's marriage broke up—and so did Liza's.

Part of the reason that the Haley marriage broke up is that their lives had become too dissimilar; Liza's need for creative expression outweighed her desire for normalcy: "I've always had a two-part dream," she was to say. "The first part was to be successful artistically. The second part was to be a normal, happily married woman. But a very strange thing happened to me—I couldn't adjust to normalcy . . . for someone in my position, that piece of paper is a terrible thing. I never in my life again want to put someone in the position of being called 'Mr. Minnelli'—except my father."

Liza kept up the incredible professional pace she had been keeping for years, and although she was just thirty-two, it began to take its toll. She collapsed during an out-of-town performance of *The Act* in August 1977; in New York in December she was hospitalized with

Robert De Niro as Jimmy Doyle and Liza as Francine Evans in Martin Scorsese's *New York, New York*, 1977.

New York, New York, 1977.

exhaustion. She disobeyed doctor's orders and returned to the show. In January, there was a fire in her apartment (reportedly caused by her smoking in bed) and she ended up back in the hospital being treated for smoke inhalation and a lung infection. She would miss over two dozen performances due to illness before *The Act* closed.

Articles began appearing, in women's magazines as well as the tabloid press, suggesting drug and alcohol use by Liza and asking questions like "Liza Minnelli: Is She Burning Out Like Judy?" Her friends became more and more worried by the new rumors of drug use; Liza seemed to spend a great deal of time at trendy Studio 54, where cocaine was the drug of choice. A story made the rounds about Liza getting up to say a few words at a party, appearing obviously under the influence. Someone in the crowd called out, "You're getting more and more like your mother, Liza." Liza, it was said, ran from the room in tears.

She continued to work, not lessening her pace one bit. She won another Tony Award for *The Act,* then began planning a national tour for the rest of 1978 and 1979. Despite her comments that she needed a career more than a normal life, she was falling in love with the New York stage manager for *The Act,* Mark Gero, a handsome, brooding twenty-seven-year-old Italian. Mark had proposed to her early on, but she resisted. Her divorce from Jack Haley would not be final until April 1979, and she was afraid of another marriage commitment. Mark pressed her, and she continued to fight the commitment until she discovered, late in 1979, that she was pregnant.

Her outlook changed. "I was so anxious to grow as an artist—period. Now, I'm even more anxious to grow as a human being. I suppose age and maturity have a lot to do with that feeling, but, finally, there's more to my life than just show business."

Liza and Mark were married on December 4, 1979. A week later, Liza lost her baby. She used all the courage she had learned being Judy's daughter: "You can't give way to despair," she said. "What works is being able to bounce back. Resilience. That's what does it."

Liza and Mark settled into their New York apartment and scaled down their activities. For Liza, it was almost a semi-retirement. But she couldn't stop working altogether. She appeared with her friend Mikhail Baryshnikov on a TV special, and agreed to play a supporting role in Dudley Moore's film *Arthur.* It was a pleasure for her, filmed in New York, and her only concern was whether her part were so small it would be cut out of the final film. It wasn't, and *Arthur*'s huge success brought Liza Minnelli's screen persona back into focus for millions of Americans.

In the summer of 1980, Liza discovered she was pregnant again. She had commitments to perform in Reno and Las Vegas, but complications with the pregnancy put her into the hospital, where doctors told her she would have to eliminate all activities in order to carry her baby to full term—in fact, she would have to stay in bed, much as Sophia Loren had done, for the entire duration of her pregnancy.

Liza followed her doctor's advice, and canceled her concert plans. "She's calmed down a lot," a friend said. "She's determined to be a good full-time mother, and she believes that being a good mother starts before the baby is born."

In January 1981, Liza miscarried again. It was devastating to her. She had so much wanted a baby now, after having put it off for so many years. She couldn't help wondering whether the pace and lifestyle she had lived contributed to her seeming inability to carry a pregnancy to term. While in the hospital, she consented to having corrective surgery done. Her doctors told her it would still be possible for her to have children, but as she entered her late thirties, she was aware that a first-time birth at that age can be a very difficult prospect for a woman.

What lies in store for Liza Minnelli? She seems, finally, to have accepted the need in her life for domestic tranquillity. She took almost a year off in 1982, and though she returned to the

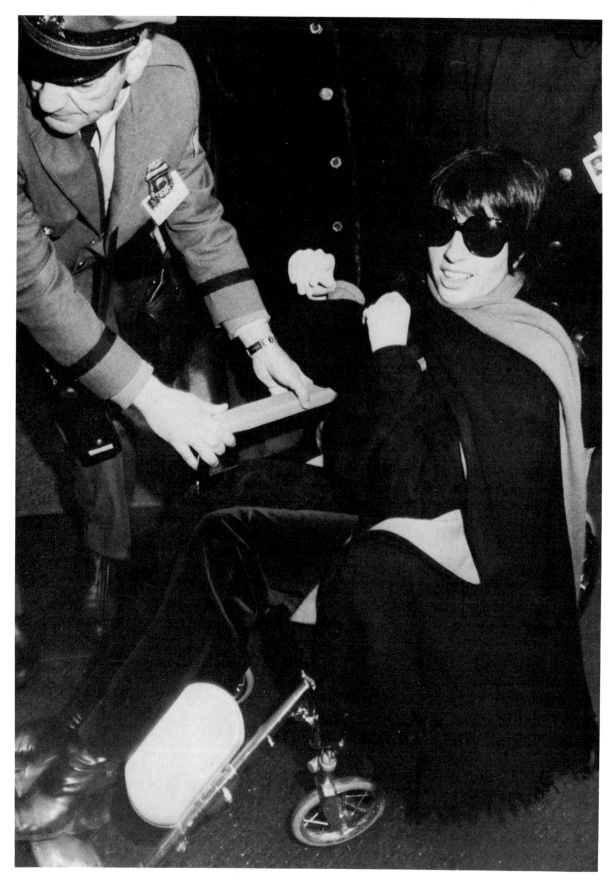

Liza is wheeled into New York Hospital–Cornell Medical Center on January 18, 1978, with a lung infection complicated by smoke inhalation after a fire in her apartment.

Mark Gero and Liza at New York's trendy Studio 54, January 17, 1979. They denied rumors they planned to wed.

Liza and Dudley Moore in *Arthur*.

Liza on tour, 1980.

Liza on stage, 1981.

Lee Minelli and Liza congratulate Vincente at his birthday tribute, February 1983.

concert trail in 1983, the frenetic pace was missing; there no longer seemed that desperate desire to please, to keep proving herself at all costs.

And she seems more and more comfortable with the memory of her mother. During a Los Angeles concert in 1981, she paused and told the audience that she would like to sing a song she had never sung before. It was a song made famous by someone whose songs she had never dared to sing. "I didn't feel I was ready and I didn't want to. But now I want to, very much. She was a showstopper and I've always wanted to be one . . . she was the best friend I ever had. This is for you, Mama."

She began a heart-rending version of "The Man That Got Away," and the Los Angeles *Times* reported the next day: "The overwhelming reception brought her to tears and was one of those genuine emotional exchanges between audience and performer that make it even worth fighting the traffic . . ."

Performing one of her mother's signature songs had a cathartic effect on Liza, further helping her along in her quest to be completely comfortable with the memory of her mother. Later in the year, she told a journalist, "Mama's been dead for twelve years—impossible to believe! I think about her at least a dozen times a day."

In February 1983, Liza performed at a birthday celebration for her father in Palm Springs, California. It was a moving occasion, as friends and colleagues of Vincente's paid homage to him as a man and an artist. Particularly touching was Liza's tribute to her dad, in which she sang for the first time two songs of her mother's from the film that brought her parents together, *Meet Me in St. Louis*.

While appearing in Houston the following month, Liza was rushed to a hospital in the middle of the night, choking on food. She was released the next day, and resumed her concert tour, which took her to seven American cities and Europe during 1983.

Although Liza resumed her hectic pace in 1983—she co-hosted the Academy Awards the day after a four-night concert stand in Los Angeles in April—there has been little talk of the "Liza is burning herself out" variety in the past year. Her friends believe that Liza may finally have accepted the joys of domesticity, and found a way to reasonably balance her love of performing with the need we all share for rest, quiet, and a good sense of our energy limits.

In her thirty-seven years, Liza Minnelli has proven that she is the ultimate survivor. She has led a life that for some people would have meant—in the words of Lee Gershwin more than three decades ago—"grow[ing] up to be a commuter to an institution." But it has not been so with Liza Minnelli. She has persevered, suffered slings and arrows with renewed strength, and emerged as her own woman. The search for herself was a long, arduous one—and is still going on—but one senses that Liza has found the peace of mind which augurs well for a long, happy life.

Liza has gone a long way toward realizing her goal not only of becoming herself, but remaining so. "I fight to be Liza Minnelli onstage and I fight to be Liza Minnelli offstage," she says. "They're trying to prove that history repeats itself, but Mama proved to me that it doesn't have to. 'Watch my mistakes,' she used to say to me. I'll never forget it. I'm not just Judy Garland's daughter. I'm Liza Minnelli.

"I'm me. I've made it on my own."

BIBLIOGRAPHY

Astor, Mary, *A Life on Film.* New York: Delacorte Press, 1967.

Bacall, Lauren, *By Myself.* New York: Alfred A. Knopf, Inc., 1979.

Bogarde, Dirk, *Snakes and Ladders.* New York: Holt, Rinehart & Winston, 1979.

Dahl, David, and Barry Kehoe, *Young Judy.* New York: Mason Charter, 1976.

Davidson, Muriel, "My Mom and I." *Good Housekeeping,* July 1968.

Edwards, Anne, *Judy Garland.* New York: Simon & Schuster, 1975.

Finch, Christopher, *Rainbow: The Stormy Life of Judy Garland.* New York: Grosset & Dunlap, 1975.

Fordin, Hugh, *The World of Entertainment, Hollywood's Greatest Musicals.* Garden City, New York: Doubleday & Company, 1975.

Frank, Gerold, *Judy.* New York: Harper & Row, 1975.

Griffin, Merv, with Peter Barsocchini, *Merv.* New York: Simon & Schuster, 1980.

Harmetz, Aljean, *The Making of the Wizard of Oz.* New York: Alfred A. Knopf, 1977.

Hotchner, A. E., *Doris Day: Her Own Story.* New York: William Morrow & Co., 1975.

Minnelli, Vincente, with Hector Arce, *I Remember It Well.* Garden City, New York: Doubleday & Company, 1974.

Parish, James Robert, with Jack Ano, *Liza!* New York: Pocket Books, 1975.

Pasternak, Joe (as told to David Chandler), *Easy the Hard Way.* New York: G. P. Putnam's Sons, 1956.

Rooney, Mickey, *I.E.: An Autobiography.* New York: G. P. Putnam's Sons, 1965.

Tormé, Mel, *The Other Side of the Rainbow (with Judy Garland on the Dawn Patrol).* New York: William Morrow & Co., 1970.

PHOTO CREDITS

ABOUT THE AUTHOR

James Spada is the author of the best-selling *Monroe: Her Life in Pictures* and *Streisand: The Woman and the Legend,* as well as three other books. His work has been serialized in *People, McCall's,* the *Ladies' Home Journal,* the New York *Daily News,* the Philadelphia *Inquirer,* the Chicago *Tribune,* the London *Daily Mirror* and by the New York *Times* Syndicate.

Born and raised in Staten Island, New York, Mr. Spada now lives in Los Angeles, where he publishes *Barbra Quarterly,* a magazine about Streisand. He is currently at work on his next book, *Hepburn: Her Life in Pictures.*